Seeing the real you at last

Seeing the real you at last
Life and love on the road with Bob Dylan
Britta Lee Shain

A Jawbone book
First edition 2016
Published in the UK and the USA by
Jawbone Press
3.1D Union Court,
20–22 Union Road,
London SW4 6JP,
England
www.jawbonepress.com

ISBN 978-1-908279-94-1

EDITOR Tom Seabrook
JACKET DESIGN Mark Case

Printed by Everbest Printing Co Ltd, China

1 2 3 4 5 20 19 18 17 16

Contents

PROLOGUE   If not for you ...   5

ONE   Subterranean homesick blues   7

TWO   Slow train coming   26

THREE   New morning   43

FOUR   Tangled up in blue   63

FIVE   Gotta serve somebody   86

SIX   I want you   119

SEVEN   You're a big girl now   165

EIGHT   Love minus zero no limit   190

NINE   Seeing the real you at last   210

TEN   Like a rolling stone   218

ELEVEN   Knockin' on heaven's door   249

EPILOGUE   It's not dark, yet ...   271

            Acknowledgments   279

I didn't know I would fall in love with you. It never even occurred to me. The room is so empty without your music. As you lie there, I cannot look, I so respect your privacy. I appear so 'orderly' as I fall apart inside. I'm wiped out, starting to nod off. Is this what love is, some deep sleep that anesthetizes without healing? God help me.

BRITTA LEE SHAIN, OCTOBER 1987

If not
for you ...

August 7 2014. Los Angeles, California. I'm on my way to a meeting to discuss the possibility of publishing a memoir about my life in the late 80s, when I was a member of Bob Dylan's inner circle. On the heels of Dylan's near-lethal lung infection back in 1997, I had written an account of my travels with the legend as a way of making peace with my long-held affection for him. But over the years, in books and on the Internet, our friendship had been mischaracterized. With some distance from the subject, the thought was that now might be the right time for me to set the record straight.

I'd never seen a Bob Dylan smile, except in photos or on the stage. Flicker of teeth. Flash of blue-eyed lightening.

It's four o'clock, 100 degrees, and I'm turning right off Laurel Canyon Boulevard when, in the crosswalk, walking spryly north on Laurel, I see Bob Dylan.

'If you were my woman,' Bob tells me, 'I'd be worth four times as much.'

I watch dumbstruck as this super-charismatic guy bearing Bob's unmistakable features, attire, and gait moves buoyantly past my slightly encroaching vehicle, only feet out of reach. My heart falls open with joy and disbelief.

Slowly I make my turn, rolling down the window, promising to speak, as he hops the curb and twirls to look at me just like Bob would have on his best days.

'Hello ...?' he smiles, playfully, assuredly, flirtatiously.

Our eyes meet.

'Britta, Britta, I love you, I love you.'

Without missing a step, the familiar icon ambles onward, looking back at me and grinning over his shoulder. I note the thick red-fringed headband, the earring, black leather vest, and the inconceivably hot billowing satin shirt. This can't possibly be Bob, I realize, because there is none of Bob's recent white-faced pallor; no sunken cheekbones, no thin Vincent Price moustache—no black cape and top hat in keeping with the current iteration of the ever-changing Bob Dylan.

No, this was the forty-five-year-old Bob Dylan I first met nearly thirty years ago, with a gleam of light shining through his soulful eyes and still emanating that spark of wit and gleeful mischievousness that mesmerized a generation.

'All of life's a chess game,' Bob confides, giving me his best all-knowing look.

Now, indeed, would be the right time for me to set the record straight.

CHAPTER ONE

Subterranean homesick blues

If my mem'ry serves me well ...

1966. UC Berkeley. Sex, drugs, and antiwar demonstrations. Back home in LA, my alcoholic mother is dying of cancer, while Daddy, suffering from delusions, is in the VA hospital, being force-fed Stelazine and Thorazine. A lonely only child from just this side of the wrong side of the tracks, who happens to be smart and pretty, it isn't long before I shock my sorority sisters by bringing home a long-haired skinny guy wearing a suede fringed jacket and riding a Harley: a long-haired skinny guy who would drown in the Russian River a few years later, on an acid trip; a tortured genius who would bring over an unlikely album to neck to in the Alpha Omicron Pi sitting room. Bob Dylan's *Highway 61 Revisited*.

I'll never forget getting high and listening to 'From A Buick 6,' 'Ballad Of A Thin Man,' 'It Takes A Lot To Laugh, It Takes A Train To Cry,' until Mrs. Axe—no word of a lie, that was the housemother's name—nose pinched at the sight of him, asks my friend to leave.

After the date, a handful of us pile into the rare campus car—a flesh-colored Mustang fastback—and head down to Edie's on Shattuck for ice cream sundaes, quick before it closes.

'What do you see in *him*?' the girls giggle at the thought of my long-haired friend, and as I sit there gazing at all their pretty faces sucking up hot fudge and cream, snippets of Dylan's 'Desolation Row' play back word for word in my head.

No use in explaining, I realize. Casanova's just being punished for going up to sorority row.

The next day I walk to Leopold's Records on Telegraph, and after comparing notes with the bearded guys who work there, I buy every one of Dylan's albums, including some bootlegs. I have a lot of catching up to do.

Bob Dylan, The Freewheelin' Bob Dylan, The Times They Are A-Changin', Another Side Of Bob Dylan, Bringin' It All Back Home, Highway 61 Revisited …

FM radio consists of only a single underground station, and while you might hear 'Masters Of War' over the AM airwaves, you'd never hear 'Bob Dylan's Dream,' and it was 'Bob Dylan's Dream' that I really identified with, or 'I Don't Believe You,' or 'My Back Pages.' Songs of hopelessness and heartbreak—the emotions I was the most familiar with. That isn't to say that the politics and poetry of 'Blowin' In The Wind,' 'Chimes Of Freedom,' and 'Mr. Tambourine Man' are lost on me. They most certainly are not. By *Highway 61 Revisited,* I've committed most of Dylan's lyrics to heart. But '115th Dream,' frenetic and crazy like a hallucination, rocks me to my roots because I'm positive I'm the only person in the world, besides the song's writer, who understands every word.

Whoever this Bob Dylan cat is, he really speaks to me. Joni and Judy and Leonard speak to me, too, as do John Lennon and Tim Buckley, but it's different with Dylan, though at the time, I couldn't tell you how. Seventeen, blue-eyed, and *Blonde On Blonde,* I'm Bob Dylan's biggest new fan.

If someone had said back then that one day I'd meet Mr. Dylan, the man, face to face, I probably would have told them, 'I want a hit of what you're tokin'.'

Dont Look Back, John Wesley Harding, Nashville Skyline …
August 1969. Hitchhiking across Western Europe with a girlfriend, rumors of Dylan performing at the Isle of Wight Festival abound, but despite the ready availability of marijuana, cheap wine, and Volkswagen vans, I'm unable to convince any of my drivers to take me there.

Self Portrait, New Morning …
1970. I see Carole King and James Taylor at the Troubadour. The next day I buy a guitar.

Tarantula, Eat The Document, Pat Garrett And Billy The Kid, Dylan, Planet Waves …
1974. The *Los Angeles Times* announces that Bob Dylan and The Band will be performing at the Forum—his first paid performance in years. I'm back in LA. Mom is indeed dead, and Daddy's living in his '64 Falcon in the Arizona desert. I'm alone, but I now have a master's degree in educational psychology from UCLA, which I'm refusing to put to good use, probably because it would have made my mother happy from whatever vantage I'm convinced she still has. Instead, I'm a secretary for an entertainment accounting firm on the Sunset Strip, where the big thrills include Steve McQueen riding his motorcycle into the foyer whenever he has an appointment, and the opportunity to review Raquel Welch's plastic surgery bills.

I call a few friends about the Dylan concert. Everyone's a taker. After filling out the necessary forms, I naively include a comment about how I'd like the best seats available—those were the days—

and mail in the check. Two weeks later, the tickets show up at my place in Santa Monica, along with a handwritten note.

Britta! Hi! Hi! Hi!

It's from a guy I knew back when I lived in the dorms at Berkeley. He always called me Brit-ah instead of Bree-tah, the way my name is pronounced.

Processed your Dylan order this morning.

I glance into the envelope. Four seats on the floor, tenth row center.

Hope you get the tickets of your dreams …

Valentine's Day 1974. The final dates of Dylan's first American tour in eight years will be recorded live for an album. The crowd is on fire. The place is packed. Electricity fills the air. Dylan takes the stage. At thirty-three, Bob Dylan has matured. He's heavier than he was in previous incarnations, and with his closely trimmed beard and mustache and thick, dark head of hair, he looks better than ever. Midway through a set that includes 'Just Like A Woman,' 'It Ain't Me, Babe,' and 'Most Likely You Go Your Way, I'll Go Mine,' a gigantic red heart is unscrolled on a screen on the back wall of the amphitheater.

I'm in love.

When the live album is released in June, I rush to the record store to buy it. It's called *Before The Flood*.

I wish I could say the 70s were one long joyride for me—all platform shoes and striped bell-bottoms—but starting with my mother's death in '71, the train I was riding on just kept getting derailed. In '72, a good male friend of mine from Berkeley is diagnosed with leukemia and dies a month after visiting me at my Santa Monica apartment. Then, in the fall of '74, after a string of disappointing relationships—many of them one-night stands—I meet Ron Lee at his plant store in Pacific Palisades. Having moved up from secretary to sales rep, I'm now pushing a line of plastic gingham flowerpots that are selling nationwide to housewives with a penchant for growing philodendrons.

When my mother passed away, I'd inherited a whopping twenty grand, and while I saved most of it, I used some of the money to trade in my Triumph Spitfire—after it had coughed and died on the 405 for the thirty-second time—for a brand new, navy blue Fiat 124 Spider. Now, cruising the boulevards, top down, from Seal Beach to downtown and back up to Malibu in search of buyers for my gardening wares, I stumble into the Plant Shanty, a small shop that caters to the likes of Walter Matthau and the Captain & Tennille, and meet the proprietor, Ron, a diminutive guy in faded denim with twinkly blue eyes and a hairdo and mustache to rival Sonny Bono's. On our first date, we stay up all night talking—this is novel for the 70s—and after two weeks of getting to know each other, we move in together.

On the surface, Ron's a simple guy, a Vietnam vet with no post-high-school degree. But he's tortured by the action he's seen, and he often wakes up in the middle of the night screaming. Pisces and Cancer—the only excuse I can come up with, besides sheer coincidence—we both have an affinity for the water. Living only a block from the beach, we meet after work every afternoon at sunset to swim, hungrily riding the waves until both the sky and the water turn black.

Ron is a Dylan fan, too, though his tastes lean more toward *Nashville Skyline* and the *Pat Garrett And Billy The Kid* soundtrack. As each new album is released, I buy it and devour it. Dylan's bleak irony and bleaker sense of humor continue to touch me. *Blood On*

The Tracks, his postmortem to his marriage—the alienation and suffering so intense—becomes an instant part of me. On one of Ron's plant deliveries, he picks up a seventy-year-old upright piano for fifty bucks and gives it to me so I can follow up on the lessons I took as a kid.

I've reached a turning point in my life. Twenty-six years old, with two college degrees, I'm still struggling financially. It turns out I'm 'too good' of a salesperson. The Beverly Hills company I work for can't ship enough merchandise to cover my sales, and even though I sell more than a thousand dollars each month in commissions, the checks that trickle in are for $250–$350.

It's beginning to sink in that all I really want to do is be a writer. I start taking extension classes in filmmaking at UCLA. One memorable seminar features four hot young directors and their first films: Steven Spielberg, George Lucas, Francis Ford Coppola, and Martin Scorsese—the latter of whom would direct the farewell to The Band movie known as the *The Last Waltz*, the highlight of which would be the closely watched Bob Dylan.

Ron says that if I want to go to film school, he'll support me, but the voice of my dead mother intervenes. *You don't deserve to go to film school*, she says. A failed actress herself, she'd never wanted me to have anything to do with Hollywood. She still lives vicariously through me, even though she's been gone more than four years. Her message persists: I have to earn the right to go back to school by making enough money to be a writer.

I choose real estate over interior decorating as my new career. Waiting to take the sales exam, I become office manager to a highly sought-after plastic surgeon whose client list includes Liberace, Henry Mancini, and Priscilla Presley. The doctor—a man who, while still in medical school, remained awake without anesthesia to direct his own nose operation—wants to perform plastic surgery on me, insisting that my nose isn't narrow enough for me to be considered a classic American beauty. He has a great sound system, though, which he writes off as an office expense, and when he isn't in, I study my real estate books while listening to Dylan's latest releases, *The Basement Tapes* and *Desire*.

The doctor's favorite Dylan song is apparently 'Lay Lady Lay.' He calls me up in the morning from his bed, and before asking me to recite his calendar he says things in his Mississippi drawl like, 'I had a dream about you last night. You were wearing a black negligee.' When I announce that Ron and I will be married on Valentine's Day '76, he brings a psychic friend of his to the office to read my astrological chart—a weathered old woman who looks like a gypsy and lives in the same Mid-Wilshire high-rise as he does, and who, according to what he told me when her dog was dying, had asked him to shoot it with some drug before the two of them shoved the poor thing down the garbage chute of the building. I have no respect for either of them—as soon as my real estate license is issued, I'll be gone—so I agree to the reading, knowing that anything she tells me will just go out one ear.

Dressed in black, her wrinkled face somber, she comes to the office that winter to deliver a report based on Ron's and my dates of birth, as well as the times and locations.

She reads my palm, her own hands shaking. 'Disaster,' she says. She's a good actress. Voice quaking, her eyes penetrate mine. 'Do not marry this man.'

I figure the doctor has put her up to it, but six months after our rainy day Valentine's wedding, my sweet, twinkly-eyed Ron dies on the back of a friend's motorcycle on Sunset Boulevard. I will spend the next years of my life in a peculiar hell, whereby I make lots of money working eighty hours a week selling property, lose all my friends because of it, and flit from one uncommitted liaison to another.

'Why did this happen to me?' I remember asking at Ron's wake. The room is filled with my closest friends—friends who even then had looked to me like ghosts.

'Because you're the only one who could handle it,' I'm told.

August 1976. *Hard Rain*. An interview with Dylan appears in *TV Guide*, of all places. When the interviewer asks him how he envisions God, Dylan responds, 'How come nobody ever asks Kris Kristofferson questions like that?'

Renaldo & Clara, The Last Waltz, Street Legal …
June 1978. Dylan performs seven nights in a row at the Universal Amphitheater. I can now afford good seats without asking for a favor. I take my boyfriend, a struggling actor and screenwriter and fellow Dylan worshipper who will leave me shortly before exhausting my savings. A somewhat scruffy but still very captivating Dylan plays 'Is Your Love In Vain?,' 'Don't Think Twice,' and the song that hits me the hardest since Ron's death, 'Simple Twist Of Fate.'

Bob Dylan At Budokan, Slow Train Coming …
November 1979. An intense but disheveled Bob Dylan performs his religious set at the Santa Monica Civic Auditorium, and while some boo and walk out, I enjoy it.

I attend a meeting of born-again Christians in Pacific Palisades in an attempt to renew my faith in life, and afterwards I'm told it's one of the meetings Dylan usually attends. I'm bored by the rhetoric, as well as the people, and I never go back. Instead, I experiment with an offbeat school of thought called Arica, and get a dog.

Saved …

December 8 1980. John Lennon is assassinated, and I take it personally. The next day, I blow off a mandatory real estate meeting to cruise the streets of Los Angeles in my latest vehicle—a mid-70s silver Mercedes Benz—wearing a black armband and buying up Beatles albums while commiserating with other devastated Lennon devotees.

Somewhere in here, I replace all of my old Bob Dylan albums because they're scratched.

June 1981. When Yoko Ono is bashed in the press for exploiting her husband's death by releasing the controversial album *Season Of Glass*, I write a lengthy letter to the *Los Angeles Times* in her defense. I'm disappointed when it isn't picked up in the 'Calendar' section that Sunday—all my previous letters have been published—but the following Saturday, my missive appears in rock critic Robert Hilburn's column.

Shot Of Love …

The early 1980s. Another relationship, another Dylan fan. I meet this guy, who is terminally handsome, while getting my real estate brokers license. A Realtor, coincidentally named Bob, he remembers Dylan coming in to buy a pick when he was working at West LA Music. His sister, Velo—short for Velocity—claims to have been Dylan's lover in New York in the 60s, and she has the stories to prove it. She drives me up to Malibu to show me the outside of Dylan's house. Later, I take others there, never dreaming that, one day, I will be a guest.

1983. My first novel, *Detours*, is completed, and within days I have an agent. The book goes out to six publishers and is rejected by all of them. My favorite rejection is from Viking Penguin: 'Fast paced and well-written novel with great commercial appeal, but not for us!' I frame it.

Infidels …

After a torrid affair with a brilliant but forever-younger man, a New York–based Dylanophile who romances me with audiotapes that include Dylan's 'Fools Rush In' and the Budokan version of 'I Want You'—I'm thirty-three, he's nineteen, and his next girlfriend will be Martha Quinn of MTV VJ fame—I decide it's time to get married, street legal, so to speak, and marry literally the next guy who walks through the door, a music producer who does mostly commercials when he's not doing drugs.

Voluntarily, I convert to Judaism—the conversion consisting of six deli lunches with the hippie rabbi, a minor oral exam, and the selection of my Hebrew name, Ruth, which, as fate will have it, turns out to mean 'Companion'—all so my fiancé's mother can watch her son smash the glass at the wedding.

This time, without the presaging of a gypsy, the marriage ends abruptly after nine months, but at least everyone's still alive.

March 22 1984. A clean-shaven Bob Dylan performs three songs, including a never-ending version of 'License To Kill,' on *Late Night With David Letterman*. He gets rave reviews, but I think he looks strange, old beyond his years, off-balance somehow, and I'm disappointed. At one point, he picks up the wrong harp, blows a few notes, and then has to wait while someone dredges up the right one. Afterwards, Dave jokingly asks Dylan if he and the band—a ragged bunch of guys I've never seen before—can come back to the show every Thursday.

Real Live, We Are The World, Empire Burlesque …

April–May 1985. After six weeks of living in my soon-to-be ex-husband's garage with only my dog, my piano, and my IBM Selectric typewriter, I find a pink stucco apartment in Westwood that reminds me of an Italian Villa. I trade my newer Mercedes in for a classic model, very deco, a '71 3.5 coupe, black on black on black. One of the positive legacies of my childhood that will come in handy along the way is the passing down to me of my father's obsession with cars.

Divorced, single, and looking, I decide to take an acting class. I've been hanging out at playwright Beth Henley's house, partying into the wee hours with a group of talented musicians, actors, and directors including Rickie Lee Jones, John Lithgow, Stephen Tobolosky, and Ulu Grosbard—Beth won the Pulitzer for her play *Crimes Of The Heart*—and after performing a few scenes at a private workshop led by her friend, actress Elizabeth Huddle, people say I'm pretty good. I pick the Loft Studio on La Brea, one of the two best acting schools in town, to try out for. The other establishment is Scientology-based, and I know that with my personality, if I get in, I'll never get out.

The Loft is run by Actors Studio and Lee Strasberg alum Peggy Feury and her husband Bill Traylor. My audition for Bill consists of telling him my life story: alcoholic mother, schizophrenic father; incest, death, lots and lots of death. I'm wearing metallic-blue nail polish, and I pick nervously at my fingers while I talk. On the spot, Bill says he'll accept me—this is not an easy group to get in with. At the time, their students include the likes of Sean Penn and Nicholas Cage. Bill teases me before I leave, 'Don't let me find out later you made this whole story up!'

To start out, almost everyone studies with Bill—a very cool

gangly character actor, now gone, who you may remember from *The Adventures Of Buckaroo Banzai*. Then, when you're deemed ready, you're moved up to Peggy's class, where the heavy hitters are. Notables in my beginner's group are Meg Ryan—no one knew who she was back then, except for the fact that she was by far the best actress—and Karla Bonoff, a successful singer-songwriter who, at the time, I hadn't heard of.

At the first meeting, Bill gives us a number of exercises to participate in, including one where you have to pretend you're at a cocktail party and mingle. When the group shifts randomly, I find myself face-to-face with Karla. She's tall and pretty, with shining dark hair and eyes the color of coffee.

'I can sing in front of 20,000 people,' she says, 'but I'm afraid to do this.'

Twenty thousand people? Who is this woman?

Karla and I are older than most of the group, and one night after class we go out for cappuccinos. Over the raucous rumble of the crowd at the Cat & The Fiddle, we confess to each other that in addition to hoping to overcome some of our irrational fears by enrolling in the acting class, we also thought we might meet a man. But the guys in our group are eighteen, married, or gay—one exotic example going on to gain notoriety as the Mexican Elvis impersonator El Vez. Instead, Karla and I had met each other.

A few weeks later, after seeing a movie in Century City, Karla gives me a couple of her albums to listen to. To my shock, they contain many famous songs, like the Linda Ronstadt hit 'Someone To Lay Down Beside Me,' except it was Karla who wrote it, and I like her more soulful version better. In fact, I've heard almost every song she's written at some time or another.

I call her up the next day: 'Oh, *that* Karla Bonoff!' We laugh.

July 13 1985. I'm invited to a going-away party in Topanga Canyon for my soon-to-be-former coke dealer. The last time I'd scored from him was in the elevator of this famous hairdresser-turned-movie producer's building in Beverly Hills.

'You're retiring?' I say. The guy's only about thirty-six. 'How'd you swing that?'

'Meeting people like you in elevators,' he grins. The door opens.

The party is strictly Fellini and includes an appearance by my very first boyfriend from when I was sixteen, a surfer-musician from Orange County who, when I knew him, drove a radioactive-orange '57 Chevy convertible with blue-tinted windows that we took to the drive-in as well as the beach. He's changed his name from Fred to Derf, because he's into numerology, and even though it was he who dumped me, he swears I broke his heart and he's never recovered. Derf starts charting out our numbers to see if reconciliation is in the stars.

I'm completely fucked-up from all the stuff being passed around when someone screams, 'Dylan's on *Live Aid*!'

A bunch of us huddle around a small TV, passing a joint, as Dylan, Ron Wood, and Keith Richards, looking as though they've been dug up from their respective graves, deliver one of the worst performances imaginable. Before staggering offstage, Dylan does wind up mumbling something audible—albeit inappropriate—about diverting one or two million dollars of the money collected for saving the lives of Ethiopian famine victims to helping farmers here in the US pay off their mortgages.

Everyone watching is disgusted by the debacle, except for me. I'm merely confused and once again disappointed. What can be going so wrong in Bob Dylan's life that his last several performances—*We Are The World*, Letterman, and now this one—have been so depressing?

When I finally gather the good sense to depart, it's dark, and I wind up driving around Topanga State Park for two hours, lost.

Maybe it's my friendship with Karla, or maybe it's just something in the air, but I pick up the guitar again and write a country-rock song about how hard it is to find a good man, or good to find a hard one, or something like that, called 'A Man I Didn't Know.' When I play it for Karla, she says we should record it. We take it to her friend Ira Ingber's studio—Ira played guitar on *Empire Burlesque*—where another friend named Karen sings lead; Karla sings backup and Ira plays the guitar. When it's finished, we will send the recording off to Nashville.

The session is great laughs, and afterwards Karla asks Ira if he has anyone to fix me up with. After running through a few rejects, he suggests his friend Ernie, who is Bob Dylan's road manager.

Whoa! I think. *Is he kidding?*

Karla, more of a classic interior decorator than I, winces and brushes off the idea, telling him Ernie's too far out. 'His kitchen looks like a diner!'

'Sounds cool to me,' I say, trying to focus on Ernie and snuff out the first spark of excitement that I might actually wind up dating someone who knows Bob Dylan. Ira tells me Ernie is a widower—an odd coincidence—and that he hasn't dated anyone in a long time. He thinks I'd be perfect for him, but Ernie is away now, with 'Bob,' in Russia, at some poetry convention. He'll have to wait and give him a call when he gets back.

Summer 1985. I land a part as an extra in *Legends Of The Spanish Kitchen*, a short film about a boarded up restaurant on Beverly Blvd, made for HBO, and directed by then record producer T Bone

Burnett, of all people, who accompanied Dylan on the Rolling Thunder Revue tour, and was instrumental, so to speak, in Dylan's religious conversion. Bored with the acting bit—as in, there's nothing to do!—I follow the sunglass-clad, charismatic T Bone around the soundstage, picking up tips on directing. My favorite castmate turns out to be Steve Hochman, a rock reviewer for the *Los Angeles Times*, who fills me in on T Bone's tight connection to Mr. D.

After the shoot, one of the film's producers pursues me. He's extremely intelligent, but no matter how hard I try, I cannot make him my type. To woo me, he comes to my Westwood apartment armed with Dylan paraphernalia: videos of *Eat The Document*, *Dont Look Back*, and Dylan's infamous 1965 San Francisco press conference. He's also managed to snag an audiotape of the unreleased acoustic version of *Blood On The Tracks*, which Karla will tell me later she once had a copy of, until someone ripped it off from her house.

The producer and I watch and listen to all this stuff, which makes for quite a marathon, and I remember thinking, while viewing the young Dylan's press conference, *Jesus, they're calling him Mr. Dylan, and he's only twenty-four!* During the course of the interview, the youthful Dylan lights himself on fire with fallen cigarette ash and spews out one-word answers that somehow say it all.

Why can't I find a guy like him, I'm wondering, while fending off my nerdy date's advances. *He* and I would get along great.

I must have crushed the producer's ego one too many times, or sent him away wounded somehow, because when he takes off that night, for the last time, he leaves all those groovy Dylan artifacts behind. As nice a fellow as he was, I'm not gonna mention his name here because I don't know what the statute of limitations is on something like this, and now, more than ever, I'd prefer not to have to give all that stuff back.

Fall 1985. The way I remember it is like this: Karla and I are taking a stroll down Melrose one balmy evening when this good-looking guy shows up walking his Irish Setter. Trying to be cool, I look at the dog. Karla says hi to the guy, and I see his dark eyes flash as we pass. Half a block later, Karla says, 'Oh my god, that was Ernie!'

'Wow!' I say. 'He's cute.' And he was.

The next day, Karla calls Ira, who has to call Ernie a second time to encourage him to call me. 'She's lively,' Ira tells him. But Ernie's off to Indonesia for a three-week vacation, so our meeting will have to be further postponed.

September 1985. My first date with Ernie. He's not just cute; he's funny, too! Sort of a rockabilly Presley type wearing tight black pants with a shiny jacket and cowboy boots. We go out for dinner. Ernie doesn't drink or do drugs. I have a glass of wine. Afterwards we take a walk down Melrose, wind up at some diner on Beverly Drive—how fitting—talking until two in the morning about life, love, love life, and death. But never any mention of Bob.

Ernie lightly touches my hand.

'I'm sorry about your husband,' he says. We're both a little misty-eyed.

'I'm sorry about your wife.'

We go back to his place, where the kitchen does, in fact, look like a diner—very cool—and by 3am we end up in his predominantly black bedroom, where a giant silver plaque akin to a framed gold record hangs commemorating the Rolling Thunder Revue, and proceed to fuck our brains out.

I think I'm in love, but in the morning Ernie's sulking.

'What's wrong?' I ask.

'You didn't have an orgasm,' he groans.

'Of course I did,' I tell him, trying to explain about how there are different kinds of orgasms—I'd thought I'd had about ten of them—but the look of disdain on his face makes me question my own veracity.

'No,' he says. 'You didn't.'

It's not until Monday morning, when Ernie gets up early to go to work, that I notice only a small portion of his spacious closet is available for his stylish wardrobe. The rest of the closet, along with a makeup table and jewelry box, is still cram-packed and intact with his dearly departed wife Grace's hats, clothes, and shoes.

The following Wednesday, Ernie takes me to the celebrity hot spot the Ivy on Robertson for dinner. As always, the food and the atmosphere are outstanding, but our communication seems a bit lacking. A psychologist will tell me later that a couple's level of communication is usually frozen at the point at which they first become intimate, which is why it's better to wait a while before having sex when you're trying to establish a meaningful relationship. When Karla asks me the next day how the date went, I tell her, 'Oh, Karla. I'd be bored with anyone.'

At least a month goes by of wining and dining and hanging out at Ernie's place in Venice—when he's not mysteriously called out of town to New York or London. His whole house is a collector's paradise, full of advertising and industrial art, and most of it is functional. A pink neon Pegasus from an old Mobil station lights up a brick wall in the den. The stereo equipment is cleverly ensconced behind old vending-machine doors, and there's a fully functioning photo booth installed in the hall.

Ernie's a great cook, too, and while I sit reading at the black Formica counter in the kitchen, he grills veal chops from Hugo's on his massive restaurant range, or mixes a Chinese chicken salad for dinner, as Aerosmith's 'Sweet Emotion' blasts through the speakers of his restored 60s jukebox, shaking the walls and blocking out any hope of conversation.

What's wrong with this picture? On paper, Ernie should be everything I want. He's attractive, generous, successful. He has a lucrative poster-printing business, in addition to being a road manager. He's well traveled and hip, though he still hasn't mentioned any connection at all to Bob, and he keeps calling me up and asking me out—an almost unheard of phenomenon in the mid 80s, as the MO for most of the guys who date me or my girlfriends is to sleep with us once and then never be heard from again.

Ernie's an idea man, but unlike most people with big ideas, he actually carries his out. He's perfect, I decide. There's something wrong with me.

September 22 1985. Without disclosing the purpose of his trip, Ernie's in Illinois, at *Farm Aid*. I watch Dylan—backed by Tom Petty & The Heartbreakers—on a TV at a gathering where everyone is expecting a train wreck. We all breathe a sigh of relief when Dylan, whose Live Aid comments may have actually spurred the event, manages to pull his caboose out of the fire and put on a good show.

Biograph …

One night I'm over at Ernie's, after work, and when we've finished dinner, Ernie, who's acting a little edgy, asks if he can move my Mercedes across the alley, because he's got someone coming over for a business meeting who has to park in the driveway. I say sure, no problem, and I go into the den to work on a script I've been writing. I'm premenstrual, in a funk, and there's a full moon out.

About an hour later, I hear some commotion in the kitchen, and Ernie comes thundering back to the jukebox to make a selection.

'He's here,' he says, scurrying away again toward the kitchen, just as 'Subterranean Homesick Blues' begins its blare.

No! It couldn't be, I'm thinking, but my pounding heart is saying otherwise. *I'm not going to meet Bob Dylan, now? Not like this, wearing dorky business attire!* But sure enough, I hear the nasal musings of the human being I admire most on the planet wafting above the music and moving closer to me as the man himself, Bob Dylan, catches up on Ernie's latest artistic improvements to the house.

Get dressed. Get blessed. Try to be a suck-cess …

Dylan walks into the room like a camel, and then he smiles. His eyes fix on the neon Pegasus above me.

'Bob, Britta. Britta, Bob.' This brief introduction by Ernie is the culmination of twenty years of near worship on my part.

I've never seen a Bob Dylan smile, except in photos or on the stage. Not the real thing. Flicker of teeth. Flash of blue-eyed lightening. A small silver cross dangles from his left ear. I black out for a second. When I come to, Ernie is escorting Bob—clad, I now notice, in blue jeans, white T-shirt, a black leather jacket, and tall-heeled boots—back to the kitchen for a conference.

I suddenly feel very tired and collapse fully clothed onto Ernie's bed. It's understood I am not to interrupt them. At some point, Bob noiselessly passes by the open door to the bedroom, on his way to use the head, and then passes back again. I see him, but I can't move.

The next morning, when I awaken, it feels like there's an electrical charge surging through the house. Bob Dylan's overflowing ashtray and half-filled coffee cup are on the kitchen table. I examine both closely, but I leave them where they are, as if moving them will dispel the fact that he's been here.

CHAPTER TWO

Slow train coming

New Year's Eve 1985. Ernie and I decide to throw a party for all our friends. Both of us, it turns out, are party-throwing fools. We stock the house with every type of food imaginable—Middle Eastern, sushi, you name it—and then cook the rest. I bake the likeness of two huge Hostess Cupcakes for dessert—knowing they will look fantastic in Ernie's pop-art kitchen—using a recipe for 'decadent chocolate cake' from the *au currant Silver Palette Cookbook* and real whipped cream for the filling. After pouring melted Belgian chocolate over the tops, I squeeze softened white chocolate through a pastry bag to make the obligatory figure-eight swirls.

The recipe has to be quadrupled, and the first four-ply batch is a failure. By five in the morning, I'm in tears, and Ernie and I have had our first fight—the kind of altercation a pop psychologist might call a kitchen sink fight, not only because we're in the kitchen but because each party throws in everything but the kitchen sink.

'I still can't believe you didn't warn me that first time Dylan was coming over. I looked so straight, he probably thought I was a creep!'

'You think he'll remember?' Ernie shouts.

I'm exhausted, and he doesn't know how to comfort me. But by six o'clock that night, I'm dressed in a dotted-swiss crinoline from rock'n'roll fashion designer Betsey Johnson and a brand-new pair of black-and-silver cowboy boots, ready to be the hostess with the mostess for the best damned New Year's Eve party anyone's ever attended.

Some sixty-odd guests arrive. Among them, Dylan's sweet, understated personal assistant, Carol Snow; the *très* alluring Dennis and Lisa, owners of Off The Wall, the hippest store on Melrose, and a regular supplier of industrial goodies to Ernie; friends of mine from Berkeley, friends of mine from Hollywood; friends and co-workers of Ernie's, like Bob Meyers, whose artistic talents are almost always tied in with any jobs that are done for Dylan; members of the band the Naughty Sweeties; members of the band The Cruzados—Charlie Quintana was the drummer I didn't recognize on the Letterman show—members of the band The Nobody's; and my new friend, rock reviewer Steve Hochman, along with his wife, whose name escapes me. Karla is there, too, with the avant-garde architect Jeffrey Daniels.

I can't remember everyone who showed up, but I know who wasn't there, though there'd been talk that he might be flying in from his farm in Minnesota. At one point, one of my friends asks Ernie, 'So what exactly do you *do* for Bob Dylan?'

'I don't know,' Ernie says. 'Paid friend, I guess. Yeah. That about sums it up.'

Around 9:30, the phone rings, and it's *him*.

'Uh ... Breeda?'

'Yeah?' My heart's a-poundin'.

'Happy New Year.'

The phrase takes on a whole other meaning when you put Dylan's characteristic inflection on it. I tell him he's missing a great party. He asks to speak to Carol.

I guess she must have talked up the party to him pretty good, because when she comes back into the kitchen—now loudly bustling with the clamor of cooking and conversation—she puts her arm around my waist and says what a terrific time she's having, and how Bob seemed a little jealous. 'I told him, wait till you see what a great girl Ernie's got for himself!'

I tell her thanks and give her a hug.

'Round midnight, Ernie breaks out the champagne. We cut into the Hostess Cupcakes, and by dawn there isn't a crumb left.

January 1986. Something's not right with Ernie and me, but he keeps telling me it's my fault, and I believe him. After all, I'm the one who's struggling financially; the one who hasn't 'made it' in my career of choice, and who has never had a relationship that lasted more than a year. He's the one who was happily married for seven years—to a saint, no less, whose shrine of clothing remains in tribute in his bedroom closet. He's the one who is not merely Bob Dylan's road manager, as originally advertised, but Dylan's advisor, his companion, his friend. He's the one who, whenever I have an idea for the script I'm working on, or for a new project, without even hearing me out, can come up with a better one.

Ernie's the one who's together. I'm not.

Late at night, as we walk our two dogs around the Marina—Rita, his aging Irish Setter, and Barky, my middle-aged Samoyed pup—I take Ernie's lack of enthusiasm for my various points of view as disapproval, and a sign that I need to shape up or I'm going to be shipped out and stay single forever.

Ernie is a product of the Holocaust. Both his parents lost their families during the war, including their first spouses. His sister is a therapist, and speaking strictly for me, I know the only reason

I studied psych was to try and make sense out of my own screwy upbringing. Sadly, his father, a beatific fair-skinned man, is suffering from Alzheimer's. Good son that he is, when Ernie's in town, he takes his parents out to dinner to the same Chinese restaurant his mother adores, every Sunday night.

It's a big deal when I am finally invited to go along. I know it's a huge step for Ernie, after losing his wife of seven years, to introduce me to his parents. People pleaser that I am, I am of course the perfect future daughter-in-law, and it's obvious that Ernie's family welcomes me.

Confirming rumors that flurried in the wake of *Farm Aid*, Dylan is rehearsing with Tom Petty & The Heartbreakers for his upcoming True Confessions tour. Ernie accompanies him to the Kennedy Center in D.C. for a televised tribute to Martin Luther King, and, true to new form, during a shared finale with Stevie Wonder and Peter, Paul & Mary, Bob once again looks uncomfortable and out of place.

Somewhere in here, there's a party at T Bone Burnett's house in Santa Monica, and it's rumored that Dylan will attend, but Ernie gets caught up at work—some printing emergency—and after I've spent half the day dressing for the event, we arrive late, to a litany of 'You just missed Bob!' By all accounts, he showed up dressed in a brightly colored shirt, wearing little gold sunglasses, and stayed for a total of five minutes. Karla, who arrived shortly before we did, met the poet for the first time.

'I've heard your records,' Dylan said to her, already on his way out the door.

'I've heard yours,' she replied.

Later, Bob tells Ernie he looked for us, and when we weren't there, he left.

February 3 1986. Ernie and Bob fly to Auckland to kick off the New Zealand leg of the True Confessions tour with Tom Petty. Ernie calls me every day or so and fills me in on minor details of the trip, such as how well the shows are being received, the recording of a new Dylan composition—with Petty producing—that will become the title song for a movie called *Band Of The Hand* directed by Paul Michael Glaser, aka Starsky of *Starsky & Hutch*, and Dylan's comings and goings, which include a surprise performance by Stevie Nicks, bar hopping, parties, and getting drunk after hours with Lauren Bacall, who's in Sydney starring in a stage production of *Sweet Bird Of Youth*.

February 14 1986. The same way it will turn out that Dylan has a thing for women named Carol, I guess I have a thing for Bobs— Besides Realtor Bob, who is out of my life at this time, and of course Dylan himself, I know at least three others: Bob the Spiritual Healer; 'R.J. Bob,' the writer; and Bob Starr, the Actor. In Ernie's absence, I decide to invite all three to Ernie's kitchen for a Valentine's Day dinner. At one point we all have a good laugh when Bob the Healer tells the story of how he was once introduced to a namesake, and the other fellow shook his hand, saying, 'I've never met a bad Bob, yet.'

While Ernie is in Australia with the True Confessions tour, his father suffers a stroke and is rushed to the hospital. His mother and sister are distraught. I do everything I can to help, but it doesn't look good for Ernie's dad. I call him and beg him to come home.

Reluctantly, Ernie leaves Australia and returns to LA, just as the tour moves on to Japan, and while his presence and expertise is needed at home in order to acquire the necessary medical equipment to move his dad back into his parents' apartment, his father recovers, at least temporarily.

Ernie arrives home with an astounding array of gifts for me, mostly clothes, from Australia and New Zealand: a dressy black leather jacket with shoulder pads, a black-and-white silk polka-dot miniskirt that I'd have never picked out for myself, and several over-sized blouses like the type of shiny shirts that Dylan has been wearing recently onstage. There is even a sexy pair of high heels, though he's mistakenly bought them in Grace's size.

'Wow,' I say, fondling what must be several hundred dollars in clothing, although the thought crosses my mind that he's dressing me. 'I've never had a boyfriend treat me like this before.'

'There'd have been a lot more, if you'd let me go to Japan.'

I practically live at Ernie's now when he's in town. Due to the pre-bubble-burst atmosphere of the market, my limited real estate efforts are not paying off. Phil Collins says in an interview that he feels privileged to get paid for doing what he loves, and I'm frustrated that as good of a writer as people say I am, I still have nothing to show for it. Ernie responds to any expression of my feelings about my lack of self-worth by turning up the stereo a little louder.

March 1986. The stresses of day-to-day life are definitely taking their toll on our relationship. Nevertheless, we entertain. Dennis and Lisa come over for dinner, and while we're discussing everything from antiques to politics—even an idea for opening a hip Laundromat on Melrose … a singles laundry joint that we're gonna call Wash-O-Rama or Posh Wash, or something—the phone rings. I pick it up. An urgent voice wants to speak to Ernie.

'Who may I tell him is calling?' I ask. We're constantly getting business calls for Bob at home, and I make every attempt to keep it professional.

'Richard Manuel,' the voice rasps. Richard is one of the original members of The Band, and while I've never met him, I feel like I must have.

'Oh, hi, Richard. Hold on a sec.' I pass the phone to Ernie. 'It's Richard Manuel.'

Ernie takes the phone in the other room. When he returns, he tells us that Richard was calling from the road, where The Band are on a reunion tour. He says it's important; that Richard needed to talk to Bob right away, so he gave him Bob's number in Japan.

Naturally, Ernie's kitchen comes equipped with an industrial-sized cappuccino machine from Italy. Over espressos, he tells Dennis and Lisa how awesome the view is from the place Bob is renting for his girlfriend, Carole Childs, up on Mulholland. Ernie says he wants to build a house up there soon.

'You'll never get to Maui if you move to Mulholland Drive,' Dennis says.

It sounds cryptic at first, but he's serious, and I believe him. If Ernie's an idea man, Dennis is a visionary. Now's the time to buy property in the most desirable areas before everyone on the planet jumps on the bandwagon.

Somehow the conversation turns to Europe—probably because of how expensive even a small apartment is there—and Ernie goes on and on about the time he and Grace, who was 'poly-orgasmic,' made love in this sweltering hotel room in London for days on end. I, a mere mortal capable of only multiple orgasms, forget the specifics, but the implication is that the experience with his wife was so powerful that it can never be duplicated. Now, squeezed into the kitchen's red Naugahyde dining booth, everyone is squirming—except Ernie.

Two days later, Richard Manuel hangs himself in his motel room in Florida. I'll never know if he spoke with Bob.

A miracle occurs. Ernie and I have dinner at Spago with his sister and brother-in-law. Afterwards, the two of us go across the street to Tower Records. In the rock CD section—CDs are new, and not that many people shop for them—we run into an old acquaintance of Ernie's named Elliot Mintz. I'm not sure how the two of them know each other, but I imagine, incorrectly, that it must have something to do with Bob.

Elliot is a dashing, attractive, well-spoken man, who, in the 60s, was the father of underground radio in LA. After an animated three-way conversation in the record store, he suggests that the three of us get together for dinner soon.

Elliot, it turns out, is what I will come to refer to later as the 'liaison to the stars.' He does publicity for the biggest names in showbiz. A disc jockey turned journalist—when he interviewed John Lennon and Yoko Ono in the 70s, they liked him so much, they sent him a ticket to Japan, where he wound up living with them for six months—he was Lennon's best friend, and he believes that had he had an opportunity to read Mark David Chapman's letters to John, he might have been able to thwart the assassination.

Dylan's received numerous threats and some very strange mail, though when Ernie asks about them, Bob's girlfriend dismisses Bob's worry about overzealous fans as wishful thinking. I suggest to Ernie that we introduce Elliot to Bob, and he agrees. But this is not the miracle. The miracle is that Elliot is a poet and a scholar. I can talk to Elliot about things Ernie can't even comprehend … like sweet emotions. Elliot is 'sensitive.' If I'm suffering, he not only relates to why, but he knows how to comfort me—sometimes with just some greeting-card sympathy and a bottle of red wine, but usually much more.

Once the three of us come together, my relationship with Ernie works—all except for the sex part. Every Friday night, Elliot, Ernie, and I meet for dinner at Le Dome or some other trendy night spot, where Elliot knows everyone, or maybe we just pick up deli sandwiches, potato chips, and triple-layered chocolate cake from Greenblatt's and sit on the floor in Elliot's tree-house-like hideaway up in Laurel Canyon; whatever it is we do together, I now have someone I can talk to.

March 31 1986. Bob receives the ASCAP Founder's Award at a ceremony held at Chasen's in Beverly Hills. Elizabeth Taylor is his 'date.' Elliot Mintz does what he does best, pleasing Bob immensely. I'm supposed to pick up Ernie outside the event when it's over. I dress for the occasion, on the off chance I'll run into Bob—a second chance to make a first impression—but when I arrive, Ernie instructs me to park across the street at the Hughes Market and wait, because there are too many photographers. When he jumps behind the wheel of the car around midnight, he hands me a takeout carton of the restaurant's world famous chili.

Ernie says I'm fucked-up sexually—that I don't know how to experience pleasure. Probably, he says, it has something to do with what happened to me with my father when I was a kid—which certainly could be. I forget that, before I met Ernie, I never had any problems having orgasms with my other boyfriends; now there's so much pressure on me to climax when Ernie and I make love, sometimes I really can't perform. Ernie buys me books on sex that encourage fantasies about other people, even multiple partners, and tells me to read them.

April 10 1986. After a press conference at Westwood One with Tom Petty & The Heartbreakers to announce the upcoming summer tour—the US leg of True Confessions—Ernie and I meet up with Bob at the Mink DeVille Concert at the Palace in Hollywood. I look the part, at last, in tight black jeans with a slinky silver blouse that Ernie brought me from Australia. It's crowded and noisy, so talking to Dylan is out of the question. Everyone's staring. Ernie keeps running off to make phone calls, and it feels like I'm stranded there alone with Bob and I haven't got a clue how to be.

'He shuts down so quickly,' I complain to Ernie the next day about how awkward the whole thing felt.

'He *has* to do that,' Ernie says. 'He can't just let anyone in.'

'Oh,' I shrug. That makes sense.

'He'll do that the first four or five times he meets you. Then, one day, he'll just sit down and have a conversation with you.'

'A conversation?' A bolt of terror strikes my heart. *Me,* having a conversation with Bob Dylan? No way!

Mid-April 1986. Ernie informs me that we will be attending a birthday party for a friend of Dylan's from Minnesota named Louis Kemp. It will be held at Louis's Santa Monica apartment, and Dylan will be there. As the date approaches, I frantically shop for just the right dress and shoes, finally settling on a purple-and-black, star-patterned, faux-see-through number from Betsey Johnson and a glitter-speckled pair o' high-heels. My wardrobe, prior to meeting Ernie, has been somewhat lacking in the arena of rock'n'roll entourage member, but I'm a quick study. The coup de gras is a late-40s rhinestone necklace from the Rose Bowl Flea Market that's pretty enough to be worn by a princess.

Prior to the event, I have a conversation on the telephone with Dylan's girlfriend of record, Carole Childs—whom I have never met—in which we discuss Betsey Johnson and her success. Carole, I've been told, is an A&R person with Geffen Records who has been credited with the discovery of the band du jour, Lone Justice.

It's also Ernie's birthday right around now, so I go to Off The Wall and spring for a large basketball scoreboard that lights up and everything, which in Ernie's house will serve as a headboard.

The night of the party, I'm so nervous, waiting for Ernie to come home, that I sneak a shot of the gin he keeps in the freezer for guests. When Ernie and I arrive at the Ocean Park high-rise right on schedule, I am stunned to discover that the unshaven Dylan, posed uncomfortably on the couch, has already been there for some time. His eyes brighten upon our arrival, but he doesn't stand up.

'Bob, you remember Britta,' Ernie says, but I get the feeling he doesn't. Dylan shakes my hand. There are only a couple of people milling around, including Dennis and Lisa from Off The Wall, who have just delivered a restored soda fountain, or some such thing—a gift from Dylan to his longtime buddy Louis, who will hereafter be called Louie, since that's what we all called him.

Louie and Bob's friendship dates all the way back to Camp Herzl when they were kids. Once the tour manager for the Rolling Thunder Revues, Louie, now an orthodox Jew, has made his fortune in fish. The kosher food and the décor at the party are a little dull, but within minutes the place is jumping.

I immediately sit down to the right of a dark-haired, vibe-y young woman, introduced to me as Carol, who appears to be with

Dylan. Under his scrutinizing gaze, I engage her in an awkward conversation, presuming all the details of my earlier phone call with Carole Childs about Betsey Johnson, since this young woman, too, is wearing the trendy designer.

'I hear you have a top made out of the same material I'm wearing,' I say.

'I do,' she replies, 'but how do you know?'

'Ernie told me.'

'But how could he know? I just bought it on sale.'

Bob smirks. 'She wears it all the time,' he laughs.

I'm beginning to fluster. 'Ernie told me you wore a top just like this backstage in Australia …'

Dylan's seeming fascination with the interaction turns to glee as, red-faced, the other woman says, 'I think you've got the wrong Carol.'

'Oh, I doubt that …' I say, trying to be diplomatic, but my face is crimson now, too, as I realize she is not in fact *the* Carole—the *old lady* Carole, as her younger namesake has the nerve to call Carole Childs—but another woman Bob sees with the same name.

I swallow my embarrassment along with some champagne, and as the place fills up I grow more comfortable. At one point, Dylan and Dennis get into a thing about my sparkly shoes. Dennis says they look like Dorothy's shoes from *The Wizard Of Oz*.

'Yeah,' Dylan says, looking me over, upside down, and backward, 'why don't you click 'em together?'

Ernie and I tell Dylan about this 1959 Cadillac Eldorado-Biarritz convertible we went to see in Watts earlier in the day.

'What condition?' he wants to know.

'Supposed to be good,' Ernie says.

'Got all the parts?' He looks at me.

'Yeah.'

'What color?'

'Black with white leather interior,' I tell him. The three of us are standing in the tacky kitchen of the former low-income apartment turned co-op, drinks in hand.

'You wanna go in on it?' Ernie asks.

'Maybe … maybe not.' Dylan replies, flirting with me. 'You two'll wanna be in the back seat all the time, and I'll always end up drivin'.'

'How 'bout if you two sit in the back with your feet up, and I drive?' I suggest.

Dylan gives me the once over, one more time with feeling. 'Well, OK then. It's a deal. I'll go in on the car with you,' he says to Ernie, ''long as *she's* drivin'.' He rubs his lower lip between his thumb and index finger, then, fixes his gaze on me. 'But we'll keep it at my place.'

As the evening wears on, character actor Harry Dean Stanton shows up with the immaculate but painfully thin beauty Michelle Phillips, of the long defunct Mamas & Papas. Someone unveils the cake. It's an actual-size portrait of Louie's face—Ernie's idea—from the best bakery in town.

'Looks just like him, doesn't it?' I say to Dylan, and he nods his approval, but Louie doesn't believe in cutting anything with your picture on it. As the guests' watery mouths hang open, he wraps the luscious pastry in tinfoil and shoves it in the freezer. *Too bad*, I'm thinking. I wanted to see if Ms. Phillips would have her cake and eat it, too.

Ernie and I decide to bail with Dennis and Lisa and get some real food at Charmer's Market, the ultra-chic, pre-marriage Sean Penn and Madonna hangout with the flavored martinis. At the door, I'm surprised to discover that the now well-meaning Bob Dylan has showed up to say goodbye. When I smile and tell him how good it was to see him, again, he puckers up, leans forward on his toes, and kisses me. On the lips. Goodnight.

It's the kind of kiss you give a friend or family member to let him or her know you adore them, and that's how I take it. Bob likes me!

Later, back at Ernie's under the dim glow of the advertising signs in the kitchen, I stand munching a handful of hot cashews from a tall red vintage vending machine. I'm savoring the thrill of Dylan's kiss when it hits me: we're going to be seeing a lot more of Bob Dylan around here.

Ernie and I decide to throw another party: a junk-food party, in celebration of his thirty-sixth birthday. This is when Ernie and I are at our best—co-creating some cool event for our friends' enjoyment. Ernie's gonna cook hotdogs and hamburgers on his indoor grill. All the vending machines will be filled with candy or nuts. The popcorn machine is already in prime working order. He'll whip up chocolate malts on his Hamilton Beach shake-maker, circa 1950, and we'll have do-it-yourself hot fudge sundaes for desert.

'Do you think I should invite Bob?' Ernie asks.

'I like the guy, myself,' I say.

'Yeah, but Bob can pull a room like nobody I've ever seen. He can actually ruin a party.'

For a second I relive the powerful energy drain I felt the first time I met Dylan.

'Whatever you want to do, Ernie,' I say. 'It's your birthday.' But I know I'll be disappointed if Bob doesn't come.

The guests start arriving around eight, and soon the place is really rocking. Elliot Mintz shows up with Sean Lennon. Al Kooper, guitarist and founding member of Blood, Sweat & Tears, is there, and Stan Lynch—the drummer for the Heartbreakers—is making his beguiling presence known, prompting Karla to share with me the old music-business love-life adage to which she and her girlfriends adhere: 'Stay away from drummers.' There's a rumor circulating that a bunch of people from the Rolling Thunder Revue are going to drop by, too, after the Bobby Neuwirth concert at McCabe's Guitar Shop in Santa Monica.

The place is jam-packed. At one point Ernie introduces me to this smart energetic Jewish woman wearing a white sailor suit and a Greek fisherman's cap. Her hair is a whiter shade of platinum. Her impeccably manicured nails are painted a lurid red. She's sexy, edgy, and pretty, and her accent is strictly New York.

'Britta, I want you to meet Carole Childs,' Ernie says, and I almost faint dead away.

'*The* Carole?' I take him aside. She's not at all what I'm expecting.

'Yeah, why?'

'Oh nothing,' I say. 'I just wondered.'

Around 11:30, Dylan arrives, looking like a terrorist in a hooded gray sweatshirt. I greet him at the door and escort him to Ernie.

'What can I get for you?' I ask.

'What d'ya got?'

'Everything.'

The nuance of my unintentional choice of words is not lost on him. I give him the rundown.

'I guess I'll take a beer, then,' he laughs, before going outside to move his car.

The industrial refrigerator in the kitchen looks like it was salvaged from a Korean market, despite the fact that Ernie's had a sign painter redo the logos. I slide open the glass door and retrieve a bottle of beer. After what seems like an hour, I notice Bob standing outside the kitchen door, talking to Al Kooper.

'Here's your beer,' I say.

'Have you got something a little harder?'

I think fast. 'There's some gin in the freezer …'

'OK.'

The next day, Ernie will show me where he keeps a stockpile of pint-size Wild Turkey bottles as well as several cartons of Kool cigarettes for Bob, but for now, I pour Dylan this huge bar glass filled with gin and swig from it myself on my way back to the door.

'Here ya go …'

I wait and watch him take the first sip to make sure it's all right before leaving to attend to my other guests. Bob gives me the nod. My high-heeled feet carry me back into the party, but they're not even close to touching the floor.

At one point, I catch Sean Lennon by the CD player, mimicking the blues guitarist Albert Collins, except Sean's not literally singing, he's making these kind of guttural noises that capture the rhythm and intent of the music perfectly, and right then I think that one day he could be a bigger legend than his dad.

Later, Dylan's moved into the kitchen, and is standing at the counter, talking to my exercise buddy, Sandy Gibson, a music supervisor for the movies. I've been working out five times a week at this private establishment in West Hollywood that caters to the likes of Dyan Cannon, Pia Zadora, Laura Dern, Mrs. Michael J. Fox—you name it—and the skin-tight red-and-black leopard jeans I'm squeezed into bear testimony to the fact that, at thirty-seven, I'm in pretty damn good shape for my age. The owner of the studio and her husband are at the party, too.

As I'm passing through, Bob stops me.

'*Breeda*, you got a match?' He's smoking cigarettes, and someone's passing a joint. Neuwirth has arrived with the other members of his band, which has given the shoulda-been-waning-by-now party a shot in the arm.

'I could cut a record in here, tonight,' Bob says to me.

'Yeah,' I say, 'and call it the kitchen tapes.'

Bob likes this joke, and after a second or two, he volunteers, 'I'm ready. And you're ready, too.'

People have shown up with gifts, but Ernie, whose apparent interest in nostalgia does not make him sentimental, will give most of the presents to me. In the days and weeks following, I'll retrieve birthday cards from Elliot, Sean Lennon, and others from the trash.

As Dylan's leaving the party, T Bone Burnett corners him at the door. 'Let's get together and have some fun,' T Bone says.

'Yeah, fun …'

Dylan rolls the word over in his mind for a while, but he can't quite fathom it. He shakes a friendly finger at me. 'I'll see *you* tomorrow.'

CHAPTER THREE

New morning

Ernie needs to drop 'something' off at Bob's, or to meet with him about 'something.' If this all sounds pretty vague, it was. There was a lot of secretiveness surrounding Dylan, and as close as I was to the action, I'm sure I didn't know the half of what was going on.

I'm excited. I've never seen Dylan's place in Malibu before, except from the outside. I dress in a pair of black-and-white Dalmatian-print jeans and the black-and-silver cowboy boots from New Year's Eve. It's a sunny Sunday, and the drive up the coast, with the top down, wind whipping, is exhilarating. The ocean is gleaming a rare turquoise, and the salty air clings to my skin.

Dylan lives in an exclusive area called Point Dume, a rocky promontory that juts out into the Pacific at the north end of the Santa Monica Bay. I grew up knowing the area as Point Du-*may*, but most people have come to pronounce it Point *Doom*. We make the requisite left off the highway and find our way to the house. I don't tell Ernie I know where it is—you can't see anything from the street anyway.

Once inside the property, I'm surprised to find that there's a guard tower with a real live security guard inside. The guard phones the house, and Dylan—or his personal assistant, Carol Snow, who lives in one of the various structures on the land—gives the go ahead. After weaving our way through the unusual but beautiful landscape—the rumor is that Dylan had a lot of the trees flown in when he built the place—we pull up in front of an unpretentious, ranch-style hacienda. A relaxed Bob Dylan, dressed in sweat pants and a flannel shirt, steps out to greet us.

'Hey, Breet. How ya doin'?'

The interior of the house is spread out comfortably, not overly decorated. It's in a kind of nouveau-country style, inviting and peaceful at the same time. Dylan offers us some tea. He's quit coffee for the time being, but it's up to me if I want some. He sits at the breakfast table, leans back in his chair, appraising me.

'Where'd you get them boots?' he asks, his eyebrows rising.

'Privilege,' I say.

'Privilege?' his forehead wrinkles.

I enjoy his reaction to one-word responses. For once he's on the receiving end.

'You ever heard of the Westside Pavilion?' I ask.

'Nope.'

I explain that Privilege is an expensive shoe store in this new shopping mall in West LA—they've got other stores in New York and London—and that the black-and-silver pair I'm wearing are a bargain at about a hundred bucks.

'I'm gonna get *me* a pair.'

I tell him these are women's boots, but I'll keep my eye open for him in the future. He suggests I take a walk around the property—to 'break 'em in'—while he and Ernie have their say.

I'd love to, I say, paraphrasing a line from *Rebel Without A Cause*—the scene where James Dean and Natalie Wood have been holed up in the mansion too long and decide to go out and 'explore.'

It's rained recently, so here I am tromping through the chaparral around Dylan's fourteen-acre backyard above the Pacific in my new boots, trying not to step in any mud. The scent of wild roses, rosemary, and sage makes me high. I pass by a huge, hand-dug swimming pool with a black bottom and rocks and trees and all kinds of cool shit growing in it.

The first structure I come to is a dilapidated wooden shed. The door's open, and I go in—well, I told him I was gonna explore. The floor is rotting, and there's all these old wooden steamer trunks inside, some of them open with clothes and costumes spilling out. I pick up a hat. It's Russian or German, with emblems and embroidery on it like it belonged to royalty. There's a fur coat molding on a hanger.

After a few suffocating minutes I step out into the bright light of the afternoon and continue my journey, eventually coming to a tall thicket of bamboo. It takes me a second to realize that this huge smooth tree trunk on the ground near the path is a bench. I lie on it, savoring the warmth of the sunshine on my face and chest and marveling at the considerable circumference on the stocks of bamboo. I feel as though the log I'm lying down on is pulling me into it, wrapping me up with invisible roots and holding me there, and it's a while before I can get up.

As the afternoon begins to pale, I find my way to the ocean side of the property, one of the only places where you can see the sea's blue-green gleam. A large hammock is stretched between two pines, and I spend time swinging on it, staring at the big blue and breathing in the heady salt air, wishing, hoping, praying I might never have to leave.

Working my way back toward the house, I come across a large wooden wagon, almost a cabin, and I climb in. The wood smells good, and there are windows cut out of the sides that frame the view. When I get back to the main house, Dylan will tell me it's an old circus wagon, but for now, I rest on the well-worn plank bottom and wonder if people feel this good when they meditate.

Ernie and Dylan are waiting for me. I tell Bob how much I love the property, about the shed with all the old clothes …

'Did you go through everything?' he asks, testing me.

'Yeah.' I admit it.

'I figured you would.'

… and the bamboo grove …

'The stocks are so big!'

'Them plants there's about a hundred years old,' he says. It's hard to believe I'm talking with the Poet Laureate of the universe. 'Ordered 'em up special when I moved in.'

… and the wagon …

'Where'd you get that ring?' He nods me toward him. Taking my hand, he holds it up close to his face for a better look. The warm feel of his breath on my skin paralyzes me.

It's a man's ring, old, rose gold, fourteen karat, very ornate, with a shell scroll detail, a ruby, and the Chinese style letters 'J.F.' I'd discovered it in Grace's jewelry box in Ernie's closet, and Ernie said I could have it. I wear it on my middle finger because I read somewhere that people who wear rings on unlikely fingers tend to have more power than those who don't.

'Ernie found it in the street,' I murmur. 'When he was a little boy.'

'Is that right?' Bob gazes up at me, still holding my hand. 'What's it stand for? Janet Feinstein?'

Ernie and I are out front in the Toyota, ready to leave. Dylan rests his elbows on my windowsill. Chin in his hands, he looks at me.

'You can come back, anytime.'

'Great,' Ernie says, joking. 'She'll be back tomorrow.'

When I go to my workout session on Monday morning, the party is the talk of the exercise studio.

'How come he's aging so badly?' the owner asks of Dylan.

'I don't know,' I say. And, at that time, I didn't. Now that I know him, he doesn't look that bad to me.

But Sandy, who'd spoken at length with Bob at the party, volunteers, 'After forty, you get the looks you deserve.'

Venice, California, 1986. The rumble of a motorcycle in the driveway. It's a Sunday, a wintery, but sunny beach day, and a disheveled Bob Dylan, clad in pale-gray hooded sweats and aviator sunglasses strikes an incongruous pose on his big black Harley Davidson—leather seat and saddle bags gleaming—as he dismounts in front of the pink concrete wall that encloses Ernie's cactus-filled yard. Ernie's been watching a football game in the bedroom, but he quickly rises to attention. Bob wants to take a stroll down the boardwalk, and naturally he can't do something like that alone.

The three of us shuffle speechlessly along the crowded beachfront, collars and hoods to the wind, catching only the occasional glimpse from those particularly well-attuned passersby. Back at the house, while Ernie loads up one of his hundred different CDs, Bob and I are standing at the kitchen counter, talking about the pros and cons of vinyl. Bob doesn't like the sound of CDs. 'Too clean,' he says, and I agree. It's then that I notice his body language is speaking volumes. We're next to each other, facing at right angles, and his hips are rocking nervously toward mine.

Ernie's return quickly breaks the spell, and after giving a brief but intent listen to Professor Longhair's *Rock 'N' Roll Gumbo* CD—'Who's this?' he wonders—and checking out the cover, Bob's outside, mounting his bike.

On Wednesday, Dylan calls. He wants to go see a movie called *Crossroads*, directed by Karla's across-the-street neighbor, Walter Hill. The film is playing in Marina del Rey, so Ernie and I are the logical escorts.

Offstage, Bob seems only to possess a few articles of clothing: black jeans, black motorcycle boots with two-inch heels to make him look taller, light gray sweats with the essential hood, a white T-shirt, and a black leather jacket. Invariably, he shows up wearing some permutation of those. This night, it's the hooded gray sweatshirt with the black jeans. We ride in Ernie's white early-80s Celica, which he has had chopped into a convertible years before Toyota will come up with the idea.

The theater is nearly empty, and if you've seen the film, you know why. We find three seats near the front in the center. Bob sits down in the middle. As we wait for the curtain to rise, Ernie runs out to get popcorn and drinks.

Bob's leaning my way, and I can feel the heat rolling off him.

'Soooo,' he says, drawing out the word as if he's singing one of his archetypal nasal lyrics. 'What do you see in Ernie?'

His question catches me off guard. Is Bob Dylan coming on to me? I stammer. 'Oh, Bob,' I wind up gushing, 'I think Ernie's the smartest guy I've ever known.'

'Smart!' Dylan grunts. He sucks his teeth, loudly. '*Ernie?*' His heated dark features darken even more.

But Ernie's your right hand man, I'm thinking. *Why are you acting like this? You wouldn't hire a dummy to do your best work.* Flushed with confusion, I try to justify my remarks, but Dylan's disappeared into his disappointment.

As Ernie returns with snacks, Bob straightens up in his seat and prepares to watch the flick. The movie is about a classically trained guitarist (played by the asexual Ralph Macchio) who goes to the Deep South in search of some mythical lost manuscripts by the legendary bluesman Robert Johnson. In a subplot, his blues-oriented road companion sells his soul to the devil. I'm so concerned that I've offended Bob, and that our budding friendship has been nipped irreparably, I can barely focus on the screen.

Before the end credits finish rolling, Bob, Ernie, and I have dropped into a nondescript mall deli for a bite to eat. Despite my worry, I'm curious as to how someone as famous as the great Bob Dylan is able to go anywhere at all without being recognized, let alone mobbed, yet here we are seated in this gaudy plastic bourgeois dump. It's at this moment that I pick up my first lesson in celebrity protocol: The 'celeb' sits with his back to the entrance. Who knew? This works out well for me, because I prefer to see and be seen.

Ernie orders up some pastrami and fries, and the three of us eat quietly, undisturbed. Bob seems to have reverted to a more neutral position in my regard—amicable but disinterested. For days afterwards, I weigh everything Ernie does, and it all seems pretty stupid to me.

Another sunny day in Malibu. Carole Childs is fixing lunch. Sam Shepard is interviewing Dylan on the porch. I'm outside, nearby, fooling around with my camera, but Dylan ducks or turns away every time I focus in his direction. After the playwright leaves, Dylan tells me that the Indians say each picture takes away a little bit of your soul.

You must have hardly anything left, I think.

I'm not sure, but this may have been one of the times Bob and I talked about real estate. Bob owned quite a few properties all over the country, but he bemoaned the fact that over the years his managers had talked him out of some of the more charismatic opportunities in favor of safer choices. He describes in detail a soulful spread in

Trancas that he still regrets having let go, adding that he doesn't want that kind of thing to happen again.

At the time, I was representing a client who had an eye for Hollywood landmarks in decay. My guy would purchase the structures at near giveaway prices, then spend his investors' millions refurbishing them to their original glory before selling them at a hefty profit. One such building was the old art deco Bekins Storage facility on Highland Avenue in Hollywood. I'd gone to see it with my client, and I was sure it would make an incredible loft conversion. There was even a speakeasy with the original red-cushioned booths on the top floor, and the thought was to turn it into a private club.

Dylan makes it clear he'd be interested in investing in the property. All I have to do is set up an appointment.

One night, Ernie and I are up at the Malibu house, and I ask Bob if I can see his artwork. One of his charcoals is going to be sold at an auction to raise money for the Live Aid Foundation. He walks me into the kitchen, of all places, where a work in progress rests on an easel near the sink.

It's a man's face. I don't know whose. But, unlike the simple drawings that had just appeared in *Lyrics 1962–1985*, here Bob's attention to detail and bold strokes have exaggerated the fellow's features in such a way that even though I don't recognize the guy, it's like he's right here in the room.

'Wow!' I say. 'You're really good!' Then, in a bold move of my own, I reach out and fondly squeeze Dylan's arm. To my horror, his spongy flesh feels lifeless. Dead. Like there's nobody there.

Mid-April 1986. The newspapers report that Bob has flown to New York with Julian Lennon, John Lennon's eldest son, but I think it was just coincidence that they were on the same plane. Since hooking up with Elliot, both the bewildered Julian and the enigmatic Sean Lennon have been regular guests at Ernie's house. Later, Julian will forward an autographed photo of Bob and him taken at the airport with the intention that it be delivered to Bob. But like so many of the items sent to Dylan from all over the world, it gets lost in the shuffle. I retrieve it from obscurity at one point, and report its existence to Bob.

'You keep it,' he says.

April 1986. Dylan is recording at Skyline in Topanga Canyon, which requires Ernie's presence at several all-night sessions with Al Kooper, Ira Ingber, T Bone Burnett, and Steve Douglas, among others. One of the mornings, Ernie tells me, Dylan requests dinner at 4am. Ernie's thinking pizza—something easy, since he's the one who'll have to go fetch it, and after all, it is the middle of the night. He'll just drop down Topanga Canyon Boulevard into the Valley a mere hour-plus sojourn.

'What are you in the mood for?' he makes the mistake of asking.

'Sure could go for some chicken and vegetables,' Bob says.

Chicken and vegetables at four in the morning? Ernie winds up in Santa Monica at Zucky's Delicatessen killing an extra forty minutes waiting for the chicken to cook.

For weeks after, whenever the subject of getting or cooking something to eat comes up around the house, either Ernie or I will invariably volunteer, with a laugh, 'Sure could go for some chicken and vegetables.'

One morning, at dawn, I wake up, and Ernie has brought home the heralded session saxophonist Steve Douglas. I hear the two of them say something about a song called 'Unchain My Heart.'

'What about it?' I ask sleepily from the kitchen counter, where I'm drinking a freshly brewed espresso.

'We're rehearsing it,' Steve tells me. Boy is he adorable.

'You're kidding,' I say. 'My uncle wrote that song!'

'Cool,' Douglas says. 'You should tell Bob.'

Ernie doesn't believe it, though, so that day, I have to enlist the help of my exercise pal, Sandy, who has some way of looking it up. I don't know why I didn't just call my aunt in New York. The song is sometimes credited to Bobby Sharp and Freddy James, the latter of which is one of the names my uncle, by marriage, wrote under. Both my mother and my aunt had used the last name James at various times—there is even a race horse named Maggie James after my aunt—but mostly, my uncle is known as the big-band leader Teddy Powell, and somewhere I still had the letter my aunt had sent me the day Teddy, Bobby, and Ray Charles had sat around the baby grand in the foyer of my aunt and uncle's apartment in New York working on the song.

Even after Sandy brings me the evidence, Ernie is still skeptical.

May 15 1986. Dylan lands the role of an aging rock icon in Welsh director Richard Marquand's *Hearts Of Fire*. Marquand, best known for the Star Wars film *Return Of The Jedi*, is now riding the success of his wildly popular film, *Jagged Edge*. Shooting is scheduled for the fall: Seven weeks in London and another four or five weeks in a location to be announced. Bob is contracted to write six songs for the film.

Steve Douglas's girlfriend, Jeanette, comes to LA, and Ernie and I and she and Steve hang out together. She's wild and blonde with huge breasts and has written a book of poetry. Rumor has it that, for Steve's fortieth birthday, she bought him a blow job. Steve's got a congenital heart problem, Ernie reminds me, so he's not going to be with us forever. The implication is that this woman Jeanette—who I like very much—really has her shit together.

Ernie suggests we have a four-way encounter with the couple, but it sounds too contrived for me. Planning it would take all the fun out of it, I say. The three of them come on to me one night in Ernie's hot tub, massaging my body while I float nakedly on my back. As good as it feels, I freak out, knowing in my heart that it's a setup by Ernie.

During this time, we're also hanging out with Al Kooper and his talented live-in girlfriend, Vivien. Kooper lives in a so-so high crime-rate neighborhood just North of Melrose in the front half of a duplex. He doesn't even own a car. But he's got an unbelievable record collection, and one night we go through all the albums, trying to count how many records Bob Dylan's made to date. We're all astounded to discover it's somewhere around thirty!

Kooper and I have this bond because we're like the only two white people in the world who know who Sex-Mouth Hunter is. I recount to him how my second husband was a good friend of the saxophonist Monk Higgins, and how one night Monk and his wife Virginia had talked my ex and me into taking a midnight ride down to see Bobby Blue Bland at a club called the Five Torches, in a part of LA most people don't even know exists. Naturally, my ex and I are the only white people in the crowd, and when we enter this hotbed of calamity, a comedian named Sex-Mouth Hunter is onstage, where he remains for about three and a half hours, telling the foulest, filthiest jokes I've ever heard to the most adoring, mostly middle-class, but riotous black crowd. Talk about cultural differences! His callback line is 'What's it smell like?'

I need a police escort to use the ladies room, and when I return to our table and report that the cops have told me that a lot of people in the place are packing heat, the sweet, mild-mannered, light-skinned Virginia, Monk's wife, opens her handbag to reveal a pistol.

'Don't leave home without it,' she winks.

Two-thirty comes and goes, but the booze will still be flowing at four when Blue Bland finally hits the stage.

Kooper does a great imitation of my uncle, Teddy Powell, who he remembers meeting at the Brill Building in New York City—before his own song, 'This Diamond Ring,' was a hit—when he was still just a kid knocking on doors, trying to break into the music business. He also tells the best 'meeting Bob Dylan story' ever, which is documented superbly in this very cool book he's written, *Backstage Passes: Rock 'n' Roll Life In The Sixties*. Invited to listen in on one of the *Highway 61 Revisited* recording sessions, he'd planned to pass himself off as one of the musicians—namely a guitarist, since that's his instrument—until Chicago blues superstar Mike Bloomfield arrives, shaking snow off a Stratocaster, with Dylan in tow. At that point, Kooper, who won't even be able to hear himself play, jumps in on organ.

During the mixing, Dylan advises the engineer to pump up the volume on the organ.

'Hey, man, that guy's not an organ player,' the cat who'd invited Kooper along in the first place protests.

'Turn it up, anyway,' Dylan commands.

The song is 'Like A Rolling Stone,' and the rest, as they say, is history.

I get a copy of Al's book at Book Soup on Sunset and he autographs it:

To Britta from Sex-Mouth Kooper

Then, knowing that I am an aspiring writer, he adds:

I hope your book does better than this one.

Kooper and his girlfriend are writing country songs, and I play them mine. In fact, the last known copy of 'A Man I Didn't Know' will be left at Kooper's apartment. Kooper has always wanted to produce Karla Bonoff. I make the introduction, but to little avail. He also confides that he's always wanted to produce Dylan.

Invariably, when Ernie and I go over there, Al and his girlfriend share some of their songs and writing with us. When one of his songs is used on TV—I think it was in Michael Mann's *Crime Story*—we have a listening party in his bedroom, 'cause that's where the television is.

I adore Al. He's Mr. Charisma, super-smart and hilarious, with a deeply dark wit. Some nights when we're over there, he pulls out his guitar, and the four of us wind up singing Bob Dylan songs. We shudder to think what Bob would say, if only he knew.

May 24 1986. Bob Dylan's forty-fifth birthday. There's a party out at the Malibu house. It's three in the afternoon, and Carole's cooked and cleaned and ordered a cake: lemon with raspberry filling, frilly frosting, like it's meant for a Sweet Sixteen. Ernie and I show up with one of those picture cakes like he got for Louie, only this cake is three feet by five feet long, chocolate-chocolate chip, with a full-body portrait of Dylan wearing jeans and cowboy boots. Carole's annoyed because she wants the guests to eat the cake she bought.

Louie is there with his wife—a petite Moroccan chick who's also an orthodox Jew—as are Harry Dean Stanton and Bob's personal assistant, Carol Snow. Jakob, Dylan's youngest son, is there, too, as is Samuel, his middle son. His oldest son, Jesse, is enrolled in college as a film student in New York, so he can't attend. Earlier in the day, Dennis from Off The Wall has delivered a restored coke machine to the house—Bob's gift from Louie.

Dylan sits out by the pen that encloses his two nearly two-hundred-pound mastiffs, Brutus and Baby, and their litter of puppies. It's almost as though he's in the doghouse. Lunch is getting cold. Carole sends me outside to retrieve him. I tell Bob that lunch is ready, but he doesn't even twitch. He's pushing a stick in the dirt, looking down. I've always hated it when I'm in a beautiful setting like this and I'm forced to be indoors, and I wonder what the point of being in Malibu on a sunny day is, if we can't have lunch on the deck. I join him in the sunshine.

'What's up?' I say, though it's fairly obvious he and Carole aren't getting along. When he doesn't respond, I blurt out, 'You know that song, "Unchain My Heart?" My uncle wrote it!'

A spark of life dances in Bob's eyes. 'No kiddin'?'

I mention a few other songs my uncle wrote, like the sequel to 'Unchain My Heart' called 'Don't Set Me Free,' and the Gene Autry song 'Take Me Back To My Boots And Saddles.'

'Huh.'

'So anyway, I was thinkin' …' I begin. It's a habit of mine to take on the accent of the people I'm with. If they're from the South, I'm from the South. If they're black, I'm black. If they're Bob Dylan … 'Maybe you could record "Unchain My Heart." It'd be good for my inheritance.'

'It would, huh?' he nods, mulling it over. 'Well, it's not gonna make it onto *this* album.' A sly smile curls the corners of his lips. 'The next one, though …'

'Food's on the table!' Carole is at her wit's end, standing on the

SEEING THE REAL YOU AT LAST

porch, yelling to Bob in her thick New York accent—shades of my
parents, when I was growing up, except for the dialect. So normally
abnormal. So black-and-white movie from the 1950s. So *not* how I
picture Bob Dylan's life.

The tin man in blue jeans pulls himself up, and the two of us
walk toward the house together.

'She doesn't understand me,' he says.

Barbecued chicken, tri-tip roast, artichokes, pasta. Afterwards, Harry
Dean strolls into the dining room with a fine old guitar and sings a
heartbreaking version of 'Las Mananitas,' but soon we are all joining
him in a boisterous rendition of 'Happy Birthday.'

I've brought Bob three presents, which has always been my style.
I like to watch the anticipation grow while the people I adore open
them. The first is a card I've made for him using a photograph I took
of the *Biograph* billboard at Tower Records on Sunset. He told me
he's never seen it. He loves it. The second is a vintage shirt I bought
for myself in the early 70s at an Aardvark in Northern California.
It's a bright blue bowling shirt from Bob Dillon's Mobil station in
Emeryville that I've had in my collection for years. He really loves
this. He jumps up from the table, runs in the other room, trying
it on, comes back modeling it for us all—'Hey Louie, look at the
back of this shirt!' The last gift—'You already gave me a present,'
he drawls, in protest—is a series of Edwardian masks from the New
York Metropolitan Museum of Art that he's admired at Ernie's when
I've taken mine over there; reproductions from Madame Tussaud's
collection. He loves them.

Carole sets her now controversial birthday cake—the one *she*
bought—in front of Bob, and someone pops a bottle of champagne.
The prissy yellow slices are passed around on plates after Dylan cuts

them. Most people are lusting after Ernie's cake in the other room, but everyone, including Bob, is afraid to say so. When Dylan teases his assistant, Carol Snow, with a twisted joke about how *she* should be cutting the cake, seein' as how she does everything else for him—how she's slacking off now, not working hard enough for him—she picks up a piece of cake with her fingers, walks from her side of the table to Bob's, and mushes it in his face. People think this is pretty funny, until Bob gets up with a bigger slice and slaps it over her nose … then everyone, except for poor Carole, is hysterical. Things return to normal for a split second, everyone trying to keep from cracking up, until Bob swoops up a still larger slice, circles the table like an Indian on the warpath, then plasters the gooey dessert in my face. This is really crazy-making, 'cause I'd made such an effort with my hair and makeup that I wouldn't even let Ernie put the top down on the car on the drive up. To the horror of the onlookers, most notably Ernie, I snatch a still bigger piece of cake and chase Bob around the table until I'm able to cream him with it.

As I retake my seat, Bob picks up the champagne bottle and pours it over my head. Pretending enough's enough, he sits down at his place. I steal the bottle, pour some champagne over him, then empty the rest of it over Carole's head. Carole does not find this humorous in the least, but Bob thinks it is. She sits there without saying a word until her negative vibes drive most of the guests from the room. Looking like a couple of refugees from the Rolling Thunder Revue—Bob and I wear our cake masks for the rest of the party.

Before dark, most of the group, including Ernie and I, take a walk up the property through the rose garden to see Bob's chickens. It's here that I'm brave enough to use my Polaroid to snap a picture of Dylan posing in one of the museum masks, having up to now gone pretty far out of my way to respect his privacy. His inimitable gaze peers out through the eyeholes under a towering feather headdress made of paper: Dylan, the Indian Chief.

Louie's wife, meanwhile, is snapping away like a Japanese businessman at Disneyland. She takes me aside. 'Do you have any idea how much these pictures are worth?'

Harry Dean and I are talking in the living room. I've always been a big fan, but I'm shocked at how *old* he looks. Turns out he is old. I tell him I didn't know he was a musician. He tells me he's going to be playing at McCabe's if I want to come. I say I'll mention it to Ernie, and he says, 'Oh, you're with Ernie?'

Carole has withdrawn. The boys have sneaked some champagne and are running wild through the house. By the time Ernie and I take off, huge chunks of chocolate cake are missing from the head of Bob Dylan's pastry portrait.

May 30 1986. Prince is at the Wiltern Theater, as part of what will later be dubbed his Hit n' Run Tour, since most of the shows are announced just days or hours before the actual concert takes place. Carole gets four passes, but Bob doesn't want to go. Ernie and I escort her, and while she's really getting off on the music, I spend most of the show mingling in the foyer with a growing chattering mob that prefers being outside of the music hall. Afterwards, backstage, I'm introduced to Neil Young, whose sorrowful dark-eyed gaze threatens to suck the very life out of me.

June 1986. Dylan decides to dump most of the tracks he's been recording at Skyline and use various session tapes he's accumulated over the last few years for his next album. In an interview with *Rolling Stone*, he's quoted as saying that the new album doesn't really have a theme or purpose. At some point, word gets out that he's recruiting a children's choir to sing back up on one of the tracks—a Kris Kristofferson cover called 'They Killed Him.' My big real estate client, the one with the eye for cool buildings, has a daughter, and he begs me to let him bring her to the session. I get the go ahead from Ernie, but because of a work conflict I can't be there myself. At the recording studio, the mother of the child takes so many photos that her camera has to be confiscated. The little girl, behaving like a spoiled brat, cries and causes such a fuss that she's dismissed from the session, but her name will still appear on the album.

Ernie is pissed. I'm totally distraught when I hear the reports and apologize profusely to Bob, but he doesn't seem to hold it against me. In fact, he's now looking for an album cover, sort of a '50s pulp detective magazine thing, and when I mention that I have this friend, Tony Goodstone, with an incredible collection of old movie posters, Bob says, 'Get him up here. Tomorrow.'

Tony is this heavyset actor, writer, and antiques restorer—he owns a '58 Fairlane convertible with a *working* retractable top—who I met at a play in North Hollywood. He has literally written the book on pulp art: a substantive tome entitled *The Pulps: Fifty Years Of Pop Culture*. His best friend is screenwriter Terry Southern, who wrote the scripts for *Dr. Strangelove*, *Barbarella*, and *Easy Rider*. Tony had offered to read my novel, *Detours*, which opens with a quote from the *Maltese Falcon* about 'the stuff that dreams are made of,' and the first time he came to my house, he showed up carrying a replica of the famed fake falcon wrapped in newspaper and string, just like in the movie.

Bob and Tony hit it off right away—which is one of life's great thrills for Tony—and at a meeting that takes place on Bob's deck in Malibu, the three of us sit at the round redwood table, poring over possible photographs for the album cover.

'That's the one!' Bob says, picking out a pulpy piece from the 40s depicting a sarong-clad woman bashing an urn over some guy's head.

'I'll check out the rights,' Tony volunteers.

'Let 'em sue us,' Dylan says.

June 5 1986. I'm on assignment, thanks to Ernie, who's tied up at work. Will I please go to this fancy hotel on Sunset Boulevard and pick up renowned concert promoter Bill Graham and his assistant, who are in LA from the Bay Area for tomorrow night's Amnesty International Benefit at the Inglewood Forum, and drive them downtown to the Pantry, where Ernie will meet us and the four of us will have dinner. Graham, who had been responsible for the success of both Fillmores, East and West, as well as the Winterland Ballroom, had helped further the careers of Janis Joplin, Rod Stewart, and even The Rolling Stones.

Despite his reputation for being a moody perfectionist, Bill and his assistant are extremely down to earth. I call them from the lobby, and they meet me outside the front door, where my car is waiting. A beautifully polished bus is also parked—engines running—in front of the hotel, and Graham tells me this is Neil Young's bus, and that unlike most rockers who rent their transportation, this is actually a bus that Neil Young owns—that he's fixed it up really cool, and that other rockers rent it from him.

It's a relatively clear night in LA. The city lights are shimmering, even if the stars aren't. There's a long line of people waiting outside the Pantry, but Ernie pulls some strings, and within seconds the four of us are settled at a table. I've never been here before, but it is well known for being the best home-cooking joint in the world. The atmosphere is surprisingly devoid of character, but Bill, who was raised in the old world, has some favorite dish here—like the goulash or something—that he always taps into when he's in LA, and that's why we're here.

Ernie and Bill Graham first met when Ernie started his poster business in the 70s, straight out of high school. Ernie's accounts were mostly rock'n'roll bands, the venues they played, and the concert promoters. Ernie would print the posters for his clients, then crews of guys would come in and wild-post them all over the country. When, during Graham's stint promoting the Rolling Thunder Revue, it became evident that the ever-booked Dylan needed someone sharp to handle his business on the road, Graham recommended Ernie, the enterprising young man whose ambition and execution of ideas he'd come most to admire.

Tall, dark, and Eastern European, the charming Graham entertains us all over dinner with a story about how he avoided a speeding ticket once by signing the much shorter Omar Sharif's autograph—the cop couldn't tell how tall he was because he was sitting down. When I press him, he predicts that Peter Gabriel will be the next huge sensation to rock the music scene.

Dylan and The Heartbreakers are scheduled to perform three songs at the benefit the next night, including Bob's new single, 'Band Of The Hand.' It's the hottest ticket in town, and even Graham's office will prove incapable of getting me a pass for the event.

We sip from our cups of lukewarm coffee.

'On the right night,' Graham reminisces, 'Bob Dylan is the greatest rock'n'roller that ever lived.'

CHAPTER 4

Tangled up in blue

June 9 1986. Ernie is in San Diego with Bob, where the True Confessions tour picks up once again at the Sports Arena, and 'Unchain My Heart' makes its debut.

I'm going through some serious changes. After months of negotiations, the Bekins deal has fallen through before I can even get a chance to show the building to Bob. In fact, I'm beginning to view real estate as a complete distraction from my real goals in life, but the question remains: how am I going to support myself? I've been working on this script called *Johnny Paradise* that friends tell me is pretty good, but I've yet to land an agent. In the meantime, I'm living like a movie star, going to all the best restaurants, but feeling a deep sense of spiritual unrest.

I drive up to a cabin I know of in Inverness, California, overlooking the Tomales Bay, to see if I can get my head on straight. I usually go up there with my best girlfriend from my Berkeley days—an amazing artist and one of the art directors at Fantasy Records—but this time I want to be alone. I've got to decide what I want to do about Ernie, but it's so complicated now. I'm in love with his family. I'm in love with our lifestyle. I'm in love with the idea of being in love. And then there's Bob.

A female guru of adult children of dysfunctional families will tell me, 'You can't get a hamburger at a hardware store, and if you keep trying, you're crazy.' It's unrealistic to think you can get all your needs met through one person, she says, but if you can get most of them met and fill in the rest from elsewhere, a relationship can continue to function at a fairly high level and even be a happy one. With the emotional support of Elliot and the intellectual stimulation of Bob, on many levels, my relationship with Ernie was working, even flourishing.

After a few days of solitude, I walk down to the pay phone in the sleepy little beachfront town to check in with Ernie. His first words out of the box are, 'What's your middle name?'

'Lilli. Why?'

'Lilli. OK. I'm writing that down.'

'How come?'

'Bob wants to put your name on the album.'

'What?' My heart is beating in my throat. 'Why would he do *that*?'

'He says you inspired him,' Ernie reports, unfazed.

I, on the other hand, am beyond fazed. For days afterwards, I think I've dreamed this entire conversation.

Dylan plays Reno, then Sacramento. I meet up with the tour in Berkeley. We stay at the legendary Claremont Hotel while Dylan performs two shows at the Greek Theater with Tom Petty. I have my dog with me, and that's when I learn the second rule of celebrity: the celeb does what the celeb wants. For three days and two nights, because I'm in Bob Dylan's entourage, I'm allowed to walk my eighty pound Samoyed right through the lushly carpeted-lobby of the prestigious hotel, into the elevator, and up to my room, without management saying a word.

Thrillingly for me, the first night's set includes 'Unchain My Heart.' Seeing Dylan perform at my alma mater, however, is a bit depressing. Tom Petty's set comes up first, and many members of the largely student-body audience depart before Bob even takes the stage. Has the Berkeley student population become less intellectual? Is Tom Petty—whose music and lyrics I enjoy, but come on, now—really the voice of a new generation? Or has Bob Dylan become obsolete?

June 16 1986. After a day off at his home in Malibu, Dylan is playing the Pacific Amphitheater in Costa Mesa before resuming the final leg of the True Confessions Tour, which will take him and Ernie across the country by bus and back again, with a return date of August 6th. I don't remember the specifics of the logistics, but I do know that, in typical Bob Dylan form, we are set to leave Malibu around two, for a four o'clock soundcheck, and he's running late. All I know is, somewhere around 5:30pm, Bob, Elliot, and Carole are in the back of my vintage Mercedes; I'm in the front and Ernie's driving, going eighty-five miles an hour down the left shoulder of the 405 freeway past the rush hour, bumper-to-bumper traffic. It's questionable whether or not Dylan will even make the show, but he does. And we don't even get a ticket!

When we arrive at the hotel in Newport Beach, Ernie runs off to make sure the buses are all in order. Sometimes there can be as many as four required for a gig like this, with another band as big and as important as the Heartbreakers, and of course Bob's backup singers require their own bus, not to mention the fact that, for this trip, Dylan's decided to bring along Brutus and Baby.

The second and last night of the Costa Mesa gig, Carole, Elliot Mintz, Ernie, and I, as well as Elliot Roberts and a few others, ride from the hotel to the Amphitheater with Bob on Bob's bus. Elliot

Roberts owns Lookout Management, the biggest rock'n'roll tour-management company in the country, with clients like Joni Mitchell, Neil Young, and, more recently, Tracy Chapman. He's been Bob's on-again, off-again manager for years. He's cute and funny, and definitely a Dylan fan, though he's had first-hand experience with Bob's bad side, and is now a bit skittish because of it.

Much as Bob can pull a room, to use Ernie's phrase, on this particular night he's pulled the entire bus. Everyone rides like a vacant spirit, sitting quietly while Bob invites only Elliot Mintz to join him in his private quarters in the rear of the vehicle.

After the show, Ernie and I pick Bob up in my car and drive him to the hotel. It can be the best show or the worst show ever, but when it's over, Bob will remain unruffled. Tonight's was a good show. Ernie's behind the wheel, and I'm in the back seat. Dylan's in the passenger seat, smoking cigarettes and going over some of the finer details of the upcoming tour. I hate cigarettes and Dylan is the only person who has ever been allowed to smoke in my car. Afterwards, I will salvage the two Kool cigarette butts and keep them as souvenirs.

When we pull up in front of the hotel, all the buses are lined up, doors open, engines running, waiting, and I feel a tug of sadness that soon everyone will be taking off without me. But I have my own stuff to take care of, I remind myself, and it's not like anyone's asked me to come along.

As Ernie turns off the key, Dylan turns around in the seat to look at me.

'How come *you're* not goin' with us?

When Bob gets out of the car, Ernie shows me the proposed list of names that will go on the sleeve of Dylan's still untitled new album: Tony Goodstone (you remember, he came up with the cover), Norm's

Guitars (self-explanatory), Britt Bacon (the engineer at Skyline), Susie Pullen (Bob's dresser), Tony Dimitriades (Lookout Management), Jeff Rosen (among other things, he's Dylan's archivist in New York, and was heavily involved in *Biograph*), Jeff Jones (a journalist and possible subject of 'Ballad Of A Thin Man'), Sid Fernandez (pitcher for the New York Mets), Steve Howe (a Dodgers pitcher), Rita and Britta (that's me), Harry Dean Stanton, Frank Zappa (how'd *he* get on here?), Ernie Blum (that's Ernie), and Sam Shepard (who co-wrote 'Brownsville Girl,' by far the best song on the album).

'Who's Rita?' I ask.

'My dog,' Ernie says. 'Bob was looking for a rhyme.'

There's a lot of last-minute commotion as the buses are checked and re-checked, loaded and unloaded. Bob tells someone to make sure he hasn't forgotten the shirt I gave him for his birthday. By this show, I've been told, he never goes anywhere without it.

It's late. Getting close to midnight. Dylan and I are toking on a roach in front of the Four Seasons' opulent fountain in Costa Mesa, talking to Elliot Mintz. The subject of Bob's Madison Square Garden gig comes up, and he suggests Elliot and I fly in for the show.

'When is it?' I ask.

'July 16th,' Bob says.

'July 16th?' I can't believe it. 'That's my birthday!'

'Well, then you should come, for sure,' Bob says. 'You and Ernie can stay at my place in the Trump Tower, and I'll give Ernie the week off.'

'Will you play "Unchain My Heart"?'

'Sure. And "Happy Birthday," too.'

A few seconds later, Bob's dogs have gotten loose, and he takes off chasing them.

'Let dogs run free ...' I say in parting as he collars the first one, and I regret this comment for days. Still, as I'll come to discover, it's hard to say anything at all that Dylan hasn't already said.

When Ernie calls from the road, I tell him Dylan's offer regarding my birthday.

'If I have the week off,' he says, 'I'll be damned if I'm gonna spend it around Bob!'

Ouch.

A couple of days later, when I mention to Elliot how miserable I am that Ernie flatly refuses to go to New York for my birthday, Elliot tries to cheer me up.

'You know what Bob said to me the other night on the bus when the two of us were alone in the back?' he asks.

'No,' I sulk.

'He said, There's only one person out there in the front of this bus that I trust. Do you know who it is? So I thought about it for a second and I said, Britta. And Bob said, That's right.'

Bob Dylan trusts *me*? Now, I'm elated ... ex-hil-a-rated!

July 1986. The word is out. Bob's in a bad mood when he arrives in New York. Ernie says the crew is complaining.

I talk to Bob on the phone.

'Why aren't you comin'?' he wants to know.

'Ernie insists on taking me to Fiji,' I tell him.

'Ernie!' Bob steams. 'For your birthday? Let me talk to him.'

Fiji's a nine-hour flight from LA and about a hundred million light years from New York. It's tropical and primitive and exotic, and you can scuba dive, and it wouldn't have been so bad, except that, while

Bob Dylan is performing 'Unchain My Heart' at the Garden, and could have been singing 'Happy Birthday' to me like he did for Susie Pullen in Missouri, Ernie, whose idea it was to come to the island in the first place, decides his printing business back home has to be taken care of from halfway around the globe and spends 75 percent of his vacation time on the telephone.

I wind up standing around the post office—the only place you can go to make a long distance call—waiting hours on end for the antiquated phone system to connect him. I'm beside myself. I'm supposed to be in paradise with Mr. Right, but my heart is in New York City.

Later, in certain circles, I will impress people by telling them I've been to Fiji, but the opportunity to mention casually in polite conversation that Bob Dylan once wished me a happy birthday from the stage at Madison Square Garden is lost forever.

August 1986. Karla is asked to perform at the Hiroshima Peace Concert in Japan, and she invites me along. But I don't want to go. It's an eight-day deal, and one of those days is August 3rd, when Dylan is set to do a show at the Inglewood Forum, the last LA date of the True Confessions Tour, and Al Kooper has sworn to me that he's going to join Bob onstage to play organ on 'Like A Rolling Stone.'

'What, are you crazy?' Ernie asks from the road.

Maybe, not crazy exactly, I begin to think, *but perhaps a little obsessed.*

It's one of those two-thousand-degree days in LA, and I'm wearing this skimpy gray-knit minidress—a model friend of mine gave it to me—and a pair of red three-inch high heels when I walk into Hollywood Music on Vine to talk to the promoter of the Hiroshima

Peace Concert about going to Japan. He's a short, cherubic Japanese guy with an eye for the ladies. His English is broken.

'Did Karla tell you, this really like two tours?' he asks.

'Uh, no.'

'Yes. We take opportunity show good friend Japan. So you can go with musicians to Hiroshima for many days rehearsal, or you can come with friend and us and stay in authentic Japanese hotels, visit palaces, go to Kyoto, Miyajima Island and then to Hiroshima Peace Concert at end.' He picks up the phone. 'I call Karla for you, and you decide.'

LAX is swarming with people ready to fly to Tokyo. The 'special friend' of the tour turns out to be former baseball player Reggie Jackson, who is being courted to play in Japan, and has brought along his entire family. While Karla rehearses with Eagles songwriter J.D. Souther, James Taylor percussionist Russ Kunkel, and folk-rock hero Graham Nash, in Hiroshima, I will ride the bullet train, visit shrines, dip in public baths, wear kimonos to elaborate feasts, and hike on Miyajima, a picturesque little island, where wild monkeys run rampant, and the deer come up and eat out of your hand. At an outdoor festival, I convince an ice-cream vendor to sell me this three-foot tall plastic vanilla cone that lights up, so I can bring it home as a present for Ernie. By the time my tour hooks up with Karla's at the concert, I feel like a new me.

It's midnight, and the show is in progress, with more than fifteen thousand cheering people in the crowd. Karla, who is a big star in Japan, will not be going on until four in the morning, so most of my group takes a nap. By the time we awaken, Graham and J.D. and Karla are performing in the darkness, separately and together. One of my life's great joys will be seeing my good friend, looking beautiful at the grand piano, in front of this huge enthusiastic crowd, singing 'Someone To Lay Down Beside Me,' as the red Japanese sun comes up behind the stage.

That night, the promoter throws the going away party of all going away parties for the visiting musicians. I sit shoeless on the floor at this long wooden table with Karla, Graham, J.D., Russ, the promoters, and this cool New Zealand band called the Herbs, drinking barrels of Sake, talking and laughing and getting drunk out of our minds as one exotic dinner course after another is served.

By the time I return to LA, *Knocked Out Loaded*, Dylan's latest album, has been released into the record stores, and the cover art looks amazing. Ernie hands me a copy.

'Great title!' I say.

'Yeah, well, I know where he got it.'

'What do you mean?'

Ernie cues up the 'Junco Partner' cut from the Professor Longhair CD, and, sure enough, there it is.

Oh, down the road came a Junco Partner
Boy, he was loaded as he can be
The poor man is knocked out, knocked out loaded
And he's wobblin' all over the street ...

I slip the record out to look at the sleeve. To my shock, the short list of 'Special Thanks' has been expanded absurdly to a total of 121 names, including Zucky's—the Santa Monica deli that packed his chicken and vegetables into a takeout box at dawn—Jack Nicholson, and 'Gal Shaped Just Like A Frog.' Even Marty Feldman, Bob's accountant, is on there.

'What happened?' I yelp.

'Bob thought the short list might get him in trouble.'

Debbie Gold—a really cool, really smart girl who's been in and around the music business for years—drops by, and she's furious that with all the people Bob mentioned, he left her name off the album. 'It was my idea to introduce him to the Heartbreakers!' she moans, nursing her own broken heart. But she knows that bringing her fury up to Bob will only make matters worse.

It's an hour or so before I realize that Ernie's had his own name taken off the list and replaced with that of his deceased wife's. I have no problem whatsoever bringing my fury up to him.

When *Knocked Out Loaded* is reviewed badly, the scuttlebutt among Dylan's inner circle is that Bob is angry at Columbia for failing to adequately promote *Empire Burlesque*, which he considers one of his best later efforts, so he is just going to stiff them with one lousy record after another until his contract is up.

August 1986. Bob's in England shooting *Hearts Of Fire*. Ernie doesn't go with him; he's too busy with his own business, and Bob doesn't think it's necessary. Most days, I lock myself in my apartment in hopes of completing my screenplay.

'Tell me your fantasies,' Ernie asks, his dark side pressuring me every time we make love. 'Which ones of my friends are you hot for?'

September 1986. It's our one-year anniversary. Ernie cooks my favorite dinner—veal chops from Hugo's—and presents me with a dazzling rhinestone cuff from Off The Wall. It's the kind of costume jewelry that a glamorous movie star would wear to foil a thief. Elliot is there, and it's a perfect evening.

October 1986. Production of *Hearts Of Fire* moves to Ontario, Canada, where Ernie rents a house for Dylan. Problems arise, I'm told, when Carole wants to join him, since Bob is occupied with another woman.

November 1986. My best girlfriend from Berkeley—the one who works for Fantasy Records—has scored a gig working on the Fantasy Films production of *The Unbearable Lightness Of Being*. She's been living in Paris for several months, and it is decided that I will join her there. Then, at Christmas time, Ernie will meet me in Venice, Italy, where we will proceed to tour the country together in celebration of the holidays. I have to apply for a special visa in order to fly into France, because there have been recent threats of terrorism there, as well as several bombings.

Paris is incredible in the wintertime. Can it really be the freezing temperatures and wind-driven rain that keeps the tourists away? The city's beauty seems best captured in its starkness. Each afternoon, while my girlfriend finishes up at work, I view the sunset from a different vantage: Sacre Coeur, Le Tour Eiffel, Notre Dame. In the evenings, we dine at fabulous restaurants recommended by the film's affable producer, Saul Zaentz. My friend has an apartment in the Second Arrondissement, and in the mornings we sip coffee on the balcony or wander through the open markets in search of the perfect baguette.

While she's at work I explore the numerous museums, designer clothing stores, and sidewalk cafes. One afternoon, I wander into the Centre Georges Pompidou—a structure of such mammoth proportions that it's difficult to describe. It's said that at any given time of day, more than twenty thousand people can be found milling around the art exhibits and various shops. There's a Frenchman there who speaks English, and he's following me around, begging me for a date. When he's not looking, I duck downstairs and find, to my surprise, a record store. I'm just about to leave—my girlfriend will be home from work soon—and in fact, I'm just about to get on the escalator out of the place when I think, *I wonder if they have any Bob Dylan albums?*

Minutes later, I'm sifting through a stack when I notice that the guy that's been following me is pretending to look at albums directly across from me. I'm pissed, but before I can even turn to go, a voice booms over the PA system in French, and all movement in the place comes to a halt.

'What is it?' I whisper to the guy, as the crowd begins its slow stir.

'A bomb. We have to evacuate.'

I tell you one thing: this is not America. There must be a thousand people downstairs in this huge basement of a room, and they are all moving like snails toward the only exit. The guy grabs my hand, pulls me under the record table to his side, and guides me slowly, slowly, ever so fucking slowly, toward the exit as my heart is about to make its own escape right out the front of my chest. When its my turn to climb up the moving stairs, a white-haired elderly lady with a walking cane is pushed to the forefront, and someone shoves me out of the way so she can get on first. My reaction is obviously to panic, and some of the French people click their tongues. *Fucking Bob Dylan*, I'm thinking. *I should have been out of here a half hour ago, and now I'm about to be blowin' in the wind.*

Upstairs, most people are getting in line to board yet another escalator, but this guy I'm with—my new best friend—is tugging me quickly to an elevator he knows about at the end of the corridor. As we hop in, presumably to escape to safety, I'm frantically banging on the button to shut the door when a middle-aged couple comes running up. To my dismay, my new friend sticks his arm between the doors, opens them, and not only does this couple jump inside, but a steady stream of evacuees rushes in on their heels until the bloated car will hardly close.

An eternity later, we join hundreds of people who are running across the expansive concrete plaza in front of the building to get away.

As fate would have it, the Centre Georges Pompidou does not blow up.

When I call Ernie to tell him about my ordeal, he says, 'Huh.'

Venice, Italy, is truly one of the most beautiful places on the planet. I arrive there a few days ahead of schedule, because of an impending train strike in Paris, and spend hours walking through colorful back streets, discovering the churches and piazzas and fresh loaves of olive bread most visitors to the city will never find. It's Christmas, in a Catholic country, and nativity scenes abound: Hand-carved out of wood, live puppet shows, kinetic metal sculptures of Jesus and Mary with backgrounds that change and light up—one bakery window even showcases a nativity scene sculpted out of butter. In a butcher's storefront window, plucked and feathered poultry hang in rows from hooks with large red bows tied around their necks. A kids' carnival has been erected on the oceanfront, and at night—amid the gleeful shrieks of little children—in addition to the glow of Saint Mark's Basilica, gaudy amusement park lights twinkle, lighting up the black Italian sky.

Ernie doesn't like the hotel I've picked, even though our room is right on the canals. The taxi boats make their turn outside our window, and he says it's too noisy. I don't bother to explain that it was the best room I could find that was within our budget.

On Christmas Eve we hook up for dinner with these women

that I've met. It's too crowded to get into Saint Mark's for the midnight mass, so the four of us rush to find one of the lesser known cathedrals, but they're all dark. During the day, I've bought champagne and gorgeous Italian pastries, including one called a Yule log—a chocolate cake that's been decorated to look like the wooden bark from the trunk of a tree—and as the morning sky turns pink over the canals, the girls join us in our hotel room for a decadent Christmas Day breakfast.

Ernie prides himself on being a world traveler, but after the Fiji trip that was spent in the post office, and now this one, where we are constantly on the move, I'm beginning to wonder how much of the world Ernie's traveled to he's actually seen. While this is my fourth trip to Europe, I've never been to the Amalfi Coastline. Ernie drives the narrow road that borders the sheer cliffs, at death-defying speed, so that we can make it back up to Florence in time to hook up with a guy who works for Lookout Management, and his wife, for New Year's Eve. As flashes of tourmaline seashore and ruins of castle-hotels catch me by surprise, I vow that I will come back here one day and ride a bicycle down the goddamned Amalfi coast, or walk it, if I have to, so I can take in all the beauty.

Ernie was right about the couple we meet up with, though. They're great. And New Year's Eve is a blast at Othello, a restaurant Saul Zaentz had recommended to us when my Berkeley girlfriend and I were in Europe in 1980. Just before midnight, the waiters hand out these confetti-colored wrapped candies, and after a countdown to 1987, everyone in the restaurant starts throwing them at each other. Presumably this is traditional. Naturally, I'm totally into it. On New Year's Day, as Ernie and I walk through this crowded piazza, we recognize one of the previous night's patrons at a sidewalk cafe, and when the fellow sees me, he ducks.

When it's time to leave Florence, Ernie and I have a fight because I want to get a loaf of bread, some cheese, and a bottle of wine and sit on a hilltop overlooking the tile-roofed town and watch the sunset, and he wants to keep moving. Way back in Venice, I'd discovered a mole on my chest that I didn't have the day before, and now it's growing and itching and driving me crazy. I figure I've got melanoma, anyway, and it'll all be over soon, so I give in.

In London, before our flight home, Ernie takes me to the leather district and buys me a motorcycle jacket, which I don't see as me at all, and a black suede pony number that I love and will see at the Beverly Center when I get home for five hundred dollars, and this flashy white-and-silver leather jacket with long metallic fringe that looks like something Pete Townshend would wear. There's a full-length faux-leopard coat on Carnaby Street that I want for three hundred dollars—and it looks incredible on me—but Ernie says, 'Who do you think you are? It looks like something you wear onstage!'

And, after this apparent brief lapse into fantasy, I remember who I am.

Back in LA, my Beverly Hills dermatologist tells me the mole is nothing to be concerned about, but a couple of days later, when the biopsy comes back, I get the news that it's a basal cell carcinoma, a mild form of skin cancer, and that it will have to be removed. Ernie is a mensch. He not only takes me to the doctor, but he holds my hand throughout the entire surgery, cracking jokes and making everybody laugh. My surgeon, a woman, says, 'Where'd you find *him*? He's terrific.' I think he even pays the $1,000 bill. When I return for my follow-up appointment, I'm advised by the doctor, 'Hang on to that one!'

Late January/early February 1987. Ernie needs to deliver something to Bob. I haven't seen Dylan in what seems like forever, and I'm very excited about it. We're supposed to meet him around eight o'clock up at the place on Mulholland he rents for Carole Childs. I wear black jeans, black boots, and the black motorcycle jacket Ernie bought for me in London.

As per usual, Bob is late. Ernie says that on more than one occasion during the *Knocked Out Loaded* sessions, the notion of making a short film called *Waiting For Bob* came up on those not so infrequent times when Dylan called for a midnight recording session and didn't show up till 4am. When Bob finally did show up at these sessions, it was reportedly often with a distracting girl on one or both of his arms. In fact, the word in the Dylan camp is that a recent harmonica solo that's been christened brilliant by *Rolling Stone* was actually cut together by the sound engineer after Bob went home, because at the time it was recorded, Bob was too high and sexed up on some bimbo to perform.

Now, sitting in Carole's thoroughly modern living room overlooking the whole of greater Los Angeles to one side and the vast San Fernando Valley to the other, the three of us make idle small talk while marking time. Carole shows me the invitation Bob received from Elizabeth Taylor, for her upcoming fifty-fifth birthday party in March. It's a black velvet silhouette of Taylor with what looks like a real string of pearls around the neck. Carole's all excited because she's made Bob swear he'll take her with him. She also offers to give a copy of my script to her girlfriend at William Morris once it's finished.

Around 9:30, Bob blows in, more energetic than I've seen him. Somehow, he and I wind up in a conversation, to the exclusion of Carole and Ernie. He's in the corner, in an arm chair, saying something like, 'You're a writer, aren't you?'

Somewhat stunned, I nod. Until now, I've only heard stories of how Dylan whimsically hands out highly coveted assignments to mere acquaintances he might take a liking to.

'I've got a tape I want you to hear,' he says. 'We'll have to go get it, though. It's in the car.' He's up and heading toward the front door, with me tagging along behind him. 'Maybe you can write the video.'

Say what?

Carole and Ernie view the spectacle from the couch. People can act so weird around Bob, myself included. When he's not engaging you personally, it's like you just become invisible.

I snag my jacket off the coat rack at the door and meet Dylan outside by the opened trunk of his black Mustang convertible. In the dark, he picks out a few tapes, inspects them closely, and then rejects them. Bingo. He finds the one he's looking for and slams the trunk door. After firing up a joint, the two of us linger a minute, spellbound by the sound of the wind rustling through the brittle fronds of the tall palm trees and marveling at the number of stars that can be seen from Mulholland Drive.

Back inside, Dylan notices my motorcycle jacket as I take it off. 'Where'd you get that?'

'London.'

'Huh.'

'Ernie bought it for me.' I hang it back on the rack. 'It's buffalo.'

'Can I try it on?'

'Sure.'

Bob reaches for the coat and slips his sinewy arms through the sleeves. It's nowhere near as nice as his own butter-soft leather fringed version. He tells me to try that one on. I model it for him, savoring the feel. He studies me with a discerning eye, even asks me to turn around.

'I'll trade you,' I say, half kidding.

'Hmph,' he grunts after checking himself out in the mirror. 'Maybe …'

In the living room, Carole and Ernie are still chatting away—since when do they have so much to talk about? Bob slides the cassette into the player and throws himself down on the chair. I sit on the floor below him, listening for some clues as to what I might put in a video that I can tell him after a single listen. So far, I've been lousy at my Hollywood pitch meetings, a byproduct of my charming upbringing in which whenever I said the wrong thing, one of my parents would knock me up side the head. Now I'm sitting here with three minutes to come up with a pitch for Bob Dylan.

The first few bars roll, and I'm scared shitless. It's a long, hard-rocking intro, all Stray Cats percussion and rhythm guitar, and I keep waiting for the lyrics to guide me. Dylan listens intently, his eyes searching as if he's hearing it for the first time too.

The chords repeat. Then repeat again. A guitar solo. No melody. It's a fucking instrumental! And a long one, to boot.

When the song finally winds down, Bob looks at me. 'Well?'

'It sounds kinda like a train,' I say. *Oh my God, what if I'm wrong?*
'A train? Hmmm.'

To my amazement, he picks up on it. We discuss trains, and some nuances of the music I'm not even sure exist, and it's agreed that within the next few weeks or so, I'll have a proposal for the video.

February 21 1987. Ernie and I decide to throw a Chinese New Year's Party. I concoct an elaborate invitation consisting of a small confetti-filled takeout box lined with a copy of the Chinese Zodiac and stuffed with a fortune cookie inside. When you pull out the fortune, it reads, 'Chinese New Year's party at Ernie and Britta's, Be

There or Be Square.' The return address is the Republic of China, care of Ernie's office.

I make and send out a hundred invites, including separate ones to Bob and Carole.

It's the year of the Rabbit, Ernie's year. During the course of these activities, I discover that I'm born in the Year of the Rat. Bob is a Snake.

Ernie and I have taken over the space next door. After months of arguing over his unwillingness to empty his closet of Grace's things, I lend Ernie $12,000 as a down payment to buy the property next door, so that we can break down the adjoining brick wall between the two formerly industrial structures, and I can bring over my computer and my piano, and at long last have a place to hang my hat.

A few days before the party, Dylan drops by unannounced to inspect the demolition. I'm home alone. He floats through the house like a ghost.

'Where'd you get this piano?' he asks, barely hitting on a couple of the keys.

'It's mine.'

'Hmph,' he grunts, like he's adding this information to some list he's keeping in the back of his head.

Before he leaves, he gets the bright idea to take his picture in the photo booth. We wait awkwardly for the thing to warm up. There's a box of masks and fake noses and props for people to use if they want to, but Bob merely makes a few faces and that's that. He doesn't even wait for the results.

'Why don't you climb in here with me?' he asks.

'OK,' I say, doing my best to maintain my composure.

This is not that unusual a request. I have pictures that were taken in the booth of Ernie, Elliot, and me, all at the same time, and with lots of other friends, too. I sit down, half on Bob's leg and half on the seat. Now he seems fully in his body, and his touch flushes me. He puts his arm around my shoulder. Four flashes later, we eagerly await the results.

When the pictures drop into the slot, Bob reaches and grabs them. He holds the photos of the two of us close to his chest, then studies them and smiles.

'I'm takin' *these* with *me*.'

When he's gone, I realize he's left the first strip—the photos of just him that he never even looked at—in the booth.

'Hey,' I tell him when I see him next, 'You forgot something.'

I dangle the photo strip in front of his nose.

'Oh,' he laughs, rubbing his middle finger back and forth along the stubble under his bottom lip. 'Those are for *you*.'

Ernie makes Chinese chicken salad for a hundred. We order egg roll and spare ribs and chicken wings and all the rest from the best Chinese restaurants around town. All Ernie's equipment is working, including a life-size Uncle Sam who tips his hat to you when you enter the place. The Basketball Scoreboard has been installed, lights and all, over the bed. Home: that's Ernie's side of the bed. Visitor: that's me. Period: that speaks for itself. And Ernie is still keeping score.

Bob has bought Carole a brand new Cadillac convertible at a time when Cadillac doesn't make convertibles, so it's practically one of a kind, and Ernie arranges to borrow it and have it parked in the driveway at the party with the top down, so it's like additional seating or something. Downtown at a restaurant-supply place we buy a dessert cart and I order ten different kinds of dessert to place on it, so we can roll it around the party. I even order a cake for Carole's upcoming birthday—yellow and frilly, like I know she'll like.

My best girlfriend from Berkeley has flown down, and at about 7:30 the guests start to arrive.

Dennis Hopper turns up with a female friend. 'Great place!' I give them the tour. What a nice guy. When I'd called him to leave directions on his answering machine, his entire outgoing message had been an excerpt from 'Highway 61 Revisited.'

Yoko Ono makes an appearance. 'I want to thank you, Britta, for taking such good care of Sean.'

'My pleasure,' I smile, remembering one night in particular up at Elliot's, when Sean was playing enthusiastically, vying for my attention, while Elliot, Ernie, and I were sitting in the living room, talking. Sean was so young and sweet, and we were his babysitters. He had developed a fascination with, of all things, my leopard skin pillbox hat. He snatched it off my head and ran crazily around the house, whooping and giggling, until Elliot tackled him playfully and retrieved it.

Actress/singer Ronee Blakeley, who was nominated for an Academy Award for her supporting role in *Nashville*, shows up, looking beautiful but incredibly vulnerable. Some say she still hasn't gotten over her relationship with Dylan.

Joni Mitchell is here, too! Plus, all the usual suspects. This is by far the most successful of the parties to date.

Joni and friends wind up sitting around in Ernie's den until three or four in the morning, long after Ernie's gone to bed, singing Everly Brothers songs and other hits from the 50s and 60s while I pathetically try to keep the tune.

My girlfriend from up north has never been that big on parties, so she'd left around midnight. When I ask her the next day why she went home so early, she says, 'Well, it wasn't like I was gonna wind up singing harmony with Joni Mitchell.' I didn't have the heart to tell her that she just might have.

The only thing missing from the party was Bob. But, at the last minute, after telling Ernie he was coming for sure, he'd decided to leave town and take Carole with him. Later, Carole tells me she believes Bob did this on purpose, because he knew how badly she wanted to be there. Ernie is unfazed, as ever, but I am disappointed.

March 2 1987. Bob takes Carole with him to composer Burt Bacharach's house in LA for Elizabeth Taylor's birthday party, but they have a huge fight, Carole says, because he basically ignores her.

One night, there's a birthday party for Carole at David Geffen's Malibu beach house. Geffen, a top talent manager, had co-founded Asylum Records in 1970 when he discovered even *he* couldn't wrangle a record deal for a twenty-three-year-old new kid on the block named Jackson Browne. Soon after, he signed the Eagles, Joni Mitchell, and Bob Dylan, among others. There was a rumor going around that the only reason Carole even met Bob was because she begged Geffen to take her as his guest to Jakob Dylan's Bar Mitzvah.

The party's in full swing by the time Ernie and I arrive and there's already a stack of Polaroids on the table. Carole is sifting through them.

'Look, Ma,' she says to her mother, who was flown in for the occasion. 'Could ya die? Me and Bob Dylan!' She holds up a handful of photographs that feature her with the songwriting legend. 'Who'd have thunk it?'

Dylan, who appears to be there only because he has to be, is taken aback by this scene, and can be found lurking in various corners and alcoves throughout the night.

The beach house—a pristine country cottage on the sand once owned by Doris Day—is all French doors and white decor. Floodlights illuminate the pounding surf. The guests include a young female choreographer who will turn out to be Paula Abdul, a former Mrs. Geraldo Rivera, and a bunch of semi-celebs too numerous to mention. Geffen himself is refined and charming, but a little cold.

I'm somewhat inappropriately dressed in a thigh-high black stretch number from some chic shop on La Brea, zebra-skin stockings, and the red high-heels.

Bob corners me by the stairs, admiring my effort with a sultry, 'You sure do look good, tonight.'

When everyone is seated at the large round dinner tables that have been set up in Geffen's living room for the ensuing feast, I'm taking photographs when Dylan, his back to me at the VIP table—how does he even know I'm shooting him?—turns around, gazes directly into the lens of my camera, and captures my soul.

CHAPTER FIVE

Gotta serve somebody

March 11 1987. At Carole's behest, Dylan performs a song at a gala tribute to George Gershwin at the Brooklyn Academy of Music. Other celebrity guests include celebrated song-and-dance man Tommy Tune, actor Christopher Walken, actress Madeline Kahn, dancer and choreographer Mikhail Baryshnikov, and a twelve-year-old Drew Barrymore. The song he chooses is from the 1930 film *Strike Up The Band*. The title of the song is 'Soon.'

That night, around 3am Eastern Standard Time, Carole, in her thick New York accent, leaves a message on my answering machine at my Westwood apartment, which I've sublet to a friend. She wants me to have 'Ern' call the hotel in New York, where they are staying, as soon as he gets in. She leaves the room and the phone number, and says she'll try him at home.

A few seconds later, the phone rings again.

'Hi, Breeda? Thiz's Bob. I'm just calling from New York City. Uhhh … I was trying to reach … uh … get a message to Ernie. Couple-a things. First of all, contact Bob Meyers about the T-shirts that he had made up with … uh … with Jakob's drawing on it, that he'll know about, OK? Where are those? Second of all, we want to make a T-shirt, and tell Ernie that … uh … we want … we want

Satchmo to be on it. So we want some old pictures of Satch. And … uh … it would be the same—it would be Huntz Hall, of course— and … uh … it would be … he could do the same process he did on my T-shirts, my Highway 61 T-shirts. Whatever.'

Why is he calling *me*? I can't help but wonder, as he rambles on. Now, it's like *I'm* working for Bob.

'I hope you get this whole message, I mean. If you don't … listen, if you don't … I don't even know if you're getting this message. Call … uh … Call … uh … uh … the hotel in New York here, it's the one we usually stay at. Yeah, the one we stay at. Ernie will know. Uh … what's it called? Ritz Carlton. Ritz Carlton Hotel, and … uh … have Ernie call, and … uh … call Elliot Mintz, and we can discuss this thing further. OK?'

Click. Dial tone. Ring.

'Hi Britta. This is Elliot calling. Uh … Britta … I would really like to speak with you this eve … or Ernie this evening, because it's a sensational idea and the artistic concept is difficult to explain over the telephone, but if you made contact with me personally, I'd be able to share the information with you. So call me at the hotel in New York, and I'll be able to tell you about this very original idea. Thank you.'

In the heat of the moment—namely midnight, LA time—the above matter was apparently very urgent, but I won't get the message until the next day. As far as I know, no T-shirts fitting this description were ever created, though the idea might have come up a time or two in passing, as in, 'Yeah, like the T-shirt for Satch!' Yeah.

Easter Sunday 1987. Elliot's invited to experimental drug psychologist Timothy Leary's house for dinner and invites Ernie and me to go along. Sean Lennon has been entrusted to Elliot's care and he comes along, too. I forget how we got there, but I think we must have met up at Elliot's first and all gone over there in his old white Mercedes.

It's late afternoon when we arrive, a beautiful day in the hills above Los Angeles. Barbara, Tim's wife, greets us with grace and hospitality. There are tables set up outside on the patio to take advantage of the view once dinner is served, but in the meantime, people mingle and lounge around the 50s-style post-and-beam house, drinking from large glasses of wine and munching any one of the numerous delicious hors d'oeuvres. Sean, who is now about twelve, runs off to play with the Learys' and other guests' kids.

When the sun sets, the guests are instructed to find a place at one of the outdoor tables. Ernie and Elliot and I sit down. The salad is already served, and Barbara tells everyone to start eating. There's an empty seat to my left, and to my surprise, Timothy takes it. We immediately become engaged in a conversation about education. He's delighted with my background in educational psychology, and stunned to learn that I have a master's degree in said subject, and confides in me his upcoming plans to use computers as a means of facilitating teaching to the masses.

As we speak, everything I look at starts to take on hard edges. The sky is a deep blue-black blanket that feels like it's going to crash down on me. Barbara is laughing at another table, but her laugh seems too loud. Timothy's words become an endless stream of verbiage that's drowning me. Ernie is nervously excusing himself from the table.

'Great salad dressing, Barbara!' someone howls. 'What's the secret ingredient?'

Oh my God. Elliot and I look at each other, then down at our empty salad plates. The dressing's been laced with LSD.

After dinner, Elliot and I are watching the kids play pool on a miniature table in the game room, when one of them accidentally hits Sean's forehead with a cue stick. Blood appears to gush forth from the boy's head like water from a broken fire hydrant. Panic ensues. Elliot, Barbara, and I rush Sean into the bathroom and wash the oozing but insignificant cut. When Elliot leaves the room to enlist Ernie's help, Barbara cries, 'You don't think they'll sue us, do you?'

I don't know why—then again, maybe I do—but the only thing I remember about the drive home that night is Elliot sitting numbly in the back seat of his own Mercedes, with me in the front passenger seat and Ernie—who never drinks or does drugs—stoned at the wheel, driving the wrong way down a one-way street. After we drop Elliot off, I convince the uncharacteristically feisty and overprotective Ernie to let me do the driving back to his place, reminding him that after four years at Berzerkeley in the 60s, I do at least have some experience driving under these circumstances.

April 1987. Bob is recording at Sunset Sound in Hollywood, and a big thrill for me—when I'm not at home working on my script, or on the proposal for his video—is being able to hang out during the sessions. This latest, as yet untitled album will be self-produced. Steve Douglas is there sometimes, as is Dave Alvin of The Blasters. Occasionally, Karla's old friend Danny Kortchmar plays guitar, too. I mostly hang out in the waiting room until it's time to listen.

I'm not crazy about a lot of the tunes, probably 'cause Bob didn't write them, and half the cuts I hear won't make the record. My favorite is a song previously covered by Hank Snow called 'Ninety Miles An Hour (Down A Dead End Street).'

You belong to someone else and I do too
It's just crazy bein' here with you

One night, while Ernie's Celica convertible is parked in the lot of the recording studio, a thief breaks into the trunk and steals a bunch of stuff that Ernie was carting around for Bob. I think he also takes Dylan's leather jacket and gloves off the handlebar of Dylan's Harley. Ernie spots the guy and chases him down several blocks, until the creep turns and pulls a knife on him.

When Ernie reports the bad news to Bob that the guy got away with the loot because he had a knife, Bob tells him, 'You shoulda had a gun.'

Mid-April 1987. Al Kooper plays the Roxy, and Dylan's supposed to attend. It's an incredible show, but Bob bails at the last minute.

Somewhere in here, I get a late call to get dressed in a hurry. We're meeting Bob and Carole at a restaurant in Brentwood on 26th Street. We get there late—maybe 9:30 or 10:00, even. It's a huge party of twenty or more people in a private room. There's barely time to get a glass of wine or two before Carole mentions there's another party she wants to go to. Reluctantly, Bob agrees to go.

I've never ridden in a limo before, so it's agreed that Ernie will drive the Toyota and follow us, and I'll ride with Bob, Carole, and Elliot Mintz in the stretch.

'You think this is a big limo?' Bob laughs. 'Some of 'em have hot tubs.'

'No!' I say, trying to figure out the logistics of having all that water in a car, and electric jets, too. Still, the one we're in feels as comfortable and as big as a living room.

'Sure,' Bob says, 'they come with toilets, king-size beds … tennis courts …' *Did he just wink at Elliot?* 'Small ones, though.'

Now I don't know what to think. Bob and I are sitting next to each other, riding backward, passing a joint back and forth. He's broken into the limo's liquor cabinet, against Carole's wishes, and she's giving him the evil eye. He's really getting out there. His ramblings about real estate are too convoluted for even me to understand, although I keep affirming them as if I do.

Carole and Elliot sit silently across from us, watching the show, and while Elliot seems like he's into it, I can tell Carole's majorly pissed off. Either we are smoking some really good shit or this trip is taking forever.

'Hey,' Bob blurts out finally. 'Where're we goin'?'

'To Bruce Willis's house,' Carole says smugly.

'*Bruce Willis?*' Bob says, horrified. 'If I'd a known that, I'd a never agreed to go!'

Bruce lives up one of the canyons near Mulholland, and there's been a lot of news circulating in the media about his neighbors' complaints vis-à-vis the noise at his frequent parties, and the fact that he's only a renter.

Pulling into a conservatively landscaped circular drive surrounded by massive trees and open sky, we leave behind the luxury of the limo for the crass, fully packed party situation inside the house. I duck into the ladies' room to check my hair and lipstick; Dylan has evidently walked straight through the crowd and into the backyard.

A couple of years later, I will meet Willis's younger brother, who will remember the night this way: 'I was in the kitchen mixing drinks when you guys came in, and I said to the dude next to me, Wow! That looks just like Bob Dylan! and the guy slugs me on the shoulder and says, That *is* Bob Dylan, you idiot!'

I catch more than a few glances as I pass through the bodies in search of some wine. The party is heavy on masculine energy, and without Ernie or Bob next to me, the question of my availability seems to be weighing heavily on a few too many minds. Red wine glass in hand, I, too, escape to the serenity of the backyard, where I find Bob standing alone, looking up through the towering Eucalyptus at the stars. We sit down at one of the big round metal tables that must have been set out there for just that purpose, though most of Willis's guests seem to prefer the sweaty sardine happening that's going on inside. The ground is practically throbbing from the bass on the stereo.

I tell Bob to stay put while I fetch a full bottle of red and another glass. Ernie finally finds us, and as the evening progresses, different people, all men, screw up the courage to approach the table for an audience with Bob. One guy who sits down spits out something like, 'I'm really a big fan of yours,' and I worry that Bob might eat him alive. Instead, he asks the guy his name.

'Bill, huh,' Dylan nods. 'What do *you* do?'

Dylan is ostensibly willing to carry on this perfectly mundane conversation, but within seconds Bill becomes so intimidated he flees the scene, excusing himself lamely, and never returning to the table.

I encourage Ernie to go get another bottle of wine. What am I doing? How come Ernie hasn't noticed Bob's glass is dry?

There's a flurry of activity by the back door. Willis himself is coming outside. By now, the other outdoor tables have filled up. Once word gets out, anyone with a brain in his or her head wants to be close to Bob Dylan.

Willis makes his way over to us and sits down. He's charismatic, all right, but macho to the extreme. It's early in his career—his *Moonlighting* phase—and it seems as though he's still trying to prove himself. He lays a baggy of grass on the table and rolls a nice fat joint. It's like this is the story he wants to be able to tell later … how he and Bob Dylan sat in his backyard and smoked a joint together, but whatever shit he's talking, Bob is having none of it. I'm sure Bruce tells a different version of that evening, but the way I recall it, Dylan didn't say a single word to him.

Bob must have decided it was time to leave, but while Carole and Ernie say their goodbyes, I visit the loo once again, because I don't want to have to 'hold it' all the way back to Venice, and also because I like to put some lipstick on before I say goodnight to people—and leave 'em with a good impression. When I arrive at the front door, though, there are four police officers in uniform, badges and guns gleaming in the porch light, mounting the stairs.

'Hi,' I smile at them, but I'm in shock. Elliot reaches behind one of the cops and pulls me down off the steps toward the car.

'Good night!' I sing. *Hope you liked my lipstick*.

Bob, whose sixth sense for trouble must have kicked in just about the time he gave the order for us to depart, is already firmly ensconced in the limo. The next day, reports of Willis's bust for disturbing the peace appear in the *Los Angeles Times* and on the news, but with no mention anywhere of the presence of Bob Dylan.

April 14 1987. Bob and Ernie fly to Memphis. The purpose of the trip is for Bob to sing and play harmonica on a Ringo Starr song—'Wish I Knew Now What I Knew Then'—which will never be released due to the fact that Ringo, according to his own admission, was 'under the influence' during the session.

I've submitted my video proposal to Bob, through Ernie, and am most anxious to talk to Bob about it. I trail him through the airport terminal on his way to board the plane.

'So, uh, did you get a chance to look at my pages on the video?'

The story is about an old man—Dylan in makeup—at some abandoned truck stop in the middle of nowhere, reminiscing about the time when he—Flashback: Dylan as he looks now—robs a bank and steals away on a train with his true love, only to wind up losing her and the money in an onboard shootout, so he can escape the law. I'm worried that at this stage of his life and career, Bob won't be too keen on playing an old man. But, I mean, give me a break, I didn't have much to work with.

Bob keeps a brisk stride.

'It's … uh … interesting,' he says. And the subject never comes up again.

A short while later, Bob's oldest son, Jesse, the film student in New York, will ask to borrow Louie Kemp's 1950 Cadillac convertible as a visual aid for shooting Dylan's next video, but this project won't come to fruition either.

In Memphis, Bob wants to go to Graceland, so Ernie arranges for them to take a VIP tour. They will also visit the site of Martin Luther King's shooting. The night of their return, Ernie calls from the airport.

'Get dressed, Bob and I are swinging by the house to take you to dinner.' I think Elliot Mintz was with them, too.

We meet up with Carole at an Italian restaurant on Sunset Boulevard, at the west end of the strip, and squeeze into one large oval booth. As usual, I wind up sitting next to Bob. Elliot's to my right, then Carole, then Ernie. Bob's youngest son, Jakob, is also with us. Carole is wearing these reflective blue sunglasses in the already dark room and orders a drink with a fruited umbrella toothpick in it. During dinner, she brings up the subject of Jakob not wanting to go to college.

Bob says nothing at first, but after she presses him, he responds with a shrug.

'So?'

'*So?*' Carole is livid. 'That's just great!' It seems she's anticipated his response.

Jakob's cheeks turn crimson. I hope I didn't volunteer something like 'Some of my best friends didn't go to college and they're multi-millionaires,' or 'I have a master's degree and look where it got me,' but I think I may have.

Dylan's really not interested in discussing this. After all, he just barely went to college himself. He scratches his head and makes it clear that it's Jake's life, and Jake should do what he wants with it.

'What about art school?' Carole jibes. Our table's starting to attract attention. 'Shouldn't the kid at least go to art school?'

The question hangs in the air as Dylan refuses to talk further on the subject.

Over dessert and after-dinner drinks, Dylan tells me about Memphis. He says I wouldn't believe how gaudy Graceland is, or how devoted Elvis's fans are. He says there's a trailer set up outside the grounds as you enter, with karaoke machines on raised stages where people get up and perform their favorite Elvis songs—and, if they want, they can make a CD or a video cassette of their performance right then and there. He also tells me about the balcony where Martin Luther King got shot.

'The blood stains,' he says, 'are still on the floor.'

When it comes time to order the check, the waiter who couldn't help but notice the earlier altercation approaches our table and asks Bob, 'One more for the road?' You can tell from his demeanor, this guy's been waiting tables in classy joints like this for something like a hundred years.

Bob hesitates.

'It's a long road,' the bartender advises, almost like he's Dylan's alter ego.

'That's true.'

Dylan concedes to a last round; Carole's disappeared into her soup. It is a long road.

On the way home, Bob asks us to pull over. He jumps out of the car in front of a huge mansion on Sunset, walks north a few yards to the fence, and takes a leak.

There's a party at Louie Kemp's for some visiting Rabbi to the Chabad House. If you've ever wondered why Bob Dylan appears as a guest on the Chabad Telethon, it would certainly appear that it's a favor for Louie, because Louie's a big supporter of the Chabad.

Bob picks Ernie and me up at the Venice house in his Mustang convertible. It's the first time I've been in a car when he drives, and to my surprise, he is incredibly cautious. On our way over to Louie's he takes me by this fancy shoe store on Main Street in Santa Monica. We get out and walk up to the window. Bob points out a couple of pairs of cowboy boots he wants me to come back and buy for him when the store is open. He's obviously been by here earlier. Then he points to these knee-high, white calf-leather boots with studs and fake jewels all over them for four hundred dollars and tells me to buy those for myself.

On our way into Louie's building, Bob puts on his sunglasses, even though it's already dark out.

'What are you doing?' I ask.

'You don't understand,' Bob says. 'I *have* to wear these.'

The party is teeming with Hassids and Orthodox Jews, sitting on the floor, paying homage to Rabbi Shlomo Somebody-or-other, when we enter. There's even a guy holding a guitar. Someone gives up their armchair for Bob, and he sits down. I remember this whole scene being unbearably boring, and I can't believe Dylan is putting up with it. But then again, who knows what was going on behind those sunglasses. Toward the end of the evening, the comic character actress Lainie Kazan wanders in, and when we leave, she tags along with us into the parking lot, hanging on to Bob's arm. Later, Ernie tells me she's had a crush on Dylan for years.

At some point I need to borrow a car, 'cause mine is in the shop, and I'm given Louie's candy-apple red '57 T-Bird convertible for the day. I'm shocked by how many men I meet. That night, Ernie and I toy with the idea of buying one ourselves and renting it out to single women on the prowl.

Louie buys a two-million-dollar house from me, thereby making my real estate year. After weeks of incredibly grueling negotiations, Ernie and I are invited to Louie's on the Saturday after the deal is signed, for a celebratory lunch. Louie, whose success he owes, in part, to the invention of imitation crab, corners me on the couch before we sit down to eat and says he wants me to donate 10 percent of my commission—almost $6,000—to Chabad.

I'm in shock. If he'd told me this up front, I'd have gladly done it, but now, especially after the nightmarish negotiations, it seems like a slap in the face. Because it's the Sabbath, Louie and his wife ask me—the probable goy—to turn the light switches on and off and to stick my hand down the garbage disposal when it gets clogged. Finally, when the phone rings and they ask me to answer it, I say, 'You know, everybody, I'm Jewish, too. I converted!'

When Father's Day rolls around, Carole has a brunch for Bob; she invites Ernie and me to Malibu, but once again, the two of them are going at it. It's a hot day, and Carole and I go for a swim in Bob's exquisitely sublime black-bottomed pool. As we lie on the rocks sunbathing, she tells me how cruel Bob's been to her since he decided to quit smoking. It's not like he's been physically abusive or anything—the whole relationship just sounds twisted.

Later, in the car, when the four of us are on our way out to see a movie in Westwood—I think it was *At Close Range*—I tell her about Louie wanting me to give away part of my real estate commission.

'Don't you dare give up a dime,' she says. 'That cheap son of a bitch!'

Ernie says he thinks I should do whatever Louie wants. Bob says he doesn't want to get in the middle of it.

I hit a speed bump at twenty-five miles an hour and destroy the fancy suspension in my vintage Mercedes, to the tune of fifteen hundred bucks. Ernie suggests I get rid of it. A few weeks before, it had been another two hundred for a turn signal. I'm still not sure whether I should or not. After all, the art deco–looking 3.5 was my dream car.

Ernie finds me a 1970 Mercury Cougar XR-7 convertible with a brand new Porsche paint job, gold, with a new white canvas top—a muscle car, which he says is much cooler. I reluctantly fork over the money, and a few days later, some Japanese guy who wants to take my Mercedes over to Japan gives me $11,000 in a brown paper sack.

June 1987. Bob is rehearsing with the Grateful Dead in Northern California for an upcoming US tour. I decide to combine my annual trip to Inverness with Ernie's plans to be in San Rafael with Bob. Besides, it's a good way to break in the Cougar.

Ernie, Bob, and Carole are checked into the Stouffers Hotel in Marin, where I join them for a couple of days. Bob and Carole have a suite, and Ernie and I have an adjoining room, so it's a bit like sharing a house together—a lot of running around in just T-shirts.

Or, in Bob's case, without a shirt, or maybe just in his boxer shorts. He's got a little paunch on him, and in this casual environment, I notice that his hands and toes are kind of gnarled.

When I tell Carole I've finished my script, she phones her friend at Morris and sets up an appointment for after my return. She asks me to tell her about Karla. I'm always trying to promote my friends—not just Karla but everyone. I tell Carole I like Karla's versions of her own material best, and Carole says, 'I know she's your girlfriend, but there's no way Karla Bonoff is a better singer than Linda Ronstadt.'

That's a matter of opinion, I think. But I keep it to myself. It's sort of like Bob preferring records over CDs. Carole's into commerciality; I'm not. But we agree on the band World Party.

When Bob sees the Cougar convertible, he asks, 'Where's your Mercedes?'

'I got rid of it,' I say.

Bob grimaces. 'What'd you do *that* for?'

Ernie has set the living room up with a VCR, and when Bob isn't meeting with the Dead or lounging around strumming his guitar, he likes to watch movies. Instead of renting new movies, though, he has Ernie rent *Giant*, with James Dean. Ernie and Carole have no interest in watching the classic, but I've studied film and I'm always up for a rerun of one of my favorites. Bob and I get high and stay up until three in the morning, sitting on the floor in front of the TV, mesmerized, watching the movie, until Carole emerges from the bedroom like some teenage kid's mother, yelling, 'All right you guys, break it up … it's time to go to bed!'

The next morning, over a late breakfast, Bob and I watch the end of the movie from the dining room table, much to Carole's dismay.

Since he quit smoking, Bob's eating more. He's drinking his second cup of coffee.

'You know that scene there at the end … where Dean's making his speech? That scene just doesn't ring true. You know why?'

'No,' I say. 'Why?'

''Cause James Dean was already dead when they put the voice in. That's not James Dean's voice,' he says, impressing me with this little-known information. 'It's Nick Adams.'

'Huh.'

When Dylan's interview with Sam Shepard comes out in the July *Esquire*, Bob will have said the same thing to him.

Ernie gives Bob a pocketsize German 35mm camera for his forty-sixth birthday, which we did not celebrate with him this year. It's like a four hundred dollar present, and I like the camera so much, Ernie buys me one, too. Bob and I snap the day away, and at night, while Bob is lying in his and Carole's bed, reading the autobiography of Armand Hammer, I approach him nervously to say goodnight.

'Was anyone else in your family a writer?' I ask.

'Mmmmm,' he thinks about it a second. 'I had a great uncle who was a poet.'

Before I head off to my vacation in Inverness, Ernie presses me one too many times for a sexual fantasy.

'Maybe we should get together with Bob and Carole,' I suggest, and Ernie gets mad.

Karla has given me a book called *Creative Visualization* that's supposed to make all my dreams come true. But something very strange happens when I'm in Inverness. As I sit out on the dilapidated deck of this ruin of a cabin that I rent, watching the water in the foggy Tamales Bay surging and retreating through the mist, I try to visualize myself as a successful screenwriter, taking meetings in Hollywood—my name up on the silver screen—but all I can think about is Bob. What the hell is going on? I start over, but still his visage intrudes. I write some songs on my guitar, but they all sound like bad versions of his songs. I even take a long drive up the coast, but when I get out of the car to admire the view, I discover that the sign on the entrance to the overlook says Dillon Beach!

I decide that I must have some 'work' to do in Bob's regard, some matters to clear up, before I can even think about achieving my life's dreams. I realize I've given Dylan too much power, that I'm never really myself around him; I'm so worried about saying or doing the wrong thing. I begin to visualize a relationship with him in which I can be more relaxed when we're together, so that our communication is more natural; so that we can truly become friends. I figure, if I can be friends with Bob Dylan, I can do anything.

The next morning, before I'm even out of bed, the dog is barking, and Ernie is pounding on the cabin's paint-peeled French doors.

'What's the matter?' I ask, tying my robe too tightly around my waist.

'I have to fly to LA,' Ernie says. 'A work emergency. Carole's left, too. And Bob wants you to fill in for me … to come back and stay at the hotel with him in San Rafael while I'm gone.'

This time, when I check into the hotel, I have a room of my own. Dylan's middle son, Sam, is flying in from college, where he's studying photography, and he'll be staying in the adjoining room to Dylan's suite. While Bob rehearses with the Grateful Dead, he asks me to pick Sam up from the airport in San Francisco, take him to the City Lights Bookstore, show him around the Bay Area, and drop him off at the Golden Gate Bridge, where the kid has said he wants to shoot some pictures.

Sam, at this age, is the best looking of the three sons—though this will be hard to believe once Jakob comes into his own—but he's also the shyest. The ride from the airport to the bookstore is almost painfully quiet. I fill him in on some of the City Lights history, priming him on Bukowski and Ginsberg and Kerouac before we even get out of the car. As he silently browses, I pick up two books of poems by Greg Corso, whom Dylan has touted to me. Later in the afternoon, while Dylan's middle son walks the entire length of the Golden Gate Bridge taking photographs, a strong wind blows white caps on the cobalt water. I wait in the Cougar, immersed in poetry.

I'm supposed to pick up Dylan at the rehearsal hall at six. He's told me he doesn't want to eat hotel food tonight, so, after dropping Sam off at the room, I decide to surprise Bob with something special. I drive into San Rafael, and after surveying the situation, I settle upon a fancy Indian restaurant for takeout. I order up a double helping of Tandoori chicken—just the dark meat, both Bob's and my favorite—and, you guessed it, some vegetables. I think Bob's only complaint will be that there isn't enough.

When I show up at the hall, the rehearsal is still going. I walk in on Dylan singing 'Man Of Peace,' his gravely voice etching the paint off the walls of the near-empty space.

'Sometimes Satan,' he snarls, 'comes as a man …'

Bob directs me to stop at a bookstore in town, even though it's already closed. On display in the window is his fellow folksinger and former love interest Joan Baez's newly released autobiography, *A Voice To Sing With*.

'Come back and get that tomorrow,' he says. Then he points out a bunch of other books he wants me to buy, too.

As Bob, Sam, and I dine at the Formica table in Dylan's mundane suite, I'm surprised by how reticent Sam is, even around his father, and Bob's not exactly effervescent himself. Before we are even finished eating, the kid excuses himself and goes to his room.

The subject of the Baez book comes up again.

'I wanna see what she put in there about me,' Bob says, swigging from a bottle of beer.

The next day, I drive back to the bookstore and buy all these various hardbound books—some of which I think are just decoys, so that anyone following us, or who has seen us together, won't speculate that Bob's reading Joan's book. Dylan tells me not to bring the heavy volumes upstairs in daylight, and during the evening, by the time we eat dinner and watch TV, we forget about them. Later, after Bob falls asleep on the floor where we've been sitting, I sneak down to the car and retrieve only the Baez book from the trunk. I stay up all night reading the parts about *Him*.

The next morning, while he's getting ready to leave for rehearsal—checking out his stubbly chin in the mirror behind the wet bar—I can't help myself.

'You hurt her!' I blurt out.

'She hurt herself,' Dylan says.

As I'm driving Bob to his rehearsal, top down on the Nimitz Freeway, a bunch of burly guys on Harleys pass us on the right.

'Hi, Bob!' they shout. They wave and keep going, but Bob seems nonplussed by it all.

The best thing about the Cougar, it will turn out, is the CD player I had installed in it. Without thinking, I press play on the disc that's already loaded up, World Party's *Private Revolution*, and the cut that comes up is Karl Wallinger's inspired cover of Dylan's 'All I Really Want To Do.' Ernie hates this kind of mistake. I reach for the knob to shut off the stereo but Bob yelps, 'No, turn it up!'

I didn't know then that Dylan had recorded with Mike Scott, Wallinger's former bandmate from The Waterboys, back in '85 when he was in England collaborating with Dave Stewart and Annie Lennox of the Eurythmics. I suffer through every verse until the song's end.

'*All I really want to do,*' Wallinger howls, as the keyboard fades into eternity, '*is, baby, be friends with you.*'

I couldn't agree with him more.

'Pretty good,' Bob says. 'Play it again.'

Back at the hotel that night, Dylan is listening to some very esoteric music on the boom box Ernie has left for him. Funky, bluesy, very Southern. I've never heard stuff like this before. I shuffle through the tapes, but can only remember the familiar names, Ian and Sylvia and Richard Farina. Bob tells me he was good friends with Mimi, Richard's wife.

By now, I've realized that Bob Dylan pays attention to *everything*. There's almost no topic that he can't weigh in on, and if he hasn't done so already, it's just 'cause it hasn't come up yet.

Later, when we're watching TV, *Nightline* comes on. This was at the time when Ted Koppel's contract was up for renewal, and there was actually a question as to whether or not he might quit. Apparently, his ratings were down, and ABC was having second thoughts about the program.

Bob says there's no way Koppel will quit the show. 'He's just holding out for more money.'

It's a particularly confrontational episode, though I don't recall who was on. During the commercial, I suggest to Bob that he and Baez go on *Nightline* and duke it out in public, to boost the show's ratings, and Bob enjoys this notion quite a bit.

Spring 1987. Bob buys Carole an $800,000 house in Coldwater Canyon, and Ernie and I are enlisted to go up there and wait for the telephone man or the cable guy, or both. The place is oozing charm and dripping in ivy, which in LA means it's crawling with rats, but the setting is peaceful and rustic.

Dylan is so impressed by the pest control people who do the inspection on Carole's new house—one young woman in particular—that he decides he wants to do a movie about termite inspectors. He tells Ernie to recruit me to do the research. I have a connection to the termite business, having been in real estate, so I call up some of the people I know and put together a five-page report that includes everything from the hours the inspectors work to the type of clothing they wear, the relative effectiveness of pesticides used, and a detailed description of the different types of ants, termites, and cockroaches—German, Oriental and American—that are considered a threat in Southern California. I also provide a reeling expose on rodents.

Ernie delivers the report to Bob within a couple of days of my assignment, but I never hear any more about it.

June 19 1987. There's a posthumous art opening at the Dyansen Gallery in Beverly Hills for John Lennon's book *Skywriting By Word Of Mouth*. After Yoko's press conference at Westwood One to promote it, Norm Pattiz, the broadcasting mogul, invites me to ride with him and his wife—former DJ Mary Turner—to a dinner party at Mr. Chow's in Yoko's honor. Wearing the short black-and-white miniskirt

Ernie bought me in Australia, I squeeze into the tiny back seat of his Ferrari and wind up almost sitting between the two of them. By the furtive looks Norm's giving me in his rear view mirror, I gather that, in this instance, at least, I'm making a really good impression.

Bob has declined the dinner invitation, but Carole is there, as is Elliot Mintz—and, of course, Ernie. The party is private. Upstairs. One long table with Yoko at its head. She's just returned from Russia, and in response to questions about her experience, she says she was surprised to find that Russian women have the same complaints about finding good men as American women do.

'There aren't any!'

July 3 1987. I must have done something right when I helped Bob out in northern California because it's decided that I will accompany him and Ernie on the Dylan/Dead concert circuit—six US dates starting in Foxborough, Massachusetts. And what a trip it is, literally and figuratively, to board an airplane as a member of Bob Dylan's entourage. Inquisitive, admiring, and sometimes jealous eyes follow us everywhere as we pass. On the plane, I sit nervously, reading *A Hollywood Education*, daring only scant glances at my frizzy headed, sunglass-clad idol.

I've never been to Boston, and the view from the bus is all I will ever see of the charming city. The tour gets off to a rocky start when Dylan and the Dead are booked into a Red Lion Hotel too far from the gig for comfort. Even though it's almost midnight when we arrive, and no one's eaten anything substantial, heads begin to roll on the Lookout team as Dylan, Ernie, and I are moved to a better hotel in Foxborough somewhere around three o'clock in the morning.

Dylan and the Dead have agreed to meet every night before each show and confirm the set list. But the Dead's freewheelin' spirit of adventure and Bob's penchant for playing the same songs over and over sets up an immediate conflict, and it seems clear from the outset that while the onstage impression is of communal camaraderie, offstage, Bob wants very little to do with the band.

July 4 1987. Sullivan Stadium, Maine. I am not a Grateful Dead fan, and Dylan's collaboration with them seems to me only to bring his own music down. In fact, this is my first Dead concert ever, and I am stunned by the fact that the fans on this hot July holiday have to be dowsed with huge fire hoses to keep them under control. As an energetic Dylan performs his set—with the Dead playing backup— the wet but colorful crowd, which includes topless girls riding on the shoulders of their boyfriends, scream with enthusiasm, but to me it's unclear for what.

For the first time, I watch an entire Dylan show from the stage. The vibe from the audience is intoxicating. Powerful equipment swings from the rafters. The sound is blasting. Lights flashing. Bob plays a rousing 'Stuck Inside Of Mobile …'—the first live rendition of the song in eleven years.

July 10 1987. Philadelphia is happening. Before the show, I tour the historic city, admiring its elderly architecture. Ernie's busy on the telephone, keeping tabs on his printing business back in Los Angeles. He's also busy developing an idea he's come up with that will revolutionize the way consumers buy music. He's confided in me that due to the amount of work he's accrued at home, he may not be able to go out on all of Dylan's upcoming European tour with Tom Petty.

I find the coolest Philly streets for shopping and go wild. It's a music city, and as you walk from door to door in the commercial neighborhoods, there are outdoor speakers piping rock'n'roll up and down the boulevards. I locate a shop that sells one of a kind tie-dye, by some local artist, and buy an amazing three-quarter-length jacket, black dye only on a cream background.

'What do you think?' I ask Ernie back at the hotel.

'It's OK.'

'Maybe I should get one for Bob.'

People do stuff like that for him all the time. In fact, Ernie's one of his main suppliers.

'Are you kidding?' Ernie's on hold with LA. 'He's not gonna like *that*.'

'Oh.'

I won't even wear the jacket to the show that night.

'What about these?' I ask, holding up a pair of buckskin knock-around everyday boots.

'They're not as nice as the ones I buy you.'

That afternoon, I'm told that due to another management screw up we have to be flown in to the gig at JFK Stadium by helicopter. My first and last professional flight, striking and scary at the same time. The opened door on the copter offers an uncomfortably close view of the city's residential rooftops, as well as the rocky hills—which are not hidden enough for my tastes—under a dense forest of spiky green trees. The chop-chop-chopping is ear-splitting, despite the complimentary earplugs.

In business mode, Bob and Ernie have gone ahead on another helicopter, leaving Carole and me, and a handful of others, strapped shoulder-to-shoulder into this flying tin can, praying for our mutual safety.

Highlights of the evening's show will be 'Gotta Serve Somebody' and 'Simple Twist Of Fate.'

July 12 1987. New York, New York. Carole was definitely with us on this date, as was Elliot Mintz. We're checked into the exclusive Parker Meridien Hotel. Each room comes with a view of Central Park; its leafless trees, barely budded, forming neat long rows like soldiers marching off into the horizon.

Dylan is registered under his oft-used code name, a combination of a former good friend's first name and a carefully chosen word from one of his most famous songs. Before he can even get out of the limo, he's accosted by some high-class hookers on the street. Later, upstairs, he scurries down the hall, from room to room, claiming he's being followed by over-zealous fans. He orders Ernie to call Elliot Mintz and alert security.

'He's paranoid!' Carole says, right in front of him, taking a page out of the *Who's Afraid Of Virginia Woolf?* playbook. 'Bob still thinks it's 1967.'

Tonight's show at Giants Stadium is the most exciting of the tour to date. Backstage guests include Penn from Penn and Teller; Bob's oldest son, Jesse, who I've only met once before; John Rockwell, the music reviewer from the *New York Times*; and *Miami Vice* heartthrob Don Johnson. The actual VIP area from which to view the show is small and scaffolded to the upper left of the stage.

Early in the evening, I score a perfect seat on the floor in the front, but at some point during Bob's performance, Elliot Mintz gives me a signal, and I'm told to move to the back and make room for his highness, Don Johnson, who has arrived late. Johnson's oily presence disrupts the entire ambience, as nearly everyone backstage is forced to move in order to accommodate him. He then proceeds to stand up at the rail, blocking everyone else's view, before leaving after the third song.

Still, this show with the Dead is the strongest yet, with Bob giving new life to their encore, 'Touch Of Gray'—the only Grateful Dead song I've liked in years—and his first ever live performance of the John Wesley Harding classic 'The Wicked Messenger.'

Afterwards, I gush to Ernie, 'Bob Dylan has the soul of a black man and the brain of Albert Einstein!'

'You should tell him that,' Ernie says. 'But just remember, Dylan the man and Dylan the legend are two different animals.'

There's an after-show party in Dylan's suite for his New York constituency. One long table is set up in the living room. Jeff Rosen and his wife are present, as are Jesse and Carole and all the tour regulars. Bob sits at one head, I sit at the other. At one point, there's a knock on the door: it's a guy in a wheelchair who Dylan knew growing up named Larry Kegan, a close friend who had sung with Bob back when they were 'mere mortals,' and who everyone calls Wheel-Chair Larry. Kegan was at Camp Herzl, too. Bob gives Ernie the OK to let him in.

The whole table is eating and drinking merrily, when Dylan suddenly stops the conversation about the release of his next album—which he has just announced will be called *Down In The Groove*—by nodding drunkenly down the long table at me.

'Breeda,' he says. 'Mind if I call you Rita?'

It's close to midnight as Bob, Carole, Elliot, Ernie, and I wander Manhattan in search of a drink. Bob is still sweaty from the show. He wears his trademark gray-hooded sweatshirt, and the first bar that he wants to go into refuses him service because of how he's dressed. I, like an idiot, am wearing high heels. As the five of us traipse down the humid New York sidewalks, a carload of kids come squealing by and make cat calls at Carole, who's not only in heels but also a pair of skin-tight white pants and an even tighter shiny low-cut top that shows off her ample breasts.

Bob directs us to the children's petting zoo after I say I've never seen it. We're all hanging out in the quiet of the moist night air, in awe of the llamas, when another carload of creeps comes careening by, whistling at Carole and disturbing our peace. Bob goes ballistic.

'That's it!' he yells at Carole, 'You're going home!'

For all the back and forth between the two of them, when Bob lays down the law, it's game over, and Carole gets this better than anyone. Before I know it, Ernie has secured a horse and carriage, and Bob puts the much chagrinned Carole on board, handing her a hundred bucks to get back to the hotel.

Both Bob and Elliot know I've never truly seen New York, and they're getting a kick out of showing it to me. Bob suggests we go to the bar at the Algonquin Hotel. On the way we stumble upon a place that's being used to store magic-show paraphernalia. The guard sees us peering in the windows and opens the place up. If he recognizes Bob, he keeps it to himself. The four of us hang out a while, playing like children in these grown-up toys—velvet-lined coffins and a human-sized wooden closet with nails in the door so that when you close it, they poke your eyes out.

'Hey Breeda, come over here,' Bob beckons. He wants me to climb into the large wooden crate where the magician's assistant always gets sawed in half.

The bar at the Algonquin is all dark wood and mirrors. While Ernie runs off to use the phone, Dylan and Elliot fill me in on the literary history of the place, Dorothy Parker, et al. I think Bob even mentions Faulkner. The three of us are camped out in a corner booth, drinking martinis, when the subject shifts to show business. Dylan tells me that Elizabeth Taylor is the very definition of celebrity—she's so elegant and poised—and that Bette Davis is the greatest lady he's ever met. He says he wants to have a dinner party when he gets back from Europe at the end of the summer and invite Miss Davis along. She's getting 'up there,' he says, and he'd like to see her again before she dies.

'Just a small party, though,' he adds. He tilts his chin downward, raises his eyebrows, and looks me in the eye. 'Maybe just five or six of us. Elliot, you can arrange that, can't you?'

'Of course,' Elliot says.

Three martinis apiece later, we wind up closing the bar. As we stroll down the wide sidewalks, passing a joint and window-shopping our way back to the hotel, a police car slowly cruises past.

'Uh oh,' Elliot says, 'don't look at them.'

The cop car spins a u-ey and screeches to a halt at the curb next to us.

'Oh, *man!*' Dylan moans. He has this way of saying this favorite phrase of his so that the 'a' in man is drawn out for at least two seconds, maybe three.

The cops jump out of the car.

'How you folks doin' tonight?' the policeman with the ticket pad in his right hand says with an accent that would make Sly Stallone proud. His gun glistens in the glow of the street lamp.

Oh, Jesus. I grind the joint into the cement wall behind me. Tamping the tip out with my bare fingers, I slip the roach into my purse.

'Hi,' Ernie says, pushing to the forefront, but the cops are not interested in Ernie.

'You're Bob Dylan, aren't you?' the one with the pad asks as he moves up on Dylan.

Bob grunts.

'You think I could have your autograph?'

We all think this is pretty funny, even Bob, and as Bob scrawls a few words across a blank ticket, the cop tells him that the local radio stations are saying that the show tonight was great, and that he personally likes the ill-received *Knocked Out Loaded*, and that back home in his apartment he has a video tape of *Renaldo & Clara*.

'Yeah?' Dylan snickers. 'I'd like to see a copy of that myself.'

On a whim, Dylan decides we should walk to Paul Simon's place, but by the time we've trudged more than two-thirds of the way there, he changes his mind. When we get back to the hotel, he will have me call Art Garfunkel instead. Art's wife will answer groggily, and even after I tell her it's *Bob Dylan* calling, she will insist that Art is not awake now.

Around 4am, Dylan, Ernie, Elliot, and I limp into the surprisingly busy Stage Deli for pastrami sandwiches and french fries. At this hour in New York City, clearly everyone is anonymous. Bob has Ernie call Carole to see if she wants to join us, but she's asleep and pissed off and tells Ernie to tell Bob to go fuck himself.

July 19 1987. Eugene, Oregon. Carole is definitely not with us now. In fact, I'm the only woman on this stop. Bob and I are alone on the bus for the first time. We're sitting across from each other in his private lounge toward the back, smoking a joint and talking about how, when he played Oregon in the 60s, counterculture superhero Ken Kesey put acid in his iced tea without telling him, so that when he walked out onto the stage, his whole vista of the audience was broken down into cubes.

'I went ahead and played anyway,' he tells me. 'And people said I was pretty good.'

He's surprised that I don't know about Wavy Gravy, the political peace activist who dressed like a clown, or the Merry Pranksters—a band of Kesey fanatics dedicated to promoting the use of psychedelics, who stopped by his house once to pick him up in their magic bus— or that famous avant-garde photography and art magazine from the 60s, *Réalités*.

Suddenly, Bob gets the idea that I should go out and count the number of steps from our bus to the stage, because he's blind as a bat, he says, and it helps him when he makes his entrance to know for sure how far he's got to go. I don't know if he's playing with me, or if he always does this, or if it's a brand new thought that just popped into his head, but after counting something like four hundred steps, I return to the bus to find him parading up and down the vehicle's narrow aisle wearing the three-quarter length tie-dye jacket I bought in Philadelphia, and gazing at himself in each of the bus's mirrors.

'Where'd you get this coat?' he wants to know.

'I can't leave you alone for a second,' I tease him. 'Philly,' I shrug.

'*Philly*? Did you get me one?'

'No. Ernie said you wouldn't like it.'

'Ernie doesn't know what I like,' Bob growls, looking me dead in the eye. '*You* know what I like.'

Me? Is this for real?

The Bob Dylan is standing just a foot or two in front of me— within hugging distance—dressed in my coat, looking at me with his sad but beautiful blue bedroom eyes, telling me that *I* know what he likes. My heart is pounding like an Iron Butterfly drum solo.

I speak hesitantly, knowing that the next few words out of my mouth have the potential to turn my world, as I know it, upside down.

'Ernie says he doesn't think he's going to be able to stay out on the road with you in Europe this summer,' I begin. I'm nearly whispering.

Bob's eyes burn holes right through mine.

'Guess I better take *you* with me, then,' he says.

At the soundcheck, I feel completely overawed for the first time by Bob's celebrity status, my association with him, and the notion that he and I have developed some kind of special relationship. Ernie is off working, and I don't really have anyone else on the tour to talk to. I wander the vast stadium feeling isolated and precarious, like a Ming vase balanced on the head of a pin.

The Dead have always given me the creeps, anyway, and now I don't know whether it's because they're aware of how close I'm getting to Dylan or what, but they all shine me on like I'm some bimbo. Even Bill Graham seems unfriendly all of a sudden, telling me he didn't recognize me as I walk by, and I wonder if it's some new look I've taken on.

Ernie's the only one who doesn't seem to notice. I corner him at the hotel.

'Bob invited me to go with him on the Europe tour.'

'Great,' Ernie says. And he means it.

'I'm not sure if it's great, or not,' I say. 'I mean … I have my script to contend with. Finding an agent and stuff … I don't know.'

What I *do* know is I'm afraid of being left alone with Dylan: afraid of what will happen when it's just the two of us, afraid and excited, and definitely not able to articulate it.

'Maybe it's not such a good idea,' I add casually.

'Don't be stupid,' Ernie says. 'You're a writer. This is an opportunity for you to travel with one of the world's biggest literary giants of all times. You've got to go.'

That evening, Ernie, Dylan, and I have an early dinner at an unbelievably crowded restaurant close to the venue. While Bob and I wait in the long line, warding off the hungry glances of his fans, Ernie works his magic, and before long we're escorted to a tall, round table in the rear of the restaurant, from which I'm pretty sure the previous occupants were asked to leave.

When Ernie excuses himself to make calls, Bob asks, 'Have you thought about what I asked you?'

I forget what alcoholic beverage we're drinking—some Mai Tai–like concoction in a tall glass—but he keeps having the waitress refill mine, and I keep dumping the booze in the proverbial potted palm behind me.

'Yeah …' I reply.

'Well?'

'I don't know. I've got this script I've been working on …'

Dylan swigs from his glass, then sets it back down on the table too loudly.

'Let me know by tonight,' he says. 'OK? After the show.'

'OK.'

Ernie's back. The tab's paid, but Bob wants to linger—despite the fact that we're running late—and talk about the European tour, which is scheduled to begin in Israel in September.

'Before Tel Aviv …' Bob says as he kills his drink, 'I'm thinkin' we should spend a week in Egypt.'

As the sun drops down behind the picturesque mountains, Bob and I wait for Ernie out in front of the quaint hotel by an outdoor water wheel. Various members of the entourage pass by.

'People just don't know how to act around me,' Dylan says. Shades of 'Idiot Wind.' He takes a toke and passes me the joint.

'They're afraid of you,' I volunteer. I should know.

'Why?' he asks. He seems genuinely astonished.

'Why do you think?' I say, somewhat annoyed. 'You're the fucking most famous person in the world.'

'Well, I just wish they wouldn't do that,' he grumbles.

The weedy field behind the hotel turns gold with the sun's last light. Florescent hot pink streaks the turquoise sky. I'm a sunset junkie.

Bob deciphers my longing glimpses.

'Let's you and me walk around the back there and get a better look.'

Autzen Stadium, Eugene. By now, I find the Dead's solo set so boring that I listen to it from the bus. Once Dylan is up, however, tonight's show offers several surprises: 'Watching The River Flow,' 'Dead Man, Dead Man,' 'Rainy Day Women,' and 'Heart Of Mine.'

Bob's voice warbles across the venue.

If you can't do the time, don't do the crime ...

The stadium's huge light boards project Dylan's spirited performance, breaking down his larger-than-life image into cubes.

After the show, Bill Graham informs Dylan that there's an empty seat on the private plane that's been chartered to carry the Dead to the next gig in Oakland. He urges Bob to take it. But Dylan is superstitious—maybe he can even see into the future—and he's not that keen on flying to begin with. A last-minute change affording him a chance to save a few hours travel time by flying on a small plane with Graham and the Dead is out of the question, and he flatly refuses the offer.

'What'd you decide,' Bob asks, the second we're alone again in his hotel room. 'You gonna come with me?'

He's pacing the room like a caged lion. He hands me a fresh drink.

'Sure,' I say, before taking a sip. But the pit in my stomach is the size of the Oakland Coliseum.

July 24 1987. Alameda County Coliseum, Oakland, California. I'm a big hit with my old Berkeley pals, as I'm able to get backstage passes for nearly all of them. Tonight's version of 'I Want You' is the best to date and will soon be the one selected to appear on *Dylan & The Dead*.

I alert my northern California girlfriend of my decision to accompany Bob on his European tour this fall.

A foghorn pierces the night like a choir of silver saxophones.

'Be careful,' she warns.

CHAPTER SIX

I want you

July 26 1987. Anaheim, California. Bob and I deplane together at John Wayne Airport. The air feels fresh for Orange County, and a sharp wind is whipping my long hair.

'Maybe one day,' I say, as we walk toward the hanger, 'they'll name an airport after you.'

'Yeah,' Bob laughs. 'Bob Dylan International. I gotta admit, it's got a ring to it.'

Tonight's concert, at the Anaheim Stadium, is the last American concert date before the Europe tour with Petty. Carole is there, and so is Elliot Mintz. Bob and I are hanging out on the bus, getting loaded, watching one of the twelve Elvis Presley movies Ernie has secured at Dylan's request for the road tour. Somewhere along the line we've acquired Neil Young's bus, and it's very cool, with deer antlers up front and center, above the driver's seat.

At one point, Bob and I sneak up to the front of the bus to check out what's happening outside. Dylan spots Elliot Mintz wearing a tan suit and white wingtip shoes, pacing in the parking lot, communicating with stadium security, a walkie-talkie pressed to his ear.

'Look at him,' Dylan snorts, really enjoying himself, 'he looks like a private detective. Check out those shoes!'

A motorcycle skids up to the curb directly in front of us and backfires. A guy is driving with a girl on the back.

'That's Stevie Nicks!' Bob shouts. He bangs his hand on the window, but she doesn't turn around. 'Go get her and invite her in!'

I press the button to open the hydraulic door.

'Just her, though,' Bob says, 'not the guy.'

Nicks climbs off the bike as I descend the stairs.

'Hurry!' Bob intones.

I wouldn't know Stevie Nicks from Grace Slick or Deborah Harry—actually I might recognize Deborah Harry—and given how much pot we've been smoking, I'm not at all sure Dylan's got the right girl.

'Uh … excuse me, are you Stevie Nicks?' I can see Bob's arms flailing frantically behind the tinted window, egging me on.

To my shock, instead of brushing me off as a potential autograph hound, the pretty blonde woman says 'Yes.'

'Uh … Bob would like to see you,' I nod my head in the direction of his bus. Before the female voice of Fleetwood Mac can ask about her friend, I add, ' … *only* you.'

For a few minutes, it's just me and Stevie Nicks and Bob, smoking and joking, and then someone else comes in—maybe David Kearney, Bob's acupuncturist, or more likely Elliot Roberts. But a while later, there's a persistent banging on the bus door, and I go to check it out. Outside on the curb, Elliot Mintz is standing there with an extraordinarily beautiful woman wearing these little silver antique glasses. Her chestnut hair, limitless eyes, and fine bones make me want to cry.

'Britta,' Elliot says, 'Sara Dylan is here to see Bob.'

'Just a minute,' I choke, forcing a smile. Her fragility is heartbreaking. 'I'll tell him you're here.'

Dylan escorts me back to the front door as Elliot helps her up the stairs. 'Sara, have you met Breeda?' Bob says.

She takes my hand.

'It's so good to meet you, finally,' I say. And then by way of excusing myself, I add, 'I'm Ernie's girlfriend.'

'Oh, Breeda,' Bob sighs, shaking his head, as I'm halfway out the door, 'you know that just isn't true, at all.'

R. Crumb, or a disciple of his, has done the very cool meal tickets for the gig. I go to the commissary to cash mine in and run into Ernie, who's getting tea for Bob's room backstage.

So, whose girlfriend am I, I'm wondering?

'Watch,' Ernie says. 'Bob will play "Mr. Tambourine Man" tonight, for Sara. It's her favorite song.'

Lots of people from Ernie's and my parties are on the grounds of the huge backstage lot. This is one of those gigs where there's backstage, and then there's *backstage*. Once Bob gets off the bus, he will have a small private room that's strictly off limits. Even I'm not free to go anywhere I want. Still, I'm on cloud nine and a half. I run into Al Kooper and his girlfriend, who are feeling somewhat miffed about not being able to get into Dylan's private quarters. I'm distracted, looking at the long line to the ladies room, wanting to get in there and back out again before show time, and I make the mistake of telling Al about my invitation to go to Europe.

'Look at you,' Kooper replies. 'All you can talk about is Bob. You're a climber and a gold digger, just like all the rest!'

His girlfriend takes a shot, too.

'I always knew you were a *groupie*!' she says.

A *groupie*? I'm not a groupie, am I? I mean, it's true that I have the highest admiration for Dylan's genius—as do Al and his girlfriend—but I never went out of my way to meet him. I didn't weasel my way into a recording session or talk myself into a bar mitzvah. It just happened. And now that I've met the man and hung out with him, I'm attracted more than ever to his playful character and quirky sense of humor … although I must admit I've always thought he was pretty cute, in that tortured Jewish intellectual sort of way. But a *groupie*? I'm stunned by the outburst, yet I can't come up with anything to defend myself.

Confused and wounded, I scurry away to join the dragging procession to the john. While I'm in line, the girl behind me—a young lady with dark eyes and even darker energy—befriends me with a compliment on my jacket, a very cool cowboy coat that once belonged to Davey Johnstone from the Elton John Band—a gift from my old boyfriend Realtor Bob, who had spent some time hanging out with that band when he worked at West L.A. Music. The girl tells me how she never misses a Dylan concert when he's in town, and what a huge fan of his she is.

At some venues, like this one, the best place to view the concert is not from the stage. I have a ticket for this show—and now, after washing my hands, I'm in a hurry to get to my seat.

'Maybe, I'll see you again sometime …' the girl's voice trails after me as I scramble away.

I'm standing behind the engineer's soundboard when Dylan takes the stage, his curly hair and neatly trimmed beard backlit and looking almost blond.

Bob's voice booms into the arena.

Hey! Mr. Tambourine Man, play a song for me …

Later, when I move backstage, I see Carole and Sara and all these other women watching, swaying and listening to the music, as if Dylan is singing only to them. I join in.

After the show, there's a line to get into Dylan's room, and you have to pass through a security gate before you can even wait in that line. As I'm walking between the guards, flashing my All Access Pass, the strange girl from the ladies room falls in beside me.

'Hold it!' the security guard roars.

'I'm with *her*!' the young woman protests. Her dark eyes plead with me. She grabs on to my jacket sleeve.

'No,' I say, forced to shake her off. 'She's not.' I'm frightened to realize that the girl—a *real* groupie—must have been watching me all night, and after figuring out how close I was to the excitement, she'd targeted me to get to Bob.

As I wait backstage, last in the slowly shrinking line to see Dylan, one of Bob's employees—someone who's been around forever, a longtime observer of the scene—comes over to me and chuckles.

'Did you notice Sara wasn't wearing her glasses during the show?'

'What about it?' I ask.

'Bob doesn't let her wear her glasses when she watches him, 'cause he doesn't want her checking out all the other women.'

By the time I get in to see Dylan, it's just me and him and the acupuncturist in the room. This could be the last time we're together before Tel Aviv ... if I don't back out.

Bob is sweaty with a towel drooped around his neck, looking tired and drinking from one tall rum drink-filled glass after another.

'Soooo,' he grins at me. 'What'd you think of the show?'

Back at the security station, I wait for Ernie to bring the car. The strange girl from the ladies room comes skulking up and joins me on my bench. She's come from the direction of Bob's dressing room, but she doesn't seem so scary now. Instead, she seems depressed.

'I got to see him,' she mumbles, miserably. 'Up close, he just looks like an old man.'

Summer 1987. Ernie has bought this metal contraption called a Band Box out of the *Recycler*. It's similar to, but better than, the one that's in the bar at this *très* cool new restaurant, Ivy At The Shore, and he plans to install it above the jukebox in his house. A Band Box is essentially an extension speaker for a jukebox. What makes it cool is the housing—a rounded miniature stage concealed behind lavish velvet curtains. In the 50s, if you dropped a nickel in a jukebox to play a song, the curtains would open to reveal seven four-inch-tall male puppets, swaying and seemingly playing musical instruments along to the music. This Band Box is even cooler than most that you might come across—if you were lucky enough to find one in the first place—in that, instead of little men playing the music, it's monkeys. Our friends at Off The Wall will say that Michael Jackson has been looking for one like this for years.

The Band Box needs to be revamped, and I suggest to Ernie that we make a short film about the restoration. I write an insane script called *Billy Buys A Band-Box* and recruit everybody I know who has any experience at all with filmmaking, including some of Ernie's closest friends. I am writer, director, producer.

The woman who is most helpful to me on the project is Ernie's late wife Grace's best friend, an incredible artist named Nicole. Her boyfriend, a weak but talented Central American guy, becomes the film's nerdy star, but his voiceover narration will be read by my actor friend Tony Goodstone, doing his best Humphrey Bogart.

One day, as I'm trying out a new camera angle in the kitchen, I find myself lamenting my relationship with Ernie to Nicole. I confess that I think Ernie's still in love with Grace, and that even though he keeps dressing me sexier and sexier, telling me what to do with my life and who and how I should be, I just can't become her.

'They were never married,' Nicole says.

The reflection in the glass doors of the refrigerator causes a flare in the lens.

'I'm sorry. What?' I steady myself on the ladder and try to keep from passing out.

'He just gave her a ring.'

At this point, I see a shrink. I've got a line on a therapist in Westwood who's about my age, Jewish, and a Bob Dylan fan. After hearing my family history and listening to my quandary about Ernie, his ex, my fears about Bob, and my wanting to stay home and work on my screenplay, she develops a genuine concern for my future psychological welfare and advises me in no uncertain terms that it would be *a bad idea* for me to go on the tour with Dylan. In the moment, I'm inclined to agree.

Carole's friend who's a literary agent at William Morris calls me in for a meeting after reading *Johnny Paradise*. I'm nervous, and I'm forced to wait nearly an hour. When I step inside the plush office, I notice a framed photo of the agent standing with her arm around Bob. The photo's facing outward on the desk, I presume, to impress prospective clients.

The script I've written is about a charismatic serial killer who gets discovered and made into a movie star, and the female private detective who tracks him down and brings him to justice. The agent says she has to pass on the effort, but tells me I'm a good writer, and she'd be happy to look at anything else I come up with in the future.

Mid August 1987. Dylan calls from his farm in Minnesota.

'What are you up to?' I ask.

'Readin' and writin',' he says. 'What are *you* doin'?'

When I'm not reworking my script, I've been trying to write some songs.

'Singin',' I tell him.

'Singin'? What are ya singin'?' he laughs. '"Just Like A Woman?"'

We both have a good chuckle about that.

Bob tells me he's been 'swimmin',' too, but that it's hot and humid, and I wouldn't believe how big the mosquitoes are back there. I ask if he's heard about the upcoming Harmonic Convergence, and he says yeah, but he doesn't know a lot about it. I tell him I'm supposed to go out to this friend's house in the Mojave Desert—she's sort of a female witch doctor—and hang out with her on a mountaintop all day and night when it happens. I tell him there's a map that shows all the places on the planet that are purported to be the most spiritually grounded, and that Malibu is one of them. I also tell him that I've mentioned the event to Ernie and he's not interested at all.

Dylan says he's supposed to fly back to LA that Sunday, and he's worried about going up in an airplane. I tell him I'll check with my friend about it, if he wants me to, and he says he'll call me back later that day to find out what she says.

My spiritual advisor, Elaine, is actually of Jewish-Italian descent, a mother of three who I met in New York with Realtor Bob in the early 80s. It was with her encouragement that one of her sons had become my forever-younger lover shortly thereafter. Overweight, and a chain smoker, with a younger man of her own, she's recently retired from years of cooking spaghetti marinara and potato latkes to coddle herself in the California world of astrology, crystals, and new age panaceas. I call her as soon as I hang up from Bob.

'The peak of the convergence will occur between sunrise and midnight on Monday,' she tells me, between long drags. 'Hopi Indians say to use our eyes, ears, hearts and heads … our intuition … to experience total trust and achieve complete harmony.'

'We're supposed to do whatever feels best,' I tell Dylan when he calls. I've taken notes, and I repeat them almost verbatim, proud to be of service. 'Experience no fear. Surrender. She says wherever you are on the earth is sacred. If you have a strong urge to be anywhere, be there. We have to stay aware and abandon ourselves to any galactic input we may be getting.'

'I'm open to whatever messages are coming through,' Bob says.

Ernie approaches Dylan for a loan to help finance his latest business venture. He's come up with a way for people to go into record stores and make their own custom tapes and CDs. It's an expensive idea to set up, because it requires the use of satellites, but once it's in place, it should make millions.

Ernie's worked for Bob since the mid 70s, and they are friends. Ernie asks Bob for $100,000, to be paid back with interest, and a piece of the action, but to both Ernie's and my astonishment, Bob turns him down. Despite his stoicism, I can tell Ernie's hurt.

Dylan is back. He calls from Malibu at 7:30 on Saturday morning and wakes me up.

'I need you to do me a favor,' he drawls, 'and go pick up this friend of mine at the airport and bring her up here to the house.'

Since I'm deathly afraid of rejection, saying no has never been my forte. Saying no to Bob Dylan will be one of the hardest things I've ever attempted in my life.

'Uh … I'd love to help you out,' I say, 'but I'm … uh … busy, today, writing. Can you find someone else?'

'Ohhhhh … *well*, OK. If that's how it is,' he says.

'What do you mean?' I ask, my antenna for disapproval shooting up.

'I mean, if you don't want to help me out, I guess I'll have to call someone else.'

My heart is hanging upside down in my chest. I can't let Bob Dylan down, can I?

'What time does the plane come in?' I ask, shelving any plans I have to go over my script one last time before sending it out again in hopes of landing an agent.

The flight from Dallas–Fort Worth is forty-five minutes late. Bob has told me to pick up a woman named Marlene at the airport. He says she's black. 'You'll know her when you see her.' I have no idea what to expect.

A stream of grumpy passengers slowly emerges from the plane, and there are only two black women among them. The first looks like a plumber, the second a librarian, and neither answers to the name of Marlene. Just when I'm about to give up, one last passenger appears in the gangway. A striking, dark-skinned young woman, approximately five foot ten—even taller in three-inch platforms. She's all legs, and she's wearing hot pants. Gulp.

'Marlene?'

The two of us have a great drive up to Malibu in Ernie's Celica with the top down. She tells me she met Bob the year before, in Texas, when he was on the True Confessions tour. She and her girlfriends were trying to buy scalpers tickets to the sold-out show when Dylan sent one of his emissaries, probably Ernie, to fetch her. After the gig, she says, Bob begged her to accompany him on his bus to the next destination. After a lot of soul-searching—she tells me she's a devout Christian—and some urging from her friends, she agreed to go. Later, she tells me, she was horrified to learn that there was a woman on the backup singers' bus right behind them who was carrying Bob's baby, but she spent the night with Dylan anyway.

When we show up at the house, I start to leave, but Bob asks me to stay.

'What for?' I ask.

I can tell by the look on his face that he can't believe I have anything to do that would be more important than hanging out with him, and after thinking about it for a second or two, I have to agree. Still, I'm pretty much left to my own devices as the two lovebirds go off to get reacquainted. I pick a book off the shelf and sit out on the deck reading it. It's an incredible book about carnivals or circuses, or both, a large volume printed on expensive stock with the most marvelous illustrations imaginable.

At one point, Dylan comes out to check on me.

'You've never seen that book?'

'No,' I gasp. 'I love it.'

'Someone important gave it to me,' he says, wandering back inside the house.

Later, when I go in the kitchen to get a glass of water, I can hear Bob and Marlene making love on the bed in the master bedroom upstairs, and it makes me feel queasy. They're up there for hours before he comes down around three and asks me to go shopping for them at the Mayfair Market.

'I think we should have a barbecue,' he says, and at first I'm unclear as to whether or not I'm invited. He writes out a shopping list, gives me some money, and walks me to the car.

In the garage, next to Bob's well-preserved red Caddy convertible from the 70s, I notice a brand new Harley. It's maroon, tricked out with shiny studs and soft leather. He says he's got plans to beef it up even more—a custom fringe-and-stud saddle bag has been ordered, and, any day now, it'll be on its way.

'Haven't I shown you this bike before?' Bob asks, scratching his head. 'You'd love it. At sunset … down the coast … goin' for a ride. I think I'll take Mar out after supper.'

At the market, picking out groceries that I won't be eating, I'm feeling resentful. It's not like I'm on Bob's payroll or anything. I've wasted the entire day. What am I doing here?

Back in the kitchen, as I unload the stuff onto the counter from stiff paper sacks, Bob and Marlene are buzzing around me like a pair of contented honeybees. I leave the change on the counter and don't look back.

'Have a good time!' I chirp.

I'm one of those people who are driven to write. Sometimes I think it's a curse. When I'm not writing, I forget who I am.

Bob calls me while I'm at the computer and says he's looking for a hat rack. 'You know, a place where people can hang their hats when they come in the door.'

I tell him I have an old oak one from the turn of the century in my garage in Westwood that will hold both hats and coats.

'Oh yeah?'

Escape. Transfer. Save. Quit.

I drive the antique up to his house to lend it to him, but when I get there, he's not home. His assistant, Carol, accepts it for him.

Before I know it, I have an agent. In fact, I'm actually picking one from three. Since the Harmonic Convergence, I'm feeling very intuitive, so I choose the one named Erica Voltaire, because if that's not a literary name, what is? I make the mistake of befriending her. As soon as she hears about what's going on with me in my relationship with Ernie and my budding friendship with Dylan, she, too, discourages me from going on the tour.

'There's no way I can go out on the road with Dylan,' I tell my dear friend Lon Diamond, who's been staying in my apartment while I'm living at Ernie's. Lon is a writer too—a comedy writer who will go on to create and produce a hit show on Fox called *Parker Lewis Can't Lose.*

'My agent thinks my script is really hot,' I add, 'but she wants me to make a few changes before she sends it out.'

Lon cringes at the thought of my possible missed opportunity.

'What are you going to do,' he asks, 'tell your grandchildren that you could have gone around the world with Bob Dylan, but you stayed home to rewrite your screenplay?'

Lon's young and enthusiastic—one of my favorite people on the planet. He offers to take care of my dog while I'm gone. Maybe he's right.

I drive to the beach and sit on a rock at sunset. The pounding surf vibrates up through the stone, slamming me to my core. My relationship with Ernie has been tense—we're just going through the motions. Any attempts I've made to talk to him about it have been stifled with a kiss. My agent's a bit of a nutcase … who knows if she can sell my script? I've sublet my apartment for another four months, so now, other than Ernie's, I don't really have a place to live. And then, of course, there's my growing fondness for Mr. Dylan.

Behind the dim outline of Catalina Island, the sun sinks like a ship. I look up the coast toward Bob's house and feel an immediate tug at my heartstrings. Point 'Doom' is aglow in fiery red.

As usual, Dylan's lyrics come back to haunt me.

When you ain't got nothing, you got nothing to lose.

What the hell, I decide. I *will* go.

Ernie says that Dylan wants to take a cane on the trip, for walking. We go to this pipe-and-tobacco place on Wilshire Boulevard called the Tinder Box, where Bob has told him they have a good selection. I pick out one with a hand-carved wooden handle, and Ernie picks out one that's made of a Bull's penis.

'Once the cocks are surgically removed from the animals,' the guy behind the counter tells us, 'they're dried and stretched and shaped to fit comfortably in the base of your hand.'

I think this sounds disgusting.

'Where are they from?' Ernie wants to know.

'South America. But the market's drying up, so they're going to be rare. By the way, I don't know if you noticed, but no two are alike.'

Ernie puts the cane I've picked back and buys three of the bull penis canes. When we deliver them to Bob's house in Malibu that night, he loathes them.

It's three days before we're scheduled to leave for New York, before flying off to Egypt. Ernie's been working around the clock at the office, and I've been tying up all my loose ends. I'm resting on the sofa in the den with a strong cup of black coffee and a good book when Ernie comes home from work and tells me he's not sure whether or not I'll be able to go out on the road with Dylan after all.

'*What?*'

'Bob just said, today, he wasn't sure about you going, that's all.'

'You have got to be kidding me,' I say. Now that I've made the momentous decision to go with him—against my better judgment—*Bob's* undecided?

I've been doing laundry for weeks, planning outfits for everything from the desert to the snow—it's nearly a three-month tour, so we're going to be covering a lot of territory—my passport's been renewed, and most importantly I've resigned myself to putting my professional and creative life on hold. I've even had my shots, for Chrissake!

'I've never been so insulted in my life!' I yell.

'That's Bob for you,' Ernie shrugs.

Now I'm really in a tailspin. I go to bed and stay there.

The phone rings on Thursday.

'Are you packed?' It's Ernie, calling from his car.

'Yeah,' I sniffle.

'Good, 'cause we're leaving tomorrow.'

Ernie tells me Bob's put me on the payroll for the tour. I'll be receiving a salary plus a daily per diem. My official title is vague, but I'm supposed to buy clothes for Dylan—even though Susie, his costumer, will be with us—and run errands.

Ernie says we need three small flashlights, one for each of us, and one for Bob to carry, in the event of an emergency—will I get them? He also tells me not to forget to bring a hat for the sun, and to remind him to tag my luggage at home before we leave—with the Lookout Management logo, and my own individual number—so that it will be easy to identify my bags from everyone else's on the tour, let alone from all the other passengers on the various, buses, trains, boats, and planes we'll be taking.

Swollen-eyed, I roll over on the bed and stare up at the ceiling.

'Did Bob come up with a name for this tour?' I ask.

'Yeah,' Ernie says. 'Temples In Flames.'

That afternoon, I go to the Beverly Center and buy three different colors of Penlights and a Greek fisherman's cap à la Carole's, only black. I call Karla from a payphone near the pet store to say goodbye, and she invites me up to her West Hollywood Hills abode for a quick cup of coffee.

Karla is an artist as well as a musician, and her house is a masterpiece. Karla's thumb is green, too, and the view of her garden from each of her hilltop home's clerestory windows looks like a picture of heaven. She also collects pottery and Mission-style furniture, long before they will come back into vogue.

As we sit in her charming breakfast nook, sipping freshly brewed organic coffee from hand-thrown mugs, her stern brown eyes admonish me.

'You realize if anything happens between you and Bob, it will be the end of Bob and Ernie's friendship.'

She can probably tell by my expression that I haven't given the idea the slightest thought. I grit my teeth at the prospect.

'What made you change your mind?' she asks. I can tell she's worried, but that she'll still love me no matter what I do.

'Destiny?' I say, unsure.

That night, Ernie has me call my Beverly Hills gynecologist and get a prescription for Valium so we can sleep on the plane. I don't want to make the call because I've never taken it before and I'm not really a fan of the harder stuff.

'The trick to overcoming jetlag is to sleep and drink plenty of water during the flight,' he assures me.

We pull up at the pharmacy on the way to the airport. I run in and pick up a small brown vial, which contains thirty 10mg Valium—the blues, the strongest ones, the ones that are the hardest to get.

Late, late, late August 1987. LAX is a nightmare of people, and no one can find Bob. We have six first-class tickets to New York—which Ernie says were hard to find at the last minute—including one for Carole, who is waiting, furious and frustrated, with the rest of us. Elliot Roberts is there, too, as is David Kearney, the acupuncturist; Bob's son Jakob; and Stan Golden, Bob's debonair cousin, who's a dentist in Brentwood. The plane has already boarded, and the voice over the PA advises everyone in the airport that this will be TWA's last call.

'Find him!' Ernie yells at me, and everyone scatters.

For some reason—call it intuition—I head all the way back to the street and find Bob wandering, disoriented, on the sidewalk at the main entrance to the airline.

'We're gonna miss the plane!'

I take Bob's arm and steer him in the right direction. He staggers along beside me.

'You wanna go have a drink?'

The airline holds the flight nearly ten minutes for Dylan, but by the time I can get him back to the boarding area, all of our well-tagged, easily identifiable luggage is flying off to New York without us.

This is the kind of thing Ernie gets paid for: he quickly determines that there's another flight leaving from a different terminal in less than a half hour, even though only Bob will be able to fly first class. The six of us run to catch it.

We're checked back in to the Parker Meridien, and this time the Heartbreakers are checked in with us. I'm surprised to see how green and lush Central Park looks in the summer. On the way into the hotel, Bob strikes up a conversation with a street vendor who's selling hippie belts and jewelry on the sidewalk. Adding insult to the previous injury, he tells Ernie he wants to lend the guy $25,000 to get the business on its feet, and asks him to look into it.

Dylan is committed to come up with a couple of drawings to be auctioned off and used on Christmas cards for Unicef.

'Breeda,' he says, 'you look like a model.'

To keep in shape, he's had the hotel get him a punching bag for the room. Between punches, he sketches a quick charcoal portrait of me and his cousin Stan.

The night before we're set to leave for Egypt, there's a party at Dylan's business managers' fabulous apartment, with views of the Chrysler Building and the Empire State. It's here that I first learn, to my shock, that Carole will not be going on the rest of the tour with us.

'She's got stuff to do at home,' Bob says. There have been whispers that she's thinking of having a facelift.

The party's a stiff. I drink one martini after another, floating lifelessly through the fifteen or so people who have come out to celebrate. For some reason, I only feel energized, lately, when I'm interacting with Bob, and at this event, that behavior seems totally inappropriate.

Naomi, the female half of Bob's married money-management team, approaches me as I sit alone on the back of the couch, gazing out the window at the perfectly lit New York skyline.

'You OK?' she asks.

'Sure,' I smile. 'I'm just tired.' And I am.

I'm wearing a black dress made out of some stretchy new fabric that's riding up the sides of my thighs, making me feel overexposed.

'Why are *you* going on the tour?' She catches me off guard.

My heart skips a beat.

'I always worry about you girls,' she clucks. 'I worry something will happen when you get around a big star like Bob.'

September 2 1987. Bob, Ernie, Elliot Roberts, Jakob, David Kearney, Cousin Stan, and I fly off to Egypt in the morning with the whole Tom Petty Band and their wives. I've met Tom a couple of times by now, and offstage he's almost anti-charismatic. Dylan's middle son, Sam, has also joined us, as has Victor Maymudes, who was Bob's very first road manager, back in the 60s. Roger McGuinn, Bob's opening act for the tour, will be meeting us in Israel, and Jesse, Bob's oldest son, is scheduled to join the tour at about the halfway point.

I sit next to Victor on the plane. He has the looks of a Greek god who's been ravaged by two thousand years of time. He's tall, smart, and funny, but beaten. The rumor is he's left his wife and kids in New Mexico to die on the road with Dylan. He says there are worse things in the world than hanging out and picking up Bob Dylan's sloppy seconds. He tells me stories of the early days when Bob was so broke in New York he sold his body for twenty bucks a pop, and yes, he says, there really was a motorcycle accident that put him out of commission for a year or so when he was living in Woodstock.

'No heroin?' I ask, wondering about the stories I'd read over the years.

The long flight's going really fast.

'Well there was some of that, too,' Victor says, 'so everyone around Bob used the accident as an excuse to keep him down and get him cleaned up.'

At some point, Ernie requests a Valium, and I take a half. When I wake up, the plane's circling the airport in Cairo.

Egypt is my first third-world country. Dirt, dust, and poverty abound.

'Why do I feel like we've just entered enemy territory?' Cousin Stan jokes as we disembark.

Upon arrival, we are swept away in Mercedes diesel taxies to the palatial oasis on the Nile where we'll be staying.

Inspired by the ruins of an ancient culture—the structure is actually centered on a restored palace—the Marriott Hotel exudes all the amenities the twentieth century has to offer. On our first afternoon there, members of Dylan's immediate entourage gather at the luxurious Olympic-sized outdoor swimming pool to bask in the rays of a burning sun.

I'm wearing a shimmery, flesh-colored, almost animal-skin-looking one-piece with long fringe that moves when I do. The V-shaped neckline leaps off my shoulders and plunges to its death just short of my naval. This is the first time I've worn a bathing suit in front of Dylan, and I'm painfully aware of how I look every second. Bob is wearing only a skimpy black speedo. Suddenly, I feel stripped naked.

I walk to the deep end of the pool, and as Bob watches, I dive in. By the time I emerge, he is holding court over Ernie, Victor, and the Petty Band. He goes off on one of his prophetic tangents, telling us all over cocktails that he's a great believer in the sound of words, and how their derivations come to mean what they are even more than their actual definitions. He says that, in Hebrew, the word 'media' means darkness, and that since he's learned this he refuses to use the media.

'The media is the devil,' Bob says, 'and it won't be long before

all it'll take is one charismatic leader to bring the whole world to
its knees.'

Before dark, Jakob, Sam, Elliot R., Doctor K., and I hire horses and
ride across the windswept sand to the omnipresent Pyramids. Bob
doesn't want to go.

The Pyramids are haunting, even as you look right at them.
Their sheer stature is staggering, as is the notion of the manpower it
must have taken to build them. Most of the way, we are trailed by
impoverished teenagers on horseback, who insist we accept bottles of
Cokes as gifts even though we don't want them, then ask us for three
dollars each. Once we're able to lose them, we gallop across the plains
of white, watching in reverence as the hot Egyptian sun dissolves
into a puddle beyond the distant dunes.

The next day, all of us go sightseeing, including Bob. There is
hardly another soul in the main museum, where all the Tut artifacts
are being preserved. Bob and I have broken off from the rest of our
group when I notice Ernie below me on the main floor, having an
altercation with a young black man. It's clear the fellow is pleading
for an introduction to Dylan. My God, is there no place the guy can
go without being bothered?

As I approach them, I hear the kid say he's from the Midwest.

'You *have* to introduce me,' he wails, pulling out his wallet to
show his driver's license. 'My name is Bob Dylan Johnson.'

Later, Bob will tell me it's really hard being him. 'Just when you
are getting into something, all of a sudden you have to think about
yourself.'

The high point of the day will be Bob and I standing riveted—
for nearly ten minutes—in awe of a four-thousand-year-old
tambourine.

Back at the hotel, Bob models the gallibaya and kufiya I bought for him. With his dark hair and beard, he looks right at home in the long flowing white shirt and Arafat-style headdress. I'm particularly glad that he says he's fond of a hand-tooled leather suitcase I found for him. I present him with yet another walking stick, this one made from buffalo horn, and he loves it so much that he asks me to find him two more. When I go back to the room to get money, I discover Ernie, preoccupied with his business back home, hasn't had time to go out shopping for Bob.

A bunch of us attend the light-and-sound show at the Sphinx. Doctor Kearney has a religious experience. Dylan sleeps through it.

According to legend, the Sphinx was to destroy itself once Oedipus solved its riddle. The enormity of the landmark is awe-inspiring, but pollution has taken its toll. Severe erosion has defaced the wonder—a restoration is underway—and after experiencing the rampant commercialism glutting the narrow streets leading up to the monument, the show is kind of depressing.

Afterwards, we're joined by members of the Petty band and their wives at the Felfela Restaurant in Cairo, where about twelve of us laugh, drink, and feast on some of the best Middle Eastern food in the world. Our table looks like the Last Supper, with Bob, bearded and scraggly haired, playing Jesus. I'm sitting across from him. Fresh warm pita bread, vegetables, platters of fish, lamb chops, shish kabob—the food and drink just keep coming.

'Here's to Kabob Dylan,' Cousin Stan howls, raising his wine glass.

And, everyone raises a glass to Bob.

The next morning we rise early. Ernie has hired private cars to take us to the place Bob most wants to go in Egypt: Memphis. While the rest of us crawl through the ruins of tombs, sweaty faces caked with dust—even posing as mummies for pictures in the crypts—Dylan, who says he doesn't believe in this sort of thing, sits outside with his boys in the boiling midday sun. At one point he tells our guide, who has said he plans to go to Memphis, Tennessee, to erect a statue of Ramses, that maybe they ought to erect a statue of Elvis Presley here.

On the return trip, we stop at a country store for sodas. The people on the outskirts all wear black, despite the heat. Sitting on the porch before we get back into our humid vehicle, Bob and I sip from glass bottles and watch as women, overburdened in heavy black cloth, march dutifully alongside the steaming asphalt road, carrying tall baskets of God-knows-what on their heads.

'I like the notion of women doing all the hard work,' Bob teases.

Seconds later, a black carriage jerks to an awkward halt in front of the place. The horse, too hot and too old to pull its load, falls to the ground. As Dylan and I watch in dismay, the driver, an old man, beats and whips the horse unmercifully. Before we can think to protest, Ernie snatches us from the porch and hustles us off to the car.

Bob is so enamored with Egypt that we stay an extra day. Time is of the essence now in terms of making it to rehearsals for the Tel Aviv show, but when it comes time to leave, Bob tells Ernie to cancel our plane reservations. He's having second thoughts about flying, and he wants to take a bus across the Gaza Strip to Israel. Ernie, Bob's ever-faithful servant, complies without complaint.

The only bus available for this purpose is what looks to be an American school bus from the 1950s. It's been painted red but the enamel is faded and peeling. The seats are small, old, and majorly uncomfortable. The shock absorbers have evidently never been replaced, and once closed, the door will prove almost impossible to open. Needless to say, the Petty band flies on without us.

There are only two other people traveling on the bus besides Dylan's immediate entourage: a couple who appear to be American. For ten hours, the view through the grimy windows will be one of dust, dirt, and desert. Sleeping is impossible, with or without the help of Valium. I try to take a photograph of Dylan, his back wedged on the bottom of his broken-springed seat and his legs thrown over the chair in front of him, trying to take a nap, but due to the constant jouncing and jostling of the bus, his image will elude my camera.

We stop once in a parched village to use the bathroom facilities. Victor has to use a knife to pry open the bus door. The female half of the American couple approaches me in the ladies room.

'Is that Bob Dylan?' she asks. She can hardly believe her own question.

'No,' I say, dribbling the lukewarm water that trickles from the cold side of the tap into my palms and then onto my face. 'Looks just like him, though, doesn't it?'

I've popped her celestial balloon, but I'm proud of myself at how deftly I'm able to protect my hero.

'Oh, my husband's going to be so disappointed,' the woman says.

'Yeah,' I say. 'Biff's a ringer for Bob, all right. We get that all the time.'

September 4. Tel Aviv, Israel. The city is not what I'm expecting. We drive straight through the heart of it and wind up in a high-rise hotel overlooking the nearly mystical shoreline. The view from our fourteenth-story room is breathtaking. I stand transfixed by the window, contemplating the Mediterranean in all its changeable shades of green and blue as it rocks back and forth over a long stretch of what looks like white sand and pearls.

Upon arrival, Dylan is besieged by the press. The fans seem to know our floor number before we do. The hotel catches reporters with walkie-talkies hiding in the stairwells and elevators. The onslaught, Dylan will tell me later, reminds him of when he and Sara tried to honeymoon here in the 70s, and the hungry Israeli reporters and photographers ruined any chance the couple might have for romance.

'That's why Cairo was so great,' Bob says. 'There was none of that Bob Dylan shit!' Very little of it, anyway.

Now, Dylan's angry, and when one spirited journalist using the ruse of room service does find his way to his suite, he yells through the door, 'Bob Dylan is staying across the hall!'

While Ernie and I shower, our door is nearly beaten down by the press. A camera's bulb flashes four times before the photographer realizes that Ernie—standing at the open door, dripping, with a white towel wrapped around his waist—is not Bob.

Dylan's first journey to his religious homeland in more than twenty-five years is met with immediate controversy, as due to yet another alleged Lookout screw-up, he doesn't show up for a scheduled luncheon with Prime Minister Shimon Perez. Supposedly, the invitation was declined by telephone through the management company, but never confirmed by letter, and now it appears that the *arrogant* Bob Dylan has had the audacity to stand up the Israeli Prime Minister. Dylan still refuses to meet with Perez, Ernie says, because he doesn't 'feel like it,' and despite numerous apologies, Bob is never quite forgiven. A second Tel Aviv concert is canceled with almost no notice, and the Temples In Flames tour is off to a rocky start.

September 5 1987. Hayarkon Park, Tel Aviv, Israel. At some point, I've scored a gig for my northern California girlfriend to design a T-shirt for Dylan. Cleverly, she models the logo after the old 'Greetings From …' hand-colored postcards, except instead of using tourist landmarks in the artwork, each letter of Bob's name contains a glimpse of him from one of his previous album covers. It's a very cool shirt. Bob likes it and approves it, but it isn't a big seller.

Now, sitting in Dylan's hotel suite, surrounded by piles of newly silk-screened shirts—designed by someone else—the two of us lament the *official* tour logo for Temples In Flames. Dylan's bummed, and I try lamely to allay his fears. The emblem is a profile of an American Indian in full and flaming headdress superimposed on a map of Western Europe. It says 'Dylan' in large script on the feathers, with 'Petty' in only slightly smaller script below it.

'Who's Dylan Petty?' Bob sighs.

Tonight's show will play to mixed reviews. Bob is still tired from the long bus ride, and the press will interpret this as a lack of enthusiasm on his part. The 35,000-plus avid fans in the audience, who've waited decades for his return, want only to hear the long-abandoned original versions of his songs. His final encore, 'Go Down Moses,' leaves the crowd dazed and confused.

September 6 1987. Robert Hilburn shows up at the hotel for a scheduled interview with Dylan, but protocol dictates that he has to knock on Ernie's and my door first, and Ernie is sleeping. I walk with Hilburn the few feet to Dylan's suite and tap lightly on the door. There's no answer. We can hear Bob strumming his guitar inside, and when I go to knock a second time, only louder, Hilburn stops me.

'Wait,' he says reverently. 'Let him finish.'

Tues morn
Dec. 4

Britta! Hi! Hi! Hi!

Processed your
Dylan order this morning.
Hope to see you shortly –
you'll have to come over
and meet my lady – we're
getting married the 29th in
Michigan. – Hope you get
the ticket of your dreams.
as always,
Mark

Above At home after a three-month hitchhiking tour of Europe in 1970, my newly acquired Dylan poster already framed on the wall behind me.
Right The ticket note from my Berkeley pal re: Bob's Valentine's Day concert in '74—best seats ever!
Below Me in 1967, possibly in Mexico City. The Berkeley experience has yet to take hold ...

SEP   67

Yoko Ono

Yoko Ono letters, Part II.

The anti-Yoko mail begin arriving here even before her "A Season of Glass" album was released this month. Many readers were outraged that she would return to the recording studio so soon after her husband, John Lennon, was shot to death last December in New York.

"She is a fake who has been exploitive and disrespectful of Lennon's memory," snapped Alan L. De Mena, Los Angeles, in a letter that was printed May 31 in Calendar. Added Tom Myers, Ventura: "I think she is a no-talent profiteer."

Those sentiments have continued.

Argues William Marsh, San Diego, "If Lennon hadn't been killed, no one would even be talking about Yoko's album. So, why devote page 1 of Calendar to it?" Grumbles B. R. Cash, Santa Ana, "Whatever happened to good taste?"

But others have rushed to Ono's defense.

Here are excerpts from letters prompted by the hostility of the May 31 barrage.

Offers Britta Lee, Los Angeles: "I'm sick. I've just read the letters in Calendar accusing Yoko Ono of exploiting John Lennon's death. As a 27-year-old widow, the only way I could cope with my husband's death was to immerse myself in my work. I worked into the middle of the night and started again in the morning; rarely a day off . . . I became successful and earned a lot of money as well as the jealousy and resentment of former friends . . . as though any amount of fame or wealth could compensate for what I had been through.

'A Noted Artist Before'

"Yoko was a noted artist before she met Lennon. She is processing her pain through her work . . . Her inner strength which is allowing her to cope in this dreadful situation is one of the attributes which attracted Lennon to her in the first place. Surely, Lennon must have been better able to assess value in another human being than those of you who still cling to some infantile illusion about a band called the Beatles whose inception was nearly 20 years ago. Grow up!"

Adds Debbi Pascua, Los Osos: "I, too, find much of Yoko's work brutal in its frankness, but if anyone has the right to express it, she does. Out of love and respect for John and his music, I will try to be open minded and receptive to any future work by Yoko (and Lennon's son, Julian, if he does indeed enter the business). If I like it, I'll support it. If not, I won't buy it. Simple as that. No need for nasty judgments and condemnations."

Comment Jonathan Coe and Christopher Mascis, San Diego: "The letters in Calendar show how narrow some of the Beatles 'fans' can be. It's a shame that Lennon's fans fail to show his wife the compassion that the couple so avidly advocated."

Suggests Don Beckett, Cerritos:

Please see YOKO ONO, Page 5

Above My letter to the *Los Angeles Times* in defense of Yoko Ono, from the paper's June 20 1981 edition.
Right The boots I wore to Bob's from New Year's Eve 1985. He loved 'em so much he wanted a pair of his own.
Below A promotional notecard made by employer during the time I buried myself in work after the death of my first husband.

Lelah T.
PIERSON
Realtors©

BRITTA LEE
SALESMAN OF THE MONTH

Above Me and Karla in her backyard in the
West Hollywood Hills, 1986.

Opposite page Dylan in New York following the show at
Madison Square Garden, July 1986.
This page Dylan with Liz Taylor at a tribute to Bob
by the American Society of Composers, Authors, and
Publishers at Chasen's, Beverly Hills, March 1986;
the *Knocked Out Loaded* cover and record sleeve, with
special thanks to 'Rita and Britta.'

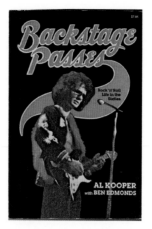

To Smith,
Hope your book does
better than this one!
Love,
St-Martin Press

Opposite page The front cover and title page of *Backstage Passes* by Al Kooper, aka 'Sex-Mouth Kooper'; Dylan onstage with the Grateful Dead.

This page The original microcassette tape containing Dylan's rambling 3am message from New York; Elliot Mintz sips red wine from a martini glass in Ernie's photo booth, 1987.

Left Bob and Tom Petty onstage at the Poplar Creek Music Theater, Chicago, July 1986.
Below The infamous 'Dylan Petty' tour laminate; the tie-dye jacket that Bob tried on on the bus, and that started the whole thing ...

Above A damaged promotional photo,
pre-signed 'Best wishes Bob Dylan.'
Below left A self-portrait Bob drew
on the bus ride between Stockholm
and Frankfurt.
Below right Bob's drawing of me and
his cousin Stan, for Unicef.

Above Dylan onstage during the Temples In Flames tour.
Right An unsent note from Bob, encouraging the recipient to 'Forgive your enemy.'

Above A photo of me in the aftermath, taken by Karla Bonoff. **Right** The jeweled white boots Bob bought me (they still fit!). **Below** A discarded satchel full of Bob's music, from the beginning of time to the mid 80s. The first song is 'Abandoned Love.'

Above Dylan outside the National Film Theatre in London, August 1986, following a screening of his film *Hearts Of Fire*.

```
              YOU CAN BLOW MY MIND
                 (If You Want To)

              Bob Dylan and Britta Lee


        My head is spinnin' round and round
        You own my heart, my soul, my skin
        My feet are flyin' off the ground
        You know I want to be with you
        And you can blow my mind...if you want to.

        People watch when we're not lookin'
        Silhouettes flashin' in the glass
        Hot is hot, they know what's cookin'
        You know I want to eat you
        And you can blow my mind...if you want to.

        I wasn't lookin' when I found you
        Now I'm blinded by your light
        I'm happy with my arms around you
        As evening's sky fades into night.

        You strike a chord in me and I just want to play it
        If there's somethin' weighin' on you, babe
        Why don't you just say it?

        The odd man out stands by the roadside
        What's he selling?  What's he got?
        The time is right for you at my side
        (Let him go now, that's his lot)
        If anyone knows about it, we do
        And you can blow my mind...if you want to.

        If I want you and you want me
        There is no room for someone else
        It's up to you to set him free
        (Lay down the cards that you were dealt)
        You know I wouldn't cheat you
        And you can blow my mind...if you want to.


                        LYRICS BY BOB DYLAN AND BRITTA LEE
                        1987
```

This page The lyrics to the song Bob and I wrote together, 'You Can Blow My Mind (If You Want To).'
Opposite page My copy of the program for the Roy Orbison Tribute Concert, as autographed by Dylan; the Certificate of Registration for 'You Can Blow My Mind (If You Want To)'; me as Dylan, Halloween 2001.

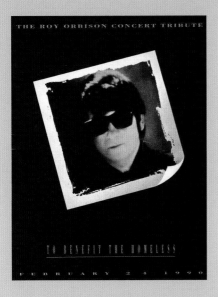

THE ROY ORBISON CONCERT TRIBUTE

TO BENEFIT THE HOMELESS

FEBRUARY 24 1990

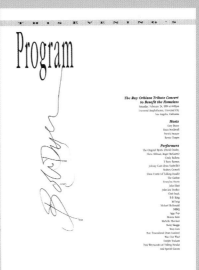

THIS EVENING'S

Program

**The Roy Orbison Tribute Concert
to Benefit the Homeless**
Saturday, February 24, 1990 at 8:00pm
Universal Amphitheatre, Universal City
Los Angeles, California

Hosts
Gary Busey
Dean Stockwell
Patrick Swayze
Bernie Taupin

Performers
The Original Byrds (David Crosby,
Chris Hillman, Roger McGuinn)
Cindy Bullens
T Bone Burnett
Johnny Cash (from Nashville)
Rodney Crowell
Chris Frantz (of Talking Heads)
The Gatlins
Emmylou Harris
John Hiatt
John Lee Hooker
Chris Isaak
B.B. King
k.d. lang
Michael McDonald
MBQ
Iggy Pop
Bonnie Raitt
Michelle Shocked
Ricky Skaggs
Steve Ciro
Pete Townshend (from London)
Was (Not Was)
Dwight Yoakam
Tina Weymouth (of Talking Heads)
And Special Guests

Certificate of Registration

This Certificate issued under the seal of the Copyright
Office in accordance with title 17, *United States Code,*
attests that registration has been made for the work
identified below. The information on this certificate has
been made a part of the Copyright Office records.

Maria A. Pallante

Register of Copyrights, United States of America

Registration Number
PAu 3-555-205

Effective date of
registration:
April 27, 2011

Title
Title of Work: YOU CAN BLOW MY MIND (If You Want To)

Completion/Publication
Year of Completion: 1987

Author
Author: BOB DYLAN
Author Created: lyrics
Work made for hire: No
Citizen of: United States   Domiciled in: United States
Year Born: 1941

Author: BRITTA LEE SHAIN
Author Created: lyrics
Work made for hire: No
Citizen of: United States   Domiciled in: United States
Year Born: 1948

Copyright claimant
Copyright Claimant: BOB DYLAN ████████████████

Copyright Claimant: BRITTA LEE SHAIN ████████████

Rights and Permissions
Name: Britta Lee Shain
Email: ████████████   Telephone: ████████
Address: ████████████

Page 1 of 2

Above Me onstage at the Levitt Pavilion Emerging
Artist Stage, Pasadena, California, September 2015.

In the couple of minutes we have together, I tell Hilburn that I'm the woman who wrote the letter he published in defense of Yoko Ono, so long ago. We hit it off, right away, finding it ironic that we would come to meet under such bizarre circumstances as standing outside Bob Dylan's hotel room door in Israel, but our encounter ends abruptly, as soon as we determine that Dylan's taking a break between riffs.

That evening, as the tour readies for the ride to Jerusalem, Hilburn presents me with a bar of soap with Elvis's image on it. He says he found it when he was out shopping and thought of me. He says, based on our earlier conversation, he had a feeling I'd appreciate it.

Ernie has arranged for four buses of the highest quality to carry Dylan and the entourage all over Western Europe. There is one bus for the Petty Band, one bus for Dylan's backup singers, the Queens of Rhythm, and another bus for Dylan's management. The best bus of all is for Dylan and his immediate family, and that is the vehicle I will be riding on for the whole of the tour.

Bob's driver is a very cool Irish guy, a former bodyguard named Jim who has most recently been a bouncer at the English equivalent of Studio 54, but who has worked in various capacities for Bob in years past. The bus ride to Jerusalem will be marred by Dylan's anger at his cousin Stan, who has taken up with a flamboyant albeit eye-catching Israeli girl and missed our departure.

September 7, Sultans Pool, Jerusalem. During the day, Bob and I go off exploring. I have more fun when I'm hanging out with him than anyone. It seems like we're into all the same crazy kind of stuff. Stuff I can never get Ernie to pay any attention to.

'Never marry anyone who doesn't share your enthusiasm,' I read in a magazine once. Dylan's enthusiasm and mine are interchangeable, synchronous:

'Look at those cracks in the paint on the wall!'

'This place has been here for a million years.'

'Longer.'

'I'm gonna take a picture of it!'

'Me too!'

On the way back to the hotel, Bob ducks into a store and buys me a hat he's seen in the window. It's black with a high stiff crest and a shiny patent leather bill—a little Third Reichian for my taste. It's not at all a hat I would have picked for myself, and I'm a little uncomfortable wearing it. Still, on the hike from the bus to the magical setting where the concert will be held, everyone compliments me.

On each date of this tour, Dylan will come up with a new set list. Tonight's show offers a vigorous version of 'Shot Of Love,' as well as a new rendition of 'Emotionally Yours.' Sometimes, I really do get the feeling that Bob's playing the show to me. He also performs the first live version of 'You're A Big Girl Now' in nine years. It's raining, and the concert ends prematurely following an electrical failure.

Kurt Loder shows up to interview Dylan for *Rolling Stone*'s twentieth anniversary issue. Dylan's sumptuous suite comes equipped with a cart that holds an ever-filled ice bucket, several different sizes of crystal glasses, and all the liquor in the world. Bob's drinking Kamikaze's, and I'm playing bartender. Cointreau, Vodka, lime juice, and lime. He and Loder sit out on the patio for four hours, talking and toking under the huge bright stars.

I can hear Bob's drawl from the living room window of our four-hundred-year-old hotel, but his words are swallowed up by my appreciation of Jerusalem's transcendent skyline as it's framed against the velvet blue sky.

After Loder's departure, Bob tells me to go wake everybody up. He wants to go to the Wailing Wall. It's 3am. Sleepy-eyed, Jakob, Sam, Elliot R., Victor, Ernie, and I join him in a late night/early morning trek from our hotel through the resplendent ancient city to the famous Israeli monument. By the time we arrive—at nearly four—only the most devout Jews are praying there.

Men and women have to pay their respects separately, and while Dylan and the other male members of his immediate entourage pray on one side of a rock ledge that divides the sexes, I will pray alone.

The wall is made up from these large, heavy, similarly sized sandstone blocks, one stacked perfectly on top of another, and the overall effect of the site—the pure power—is immeasurable. I will be struck more by the energy that emanates from this wall than from my experience with the Sphinx, the Pyramids, or any of the shrines I saw in Japan.

Up close, one can find hundreds—maybe thousands—of messages for God scrawled on tiny pieces of paper and wedged between the cracks. I'm stoned but I feel sober. *Dear God*, I'm thinking, *please let me find happiness just once—my life has been fucked up for so long. Make me strong and kind—strong and kind?— and give me the vision to see clearly.*

I'm shocked by my selfishness in the face of such wonder.

And, world peace would be nice, too.

Dylan is so taken with the wall that we return again the following night. This time, I bring my own small missive to God, which I've jotted on a page from a message pad at the Hotel. It's the last line of a Dylan song, 'Trouble In Mind,' written, ironically, during his

Christian phase. I'd recorded it earlier in the day, when Ernie was yelling on the telephone to Los Angeles about poor registration on a four-color print job, and I was on the balcony, overlooking the swaying Egyptian palms—with the muddy river running below—trying to read but not being able to, because I was so distracted by Ernie's outburst. Finally, relinquishing my book to the table, I'd stretched out under the flaming sun and opened myself up to any messages that were coming through.

I'm only happy when I'm with Bob, I realized.

Now, standing before this holy wall in the whispering breeze of the warm night air, I have a hard time making the note stick. Patiently, I squish the flimsy piece of paper between the tiny rifts in the rocks as an aged cantor's voice begins its eerie wail.

Lord, keep my blind side covered and see that I don't bleed.

CHAPTER SEVEN

You're a big girl now

Cousin Stan arrives at the hotel with the Israeli girl. She's gorgeous—big-breasted with smooth dark skin and shiny gold jewelry. But within minutes it's obvious to everyone including Stan that she's really only interested in meeting Dylan. Bob orders him to get rid of her, and Stan gets her out of Dylan's sight—not to mention his reach—fast, but he still won't be back in time to catch our bus when it leaves for Basel.

Bob and I have both brought our small cameras on the tour, and during the daylight hours on the bus, we snap pictures through the many windows, as well as a few of each other. One of my many jobs is to get his film developed, and I'm genuinely appalled by how many of his pictures are out of focus. But what's even weirder is that as good as my pictures turn out—of hotels, landmarks and even other people—the photographs I take of Dylan are almost always flawed in some critical way.

Ernie has brought along the Elvis movies and a couple of rough cuts of films that have been made by some of Dylan's friends. During the tour, Bob and I and some of the others will view an unfinished version of *Stand & Deliver*, which features his friend Roseanna de

Soto, and another as-yet-untitled film starring John Doe of the LA underground band X.

As the scenery flies by, we play chess. I think I even beat him once. Today, we've been playing and drinking and smoking pot all afternoon. Doctor K. and Victor are at the table with us, too. Bob squints at me, giving me his best all-knowing look.

'All of life's a chess game,' he confides. 'You always have to be thinking two or three moves ahead.'

Someone passes him the joint and he takes another toke. Breath sucked between clenched teeth, he nods, correcting himself.

'Five moves.'

September 10 1987. Basel, Switzerland. Somehow we've acquired a copy of the *Los Angeles Times* with Hilburn's positive interview, as well as two other papers with negative reviews of the shows in Israel. We're in Bob's room, and I'm sitting on his bed doing some of the reading while he sits on the floor shuffling through the newspaper pages spread out around him.

'I don't think everything I've done since 1965 is irrelevant!' Dylan grumbles.

'Of course, not,' I say, doing my best to console him with justified flattery.

Bob holds up a glowing article on Michael Jackson, which is accompanied by a photograph of the singer with his chimpanzee.

'Maybe, I ought to get *me* a monkey.'

During the day, I take a long walk by myself, touring as many churches, museums, and shops as I can squeeze into a single day in the antiseptic city. That night, before the show, about eight of us, including Bob, have dinner outdoors in an Italian cafe. Our white-clothed table rocks on the cobblestone plaza. Perhaps because I'm the only woman, but more likely because we both enjoy it, Bob and I almost always wind up sitting next to each other, talking.

Highlights of this evening's show, at Jakobshalle, include frisky versions of 'I Want You,' 'Trust Yourself,' and 'Seeing The Real You At Last.'

September 12 1987. Autodromo, Modena, Italy. The promo for the tour could have read, 'No two shows alike!' This is the best concert yet.

Some afternoons Dylan invites me to come back into the lounge in the rear of the bus to write down the set list, or he'll want to know what I think about the list or if there's anything special I want to hear. There's seating on either side of the aisle on these thin cushions that double as beds, in a pinch, and a TV in the corner. Farther back, behind a wall of red curtains, are Bob's private quarters.

The more time I spend alone with Bob, the more attracted I feel to him. Sometimes we just sit quietly looking out the window, or maybe he'll play his guitar. It's like there's this magnetic charge in the energy between us, and it's pulling us closer and closer.

This night, as I stand to the side of the stage, watching Bob in his high-heeled boots, he's undeniably listing in my direction—with his chest and shoulders aimed right at me—as he sings the lyrics to a song, which according to everyone present, he's never played live before …

I'm pledging my time to you.
Bob's gaze locks on mine.
Hopin' you'll come through, too …
I nearly swoon.

After the concert, Elliot R., Doctor K., and Ernie and I sit around the plush lounge of our elegant hotel while Dylan gets more and more sloshed. At one point he gets involved in a sing-along with a couple of his backup singers. Benmont Tench, the keyboard player from the Heartbreakers, is at the piano. Bob slurs his way through old standards like 'I Left My Heart In San Francisco' and new standards like 'You've Got A Friend.'

It's not long after this that the almost totally incoherent Bob Dylan falls out of his chair.

September 13 1987. Turin, Italy. Turin, Turin, Turin. Bob Dylan needs help, I've decided, and I'm going to be the one to give it to him. Having grown up in a home where alcohol abuse ran rampant, I use my psychology background to conclude that the guy has got to be incredibly miserable underneath it all to be abusing himself the way he does all the time.

I think back on all those awkward performances—*Letterman*, Live Aid—and I can only guess that he's filled with some kind of self-loathing for reasons I don't even know yet and probably will never comprehend. The road has a life of its own, and while it's been a lot of fun, the reviews have been mixed; and, back home, his career is not exactly skyrocketing.

On top of it all, I'm sure he's also unhappy because most of the people around him don't understand him—so he says. People yes him to death. But I *do* understand him—so he says—or I think I do, and this is undoubtedly why he and I seem to be spending so much time together.

The date is rapidly approaching when Ernie will have to return to Los Angeles. I'm overwhelmed by a rush of anticipation.

Late in the afternoon, after soundcheck and before the show, Bob and I decide to go for a walk.

I'm ready to go anywhere …

We find a park several blocks from the venue and wander off into the woods together. As I trail along behind him, Mr. Tambourine Man plays his harmonica.

In a thicket of tall trees, I sit nearby watching him and listening to his plaintive strains while the soft yellow sun sends spikes of light through the branches to caress him. I try to imagine Carole sitting on the ground, giving Bob this kind of attention, and I can't.

Darkness falls. We hurry to the entrance of the gig at the Palasport, where fans are already gathering. Blockades have been erected, the sidewalks roped off.

The guard asks to see our IDs.

'This *is* Bob Dylan,' I say, but the guy doesn't speak English.

Bob just stands there helplessly in his hooded sweatshirt.

'Bob Dylan!' I scream and point at Bob, who's trying to keep a straight face.

'Passes?' another guard says.

Now, both Bob and I are laughing hysterically.

Finally, Ernie, who's been looking everywhere for us, comes running up, pushes the guards out of the way, and lets us in.

Dylan will be in rare form tonight, playing lengthy and cohesive harmonica intros to rarely performed classics like 'License To Kill.'

After the show, Ernie and I go to an Italian eatery and buy tons of takeout antipasto for the bus ride—Bob has a thing for sausage— along with several bottles of Chianti. When Ernie has the time and is focused on working for Bob, he does go out of his way to make sure Dylan's pleased.

While Bob cools off in his quarters at the rear of the bus, Ernie tells the rest of us the story of Dylan's meeting with Leonard Cohen after Cohen's Wiltern Theater show in '85. He says that when Dylan complimented Cohen on the song 'Suzanne,' Leonard confessed that it took him five years to write it.

Later, Cohen told Dylan how much he liked 'License To Kill.'

'It took me five minutes,' Bob crowed.

September 15 1987. Westfalenhalle, Dortmund, West Germany. Sometimes Bob likes to ride on the other buses with the 'girls,' as he calls his backup singers, or with his management team. Jim, our driver, has brought along the *Biograph* tapes and a copy of *Lyrics 1962–1985*. Whenever Bob is off the bus—which is rarely—Jim, Victor, Doctor K., and even Ernie and I take the opportunity to sing along to all his tunes.

After tonight's show, just as we're leaving, some kid comes running up to the bus and pleads with Jim to take a tape of his music to play for Dylan. Bob gives Jim the go ahead to open the door.

'We'll give it a thorough listen,' Bob promises.

By the time the concert has ended, all the restaurants are closed. We're eating soggy leftovers from backstage and drinking red wine.

'Who's gonna be around in twenty or thirty years?' someone asks Dylan, inquiring about the current music scene.

'Tom Petty?' I ask.

Dylan thinks about it.

'Naw! John Cougar Mellencamp,' he says. 'He's the only one who's got what it takes.'

At some point, Dylan throws his chicken bones out through the moon roof. Then everyone starts doing it. Soon the rest of the food is flying out the hole.

Throw my suitcase out there, too.

Just when things have quieted back down again, Bob picks up the poor German kid's cassette and sails it through the roof.

September 16 1987. Frankenhalle, Nuremburg, West Germany. One gig after another, no hotels.

It's exhausting. Debilitating, in fact. Bob sleeps on his large bed in the rear of the bus, hidden from view by a barricade of red drapes. The underlings have bunks, one on top of another. Sometimes Ernie and I squeeze into one. I'm embarrassed, and I don't want to do it, but Ernie gets off on the thought that the other guys, especially Bob, can hear us making love. Most of the time I relish the chance to sleep alone.

Someone has bought the ancient Chinese game Go, which is supposed to be even more complex than chess. Bob and Victor trade off trying to teach me. But I never win a game.

Bob gives me a list of things to do when we get to the next stop, including a note to call his friend Joan Solomon—'even if it's in the middle of the night'—about the Big Bopper movie he wants to produce. He watches as I quickly but carefully transcribe all his thoughts, knowing that his every wish is my command, and that there will be no need for questions or corrections later. That he can consider the job done.

'If you were my woman,' Bob tells me, 'I'd be worth four times as much.'

'Yeah, I think that's true,' he nods. 'Four times.'

September 17 1987. East Berlin. Before the wall comes down. The concert was originally scheduled for West Berlin, but Bob thinks it would be cooler to play East. The change is orchestrated at the last minute, and it's anticipated that the crowd will be upward of a hundred thousand.

It takes hours to go through the checkpoint, and I sleep through most of it, but once we're inside the communist block province, it will be worth it. The architecture resembles our most beautiful public buildings back in the States—think the Opera House in San Francisco or the Lincoln Memorial—but here, all these incredible structures are laden with gargoyles and clustered together in massive plazas with statues and fountains.

As we approach the site of the show, people are already gathered on blankets, enjoying picnics and wine. There's a carnival set up on the field where the concert will take place, with wild rides and barkers' voices and flashing amusement park lights.

Dylan and I and Doctor K. disembark as soon as the bus is parked to go shop at the sideshow. The large tents are bustling with suspender-clad vendors hawking a wide variety of weird stuff. Doctor K. stumbles upon some Chinese guy with Fu Manchu facial hair. Swearing to Bob and me that he knows what he's doing, he purchases a bizarre compilation of esoteric herbs. Bob buys an octagonal wooden box.

Almost a hundred thousand people do, in fact, turn out for the momentous concert, but a scuffle breaks out between fans and security, injuring 130 of them. Due to the disruption, Dylan will play for less than an hour.

September 18 1987. Rotterdam, the Netherlands. A good place to score some dope—and I'm told someone from the Petty camp does.

That night, while Bob stays in his room, Ernie and I, along with Jakob, Sam, Stan Lynch, Benmont, and Elliot Roberts, go to an underground punk nightclub to see the local talent. Most of the time, Dylan's kids are like apparitions, hovering in the background, nearly invisible, although once in a long while one might catch the faint strum of Jakob's guitar behind a closed hotel room door.

In the morning, before I wake up, Ernie leaves with both of the younger Dylans to fly back to LA.

September 19 1987. Sportspaleis Ahoy, Rotterdam, the Netherlands. Alone at last.

I sigh with relief, telling myself I just want a chance to be on my own with Dylan, instead of having to drag Ernie around with me everywhere like a psychological anchor. In the afternoon, I take a meditative walk through the outskirts of town. In English, spray-painted on a concrete slab in an industrial park, I see the red, bleeding, florescent words, 'Risk It!'

That night, Bob ends his set with 'Slow Train,' before returning with Roger McGuinn for an encore of 'Chimes Of Freedom.'

After the show, as I'm mixing drinks for Dylan in his backstage dressing room, a woman claiming to be the late Mike Bloomfield's wife, Christiana, shows up. She's cute, with boy-short hair, kind of pixyish, and when the buses take off again, to my shock, she comes along with us, even sharing Bob's sleeping quarters.

'How come she gets to sleep with you?' I ask impetuously over poached eggs and grapefruit juice the next morning in Dylan's suite before I even realize what I'm saying. Talk about tipping my hand! How come I care so much? I have to ask myself.

'Aw, she doesn't mean nothin' to me,' Dylan says.

September 20 1987. Halle 20, International Trade Center, Hanover, West Germany. This is the last time on the tour that Dylan performs 'Slow Train.' Riding on the bus after the show, a not particularly blasted Bob is having difficulty getting the wooden top to fit on his octagonal carnival box. Bloomfield's wife sits in a trance at his side.

'Here,' I say. 'Give it to me.'

I spin the top clockwise, one section at a time, until I find the proper channel, then slip it in.

'Breeda,' Bob says, his moody blue eyes ablaze, 'you're a genius!'

September 21 1987. Valbyhallen, Copenhagen, Denmark. Rumor has it that there's a conflict with the guy who's been scoring pot for the Petty band and our camp.

'Nothing personal,' Dylan tells us to tell the guy, 'but when Bob was with the Dead, there was never a problem. They asked *him* for the stuff!' He sends one of our crewmembers back to Amsterdam to buy more dope. 'Just get it, and give it to me … whatever it costs. I don't want to be in the position of begging for weed.'

Sitting in his private quarters while Bloomfield's wife plays cards with the crew, Dylan says to me, 'You make up the set list.'

Wow! Really? Cool.

I'm chewing on the pencil, thinking of all my favorite songs of his to write down in my notebook, when I notice a new manuscript on the shelf. It looks like a screenplay. I take it down. It's the official manual for Sexaholics Anonymous!

'Someone sent that to me,' Bob says, scribbling some notes in this black book he carries with him.

'Is it any good?'

'It's … uh.' He reaches for the right words. 'Very interesting.'

When I get back to business and down to the bottom of the set list, I ask if he'll play 'Desolation Row.'

'"Desolation Row"?' he groans. 'We haven't rehearsed it.'

He can't believe that it's my favorite song of his, besides 'Idiot

Wind.' I tell him how the words played themselves back to me in my head after the first time I heard them.

'Please, perform it for me,' I beg.

And that night, with the Heartbreakers in tow and Benmont hammering it home on the keys, he does.

September 23 1987. Isshallen, Helsinki, Finland. This is Bob's first ever concert in Finland, and it may be his last. His performance is sorely lacking. I attribute the unevenness of the show to Bloomfield's wife, imagining that she's draining Dylan's energy by keeping him up all night. Three songs are played for the last time on the tour: 'Highway 61 Revisited,' 'Stuck Inside Of Mobile With The Memphis Blues Again,' and 'It's All Over Now, Baby Blue.'

A funny thing about the late Mike Bloomfield's wife is that she's rarely seen in daylight. The next morning marks the beginning of the Jewish high holy days. Over poached eggs, grapefruit juice, toast, and a side order of fries, Bob—whose real last name, as everyone knows, is Zimmerman—has me call the concierge for a list of synagogues, but they can't name even one.

'Check the phone book,' Bob says, sipping the dreary hotel coffee.

By now, I'm an extension of his ego. What's the Finnish word for synagogue, I'm wondering, flipping through the pages.

'Check under Cohen,' Bob says. 'We'll call one up and ask 'em.'

There are only two Cohens in the entire book. The first one gives me the location of the only temple in town. After clearing the directions with the front desk, Bob and I walk out of the main entrance of the hotel into the stark yellow day.

Despite the poor reception the night before, there are something like twenty fans waiting outside, and they follow us. They include one goofy-looking autograph hound with thick glasses, who attempts to appeal to Bob by saying he has everyone's signature in the world except Bob Dylan's. The further we walk, the more fans we pick up.

'Run,' Bob commands, and we do. But at thirty-nine and forty-six, we're, like, *old*, and these are a bunch of kids. We eventually wind up ducking into a drugstore, where I convince the owner to call us a taxi.

By the time the car arrives, there's something like fifty people huddled outside the glass door. Bob hustles me through them, and we jump into the cab. The driver has no idea where the address we're looking for is, nor what the word 'synagogue' means, let alone where there might actually be one, so he drops us off in an upscale, arty part of town, almost like Soho or Berkeley, where we go into a bookstore to browse.

On the way out, Dylan notices a woman standing on the steps of the place, reading a newspaper, the headlines of which are unintelligible to us except for the word 'Dylan' in bold type. She's tall, lean, attractive, and dressed professionally.

'Ask her if she speaks English,' Bob says.

She does—barely. She looks at him and nearly faints.

Bob moves in and takes over.

'Uh, what's it say, there, in the paper?' he points.

She shakes her head.

'Just the headline,' Bob says. 'Maybe you could translate.'

'No.' She'd rather not.

'Why?' he pleads.

'It's not good,' she confesses. By now we're walking down the street with her, but where are we going?

'It's OK,' Dylan tells her. 'Go on, just the headline.'

She sighs and then stops. Purses her lips. Reads.

'The God arrived! The man performed.'

'Ohhhh,' Bob laughs. 'What else?'

Her face is crimson.

'It says you would have been better off if you'd have died young like other legends—like Elvis and Marilyn or James Dean.'

Even Bob Dylan can be at a loss for words. We've stopped at a corner where there's a streetlight, and the woman hesitates before crossing. She and I have both died a little for Bob.

'You're welcome to come to my place for tea, and I'll read you the whole thing,' she shrugs sheepishly.

'OK!' Dylan blurts. 'We have time for that, don't we Bree?'

'Well, not exactly,' I tell him. We have to get back to the hotel to catch the ferry to Sweden by four; it's already two and we still haven't found the synagogue.

'Just so we keep it short,' I say.

'Yeah,' Dylan says to the woman, 'we have to keep it short.'

'Sure,' she says, and you can almost see her excitement carry her across the street toward her apartment.

The place is stark, spartan, all white, with just the yellow light of the pale Helsinki sun filtering in through the sheer curtains. One wall is a bookcase, and while the woman goes into the kitchen, Bob and I quietly peruse the shelves and find two books about him, as well as a number of his albums. It's getting late. She's taking too long. At the last minute, we've decided to have coffee. I go to the kitchen to help her and notice her nervous hands are shaking as she opens and closes the cupboard doors.

'I can't believe He's here!' she whispers.

The coffee pot, cups, and spoons rattle as she rests a tray on the long, bleached pine table before us. Over the first good cup of coffee since Modena and Turin, Bob autographs all her books and albums.

As we leave, I tell Dylan we're going to be too late getting back to the hotel if we don't start now, but he's bent on finding his house of worship. The woman gives us new directions, and this time we walk straight to it.

The synagogue is in a very old stone building with a wrought-iron fence around it. A scant number of Icelandic poppies poke their wilted orange-and-yellow heads up through the tall brown grass. The gate is locked, the building closed, and it looks like it's been like this for quite some time. But the light … the light is mesmerizing. The pinks and the grays of the old stones on the structure pop right out, and the flowers glow like magic lanterns on the lawn.

In addition to the Jewish symbols on the building's walls, there is also a sign in Finnish, but of course we can't read it.

'Oh, *man*,' Dylan says, feeling thwarted.

Enthralled by the site, we hang on the iron fence, photograph the building, and even say a few prayers. Attracted to each other and magnetized by the majestic energy emanating from the place, we dally. There's something we've both noted about the Finish language: where there's one *i*, there's two. Bob suggests I change the spelling of my name to have two *is*—Briitta—and I consider it.

Now we're really short on time. Walking. Walking faster. Sweating. *With no direction home.* Dylan has this bizarre walk: not quite a swagger, almost like Renfrew dragging a ball and chain, but, as always, I keep up.

At some point we find ourselves in a quaint little village. A gnarly old man with a bucket and a mop and snaggled teeth begs change from us.

'That's what you'd call a bad omen,' Bob says. He gives me a lecture on signs and symbols.

A few feet later, in a sunlit window, we spot a black cat. We're lost.

'We're gonna miss the ferry to Sweden,' I say.

Bob doesn't even care.

'At least we found the synagogue,' he says.

As late as we are, we can't help but pause in amazement once we come across a park with a giant outdoor chess board—a metaphorical wonder—with human-size rooks, knights, bishops, pawns, and even a life-size king and queen.

When we get back, everyone is in a panic. Our luggage has been packed for us. I race up to my room to make sure nothing of mine's been left behind.

Hundreds of people are boarding the ferry. Dylan pulls one of those acts where he disappears into himself, which draws even more attention to him. I try to convince him to be more in his body, to use his power. Consciously.

'Have you ever thought about doing Tai Chi?' I ask. But Bob's not talkin', he's walkin'—like a moving black hole—sucking up the energy of all those around him as I escort him up the stairs and onto the main deck.

Again, he's sharing his room with Bloomfield's widow, and I'm disconsolate. Obviously, he tells me, there was no reservation made for her in advance, so she's got to sleep in *someone's* room. I offer to let her stay in mine.

'Ain't nothin' gonna happen between her and me,' Bob says.

Yeah right, I'm thinking. Then why are her cheeks so goddamned pink?

Bob's stateroom is twice the size of mine. There's a view to the ocean through palm fronds and silver blinds. Very hip. We order drinks for the three of us, and I try to talk Bob into having dinner in the elegant dining room.

'What's the point of being famous if you can't enjoy it?' I ask.

'If you were with Ernie right now, there wouldn't be a problem,' Dylan sulks, frustrated by his own fame.

In the end, he relents. We go to dinner, and everyone leaves us alone, except the chef who makes a point of dropping by our table two or three times to make sure everything's all right, and that one goofy-looking autograph hunter from earlier in the day. The creep actually booked passage on the boat. Bob finally gives in and signs a napkin for him, and the guy is so grateful, I think he's going to drop dead with joy right there in front of us.

In the middle of a sleepless night, I'm drawn to the upper deck. Cool sea breeze. Black, starlit sky. Wandering restlessly, I'm feeling like a prisoner to my emotions when I discover Dylan sitting alone on a bench, in the dark, on the bow.

'I thought I recognized that walk,' he says.

Of course, he recognizes it. My gait is his. I've taken over most of his mannerisms.

'Nobody walks like you,' he says.

'Oh, *man*,' I say, with the same drawn-out intonation he would use. 'What are you doin' here?'

Wordlessly we float in the shadowy salty mist for what feels like forever before returning to our respective rooms.

September 24 1987. Sweden is all upside down. The street signs read like gibberish. Bloomfield's wife, who's really very nice, finally goes back to the Netherlands.

We check in to our hotel. Bob's flipped out. His suite number is 666. He comes into my room that night while I'm lying down, reading, and stands by my bed, lamenting the horror of such a fluke.

'You can sleep in my bed …' I say. I bite my tongue before I even finish.

Dylan considers the offer, smiles.

'Aw, everyone wants to lie down with me,' he teases, and before the door closes behind him, I realize it's true.

Bob and I start writing a song together. It's called 'You Can Blow My Mind (If You Want To).' This has got to be the all-time biggest come on, ever, for a writer. Talk about an aphrodisiac. He's written songs with Sam Shepard, songs with Jacques Levy—'Isis,' 'Hurricane,' and 'Joey,' to name a few—and now he's gonna write a song with me?

We sit on the floor while he plays the guitar. He says he wants *me* to come up with the lyrics.

I choke.

'You write the words,' I say. 'I just wanna watch.'

'I already wrote all my songs,' Dylan says, and he sounds like he means it.

That evening, as I'm sitting on a chair in Dylan's private quarters on the bus, copying down his suggestions for the set list, the sunlight comes in through the window, illuminating his complicated face, and for the first time I notice that Joan Baez was right—his eyes really are robin's egg blue.

Bob is sitting on his bed. I ask him to tell me about 'Lily, Rosemary And The Jack Of Hearts,' another one of my favorite songs of his. He says it was inspired by the French film *The Children Of Paradise*, filmed during the German occupation of France in World War II. It's the story of an enigmatic courtesan and the four men who love her: an aristocrat, an actor, a mime, and a thief. I tell him I've never seen it.

'Oh you have to see that one,' he says. 'You just have to.'

I get the feeling he enjoys being my teacher. He describes the sad story of unrequited love in detail, though I still can't find the connection back to Lily and the Jack of Hearts. By now, it's no surprise to me that a favorite film of his would feature carnival workers.

Dylan keeps a journal, and while I sit there in silent reverie, he jots down a few notes. He looks over at me and smiles.

'"Tomorrow Is A Long Time,"' he says, raising his eyebrows in affirmation. 'Put that one on the list.'

I say I don't know it.

'You don't know that one?' He's stumped. 'I think if I just play that song tonight,' he says, 'everything will be all right.'

September 25 1987. Scandinavium, Gothenburg, Sweden. Dylan's performances are growing stronger with every show. Tom Petty and his band are obvious Dylan fans, and they understand the nuances of his music—especially Benmont, the keyboard player. Having grown up playing the piano, I like to stand behind him during the performances and watch how his long, sculpted fingers dance over the keys, capturing Dylan's essence.

During the show, Dylan picks up his acoustic guitar and wows both me and the audience with a stunning version of the song I thought I'd never heard.

Yes, and only if my own true love was waitin'…

As Dylan sings, I stand in the wings, my heart *a-softly poundin'.*

Only if she was lyin' by me …

He looks across the stage at me.

Then I'd lie in my bed once again.

September 26 1987. Johanneshovs Isstadion, Stockholm, Sweden. Bob's got a new charcoal up on an easel in his room. It's a portrait of a man. No one I've ever seen. Very detailed. Very bold. Very Van Gogh.

'Wow!' I say. 'It's so passionate!'

But Dylan's in a sour mood.

'What's passion?' he growls, catching me off guard. 'A perfume by Elizabeth Taylor?'

September 28 1987. Festhalle, Frankfurt, West Germany. After the Helsinki debacle, where we almost missed the boat, Bob sends someone out to buy two $1,500 bicycles, but I'm a klutz when it comes to this sort of thing. While I could easily ride a Schwinn c.1950, these newfangled racing bikes, with their down-turned handlebars, scare me.

Bob invites me to climb on the back of his bike, and while he peddles I wrap my arms around his waist, sneaking glimpses of the German countryside with my head nestled softly between his shoulders.

'A guy could go far with a girl like you on the back,' Dylan says.

September 29 1987. Martin Schleyerhalle, Stuttgart, West Germany. On the road again.

Can you cook and sew, make flowers grow? Do you understand my pain?

After losing a couple more games of Go, I get up to clean the mess at the kitchen sink and make some tea. Bob comes up behind me to get a beer.

'You're so easily bored, you don't even pretend to be interested,' he says.

He lingers directly behind me, and the heat from his body rolls up my torso sending a quiver up my spine.

'Is that so?' I say, without turning to address him.

'Uh huh,' Dylan says. 'You're gonna get bored with me.'

That night, Bob directs the driver of the bus to stop out in the middle of nowhere, while everyone else stands by, so the two of us can listen to the frogs sing as we go for a long walk under the stars.

Bob decides he wants to make a movie about Che Guevara.

'They say you can still talk to the woman who cooked his last supper.'

He fills me in on the tragic details of the captivating hero's life: how by the end Che, who was once the champion of his country's freedom, had become a mercenary who no longer needed a cause to kill and went down to South America for no good reason and got himself slain.

'You'll do the research on it when we get back to the States,' he says. 'OK?'

Someone raises the subject of this new film that's out about violent retribution for spurned love called *Fatal Attraction*, and Bob says he can't believe they're only getting around to making a movie about that now.

'I've had that idea a million times.'

That night, Dylan sleeps on the bus with the backup singers. Victor can tell I'm bummed, and when I pass by his bunk in the early morning hours, I can see him in the shadows, patting the thin mattress with his hand.

'There's room for you in my bed,' Victor says.

Not in this lifetime, I'm thinking.

The next morning, one of the 'girls' mentions that instead of making love with one of the female singers, as I'd suspected, Dylan had too much to drink and passed out.

September 30 1987. Olympiahalle, Munich, West Germany. One of the reasons I'm getting paid on this trip is to shop for Bob, but I rarely see anything worthy, and besides, his costumer Susie Pullen is with us on the tour too, even though I hardly see her. I hit a funky part of downtown and buy Dylan two shirts of the blousy, shiny variety—like Ernie's been buying for me—and a leather vest.

For myself, I buy a black silk three-quarter-length coat, but when I show it to Bob, even though he likes it, he advises me to take out the shoulder pads.

'All the women are going around looking like football players,' he says. 'Who wants that? You don't need those.'

He's sitting on the bed in his hotel room, strumming his guitar. His earring—the one shaped like a cross—catches the light.

'You don't need to wear makeup, either,' he grunts, 'with your looks.'

Verona, Italy. Bob presents me with a gift. I figure that he must have sent Susie out to buy it for me, along with his long-standing request for baby clothes, but he says no, he picked it out himself. He's sitting on the yellow shag floor of his sun-drenched room, playing his guitar and singing the Paul Simon hit 'The Boy In The Bubble'—I'm shocked that he knows all the words—when I open the package to find a pair of denim fringed hot-pants.

'I can't wear these,' I yelp.

'Why not?'

'I'm too old.'

'Naw! Just wear 'em around the hotel room, for me,' he says. 'Go on. Try 'em on.'

I return to his room a few minutes later, squeezed into these itsy-bitsy shorts. I model them for Bob and garner his approval, but they're not really me, and I'm not comfortable enough with the way they look on me to ever wear them again.

October 1 1987. Arena di Verona. The setting for *Romeo & Juliet*.

The piazza is packed. Bob often complains that most of his fans are men, but at tonight's performance there will be an exotic dark-skinned woman practically masturbating herself on one of the metal bars meant to keep the fans off the stage. We've also received a warning from Elliot Mintz that an American fan known as Sara Dylan #2—she had her name legally changed to that of Dylan's ex—may be lurking.

When I speak to Elliot on the phone, I realize how much I've missed him.

'God,' I say, 'I wish you were here.'

I tell him what a great time I'm having. He tells me that the night before, he and Ernie went out for dinner and drank a toast to me.

Before the show, Doctor K. whips up a special brew of the herbs he acquired in East Berlin. After treating Bob with acupuncture, he presents him with a huge hot cup of this ghastly looking concoction. When the chiropractor leaves the room, Bob has me make him four cocktails—Kahlua, cream, and VSOP, his drink of the week—and he performs brilliantly. The set includes some extremely effective harmonica solos, and the song I can't help wishing is for me, 'I'll Be Your Baby Tonight.'

Afterwards, on the bus, as we're all sitting around eating more Italian sausage and antipasto and drinking our favorite '86, which Bob has dubbed Chernobyl Red, Doctor K. suggests that the herbal tea must be the reason Bob performed so well.

Bob agrees enthusiastically and gives me a sly look.

'What'd you put in there, anyway?' he asks, listening attentively to the chiropractor's every word.

When I get up to use the bathroom, I notice the teacup—still overflowing with the gruesome potion—resting, untouched, on the counter of the sink.

October 1 1987. The Paleur, Rome, Italy. We're staying in a glorious modern hotel with views of ancient architecture. There are Botticelli-like paintings on every floor, and Bob and I run around in the middle of the night photographing them. Bob's eldest son, Jesse, is scheduled to fly in and meet us, and I'm worried about what he will think when he sees how close his father and I have become.

Before the concert, an urgent call is directed to my room. Jesse's plane has been detained. It took off from Kennedy but then developed engine problems and was forced to turn back. Jesse's too shaken to board another one. He cancels his plans to join the tour.

Elliot Roberts, Cousin Stan, Doctor K., and I have dinner at the world-famous Italian restaurant Alfredo where the rich cream sauce is said to have originated, but I have to bring Bob a doggie bag filled with the luscious stuff because he doesn't want to go out.

The next day, Benmont and I visit the Sistine Chapel with Mike Campbell and his wife. Benmont's cute and intelligent, with a droll sense of humor. I think he likes hanging out with Dylan as much as I do. The Campbells, too, are sweethearts. Mike and his wife have spotted a pair of boots by a famous Italian designer in a window somewhere that they think I would like, and while we wait in this seemingly interminable line to get a peek at Michelangelo's triumph, they give me directions on how to get there.

After the show that night, Bob and his immediate entourage are invited to an Israeli dignitary's home to celebrate Rosh Hashanah, but Bob says he doesn't want to go. I have to talk him into it—the perks of fame again. He reluctantly gives in to me, and it turns out that the evening will be one of the high points of the tour. On the way, in the car, as I sit next to the legend in the back seat, Dylan reads from the Bible he usually keeps on the bus next to his journal.

The Italian home is palatial. The art collection, which includes every master from Picasso to Man Ray, is priceless. To accommodate the holiday feast, separate tables for men and women are set up in orthodox tradition in a large downstairs dining room with mural-covered walls. Crusty bread, fresh greens, soup, pasta, and roast meat.

I get along well with the other women I'm with, but I'm longing to be sharing the experience more intimately with Bob. Throughout the night, whenever I look over at him, he's looking at me.

'You really handled yourself well in that situation,' Bob comments later. 'I could a never taken Carole to anything like that.'

Then why are you with her, I wonder.

Back at the hotel, he unveils a framed eight-by-ten glossy of Sara and him and all the kids that he's been carrying around in his suitcase the whole time and props it up on the round breakfast table near the entry. We're watching *Raiders Of The Lost Ark* in Italian on the carpeted floor in front of the TV. I can feel the temperature rising between us when the phone rings across the hall in my room. I run to catch it—typically, calls for Bob are screened through Ernie's room.

It's Carole.

'Where are you?' is all I can think to ask. Now my heart's racing—not only from the run but out of the fear of being found out.

'Home.' It sounds like she's chewing gum. She cracks it.

'Why aren't you here?' I ask, sensing that the inevitable is about to occur between Bob and me. It seems like a reasonable question, and my tone demands the real answer.

'I wasn't invited,' she says. Not *invited*?

'Why?'

'I don't know. You'll have to ask *Him*. Anyway, I've made an appointment to get liposuction, and I want to find out if Bob will give me the money for it. Is he around?'

'Uh … sure.'

I have the hotel transfer the call.

I sit back down on the floor in Bob's room while he and Carole duke it out over whether or not she should have the procedure. I can't believe that he didn't invite her to come with him to Europe … and that she would put up with it. What kind of a relationship is *that*?

Bob rejoins me in front of the set.

'What's she need plastic surgery for?' he asks. He plays with my hair, pushing it behind my ear to look at my face. He tells me he likes the way my hair hangs down and the fact that I don't wear much makeup.

'You walk like me,' he continues. 'You talk like me. Our hair's even the same color …'

'Mmmmm,' I shrug, keeping my eyes on the screen.

'You don't need any surgery.'

'I wouldn't do it, if I did,' I say.

'I'm not gonna pay for it,' he says.

Before Harrison Ford can rescue Karen Allen from the snake pit, Bob pulls me closer and kisses me.

Previously, Bob's told me that he's against 'going all the way.' He's convinced it's what makes the women go crazy. Now, roiling in a haze of marijuana smoke and flickering television images, with our fervor finally free to ignite, our bodies practically melt into each other.

Abruptly, Bob backs off. He's thought twice, and it's not all right.

'It's the High Holy Days,' he groans. 'And Ernie's my friend!'

CHAPTER EIGHT

Love minus zero no limit

October 4 1987. Arenea Civica di Milano, Milan, Italy.

Tonight I'll be staying here with you.

Without even entering me, Bob Dylan's the best lover in the world. He's definitely present now. His body is perfect, and I can see why he wants to use it all the time. Just feeling him rising and lowering on top of me, I can come a thousand times. Ernie would have a heart attack.

'So ... uh ... the High Holy Days are over,' Bob announces, as we wrestle ardently on his bed. I'm awash in his sensuality. His eyes embrace me. His fingers find me. Even his earring softly strokes the skin on my cheek. He waits until our bodies are slip-sliding with sweat.

'Should I take you now, baby? Should I?'

Maybe it's Bob's own warning coming back to haunt me, or the myriad stories of his many indiscretions, or even rumors that he'd been a male hustler back in the day—not to mention the fact that we were now living at the dawn of AIDS—but as I nearly drown in a sea of self-abandonment, an infinitesimal spark of self-preservation prevails.

'No,' I murmur.

Bob rolls over on his side next to me, his hands dancing delicately over my flesh, as if he's trying to divine the secret to some great mystery through the tips of his fingers. He's not disappointed. Maybe he's even relieved.

Bob's shows are getting better and better, and now more than ever, it feels like he's playing them to me—not even focusing that much on the audience, but facing more toward my backstage vantage point as he performs. His onstage energy is strong. He looks healthier, and he's in a better mood.

The acupuncturist takes the credit. Bob even has him do a treatment on me. I'm lying on the table draped in one of Bob's long white satin shirts, when Susie Pullen presents me with a cool pair of leopard-skin stockings. She also has a new Italian baby outfit to show Bob.

Seconds before showtime, Dylan and I fall back down onto the bed.

'There must be a hundred ways to do it,' Bob whispers. 'Would you like to learn them all with me?'

During a hotel-room strum on his guitar, Bob tells me his whole Christian phase was inspired by his divorce from Sara.

'I knew it was my fault,' he says. 'I knew I'd done wrong. You see, there's just women you have to fuck because they demand it.'

He says his now infamous motorcycle accident happened one morning when he came over the top of a hill and was blinded by the sun. It was a crazy time. Hard on his marriage, too. People would just show up on his lawn in Woodstock.

'They came all this way, you see, and they'd say, I've come from Paris or Istanbul or Detroit … so you have to talk to me. And I would.'

Bob takes my chin in his hand and kisses me.

'You understand me, huh baby?'

As the two of us cling to the buttons on each other's shirts, overlooking a bridge or a stream or a new-mowed lawn, Bob tells me about everyone he thinks is important, from Jacques Prevert to Jacques Cousteau. He talks about Olof and Odin and the theory of Viking architecture. Salman Rushdie and Haile Selassie. Modigliani and the meaning of Manna. He says we should buy a book on the Dadaist painter George Grosz while we're in Europe, just so I can check out the artwork.

Bob confesses that he gets freaked out whenever he has to shake hands with a stranger.

'You should avoid doin' it,' he warns, 'at all costs.'

He has me make a note about Paul the Apostle.

He says that we should write a movie called *Nazi Whores* about the Jewish women who escaped the concentration camps. I write down our casting suggestions: Cher, Sissy Spacek, Jessica Lange, Debra Winger, Theresa Russell, and Melanie Griffith.

Possible character's names will be Gertrude, Inger, Stephanie, or Gerta.

Miscellaneous notes for the day read 'El Che Productions.'

As we straighten up our room, Bob tells me William Burroughs's house is always a mess. He mentions that the movie *Billy Two Hats* inspired 'Brownsville Girl,' the song he wrote with Sam Shepard. And that *Shot Of Love* is his favorite of his own albums. He thinks it's funny that a school like Berkeley or Harvard would teach a course interpreting his lyrics.

'Sometimes I just throw in a word 'cause it sounds good,' he laughs.

Bob has an idea to bring back patched jeans, 'like they wore in the 60s.' He says he knows a seamstress who'd be perfect for the job. My notes will include phrases like 'Sexland Weirdness' and

'Project Lace.' He tells me the reason the acoustic version of *Blood On The Tracks* had to be scrapped is because his brother, who's an accountant, told him it would never sell.

He also has an idea to stage a reenactment of the Last Supper.

Bob's got this twitch. Sometimes his whole body just starts shaking. That's usually when he gets up and begins shadowboxing his way around a room. I catch him looking through my just-developed film with greasy fingers.

'These look like my pictures,' he says.

They don't, because his rarely come out, but I can't help feeling that we see a lot of things the same way.

'You're the kinda girl worth marryin',' he confides, and hope tingles me to my bones.

That night, I write in my journal:

I didn't know I would fall in love with you. It never even occurred to me. The room is so empty without your music. As you lie on the floor I cannot look, I so respect your privacy. I appear so 'orderly' as I fall apart inside. I'm wiped out, starting to nod off. Is this what love is, some deep sleep that anesthetizes without healing? God help me.

Messing around over well-done french fries, rare burgers, and black coffee, Bob and I collaborate on two new songs, 'She's So Heavy' and 'Victor's Song.' I write a poem about us called the 'Point of No Return,' and Bob says, 'It's not bad.' I don't show him 'Honey, You Can Do Anything,' or '36 Chromosomes,' in which, even though, technically, we haven't consummated our relationship, I'm irrationally praying I won't get pregnant.

In the middle of the night, I wake to find Bob rolled over on his side, looking at me. By now we are together every night.

'What are you starin' at?' I say.

'You are so fine,' he says, 'just lookin' at your face brings me pleasure.'

'People say I look like Jane Fonda,' I tell him.

'Jane Fonda!' he nearly spits. 'You're better looking than Jane Fonda.'

'You're better looking than Bob Dylan,' I tell him.

He gets a big kick out this.

October 5 1987. Piazza Grande, Locarno, Switzerland. From the time we wake up in the morning, Bob's back is bothering him. I tell him he should stop wearing the motorcycle boots with the tall heels—he even wears lifts inside those—because with a heavy guitar strapped over his shoulder during his performances … well, it's no wonder his back is always out.

We're in his dressing room, seconds before showtime. Bob is tying on this Middle Eastern–looking headdress he's been wearing at all the shows—undoubtedly an artifact of his costumer's visit to Egypt—which according to some newspaper reports looks like a dead animal swinging from his head.

'I'm so proud of you for stopping smoking when you did,' I say.

Bob shoots me a look.

'I'm gonna start, again.'

This show is one of the best yet, except I hate the fact that Bob performs 'Frankie Lee And Judas Priest,' with its moralistic conclusion that one shouldn't hang out where they don't belong. And I can't help feeling guilty.

That night, in his room, we lie together on the bed, sticky skin clinging, watching fireflies as they flit magically on the ceiling. Even on our sides, our bodies are a perfect match. I toy with his earring.

'Ernie's not a very good lover,' I confess, although the problem is more spiritual than technical.

'Why not?' Bob laughs. 'He's read all the books.'

Dylan and I sleep through the entire night, entwined—first me behind him, then him behind me, our arms encircled around our waists, our hands over our hearts.

Victor and I are looking at some of the pictures I've had developed. One in particular of Bob.

'I think we should use it as an album cover,' I say.

'*We?*' Victor admonishes me. 'I'm starting to get a bad feeling about all this,' he warns.

'I meant it as someone who works for Bob,' I say, flustered, trying to explain.

'I just know, *I'm* not part of any *we*,' Victor says.

Dylan and I are looking in a store window at three different pairs of these one-of-a-kind, handsomely detailed shoes. All Italian leather, with hand tooling and woven laces.

'It's like an art installation,' I say.

A couple of doors down, Bob points out a bracelet on the wrist of a mannequin—gold, with ruby hearts and diamonds. Too rich for my tastes.

'Should I buy that for you, baby?'

'*No!*'

October 7 1987. P.O.P.B. Bercy, Paris, France. Dylan is sick. He claims Roger McGuinn gave him a cold when the two of them sang 'Chimes Of Freedom' into a single mic a few nights before. He's also disgruntled because French ticket sales are slow, and plans for a second concert have to be canceled. We stay in bed for twenty hours.

We bundle up in the afternoon to take a stroll down the Champs-Elysées. Dylan buys art supplies. As we sip espresso at a sidewalk cafe near the Arc de Triomphe, he tosses a hunk of his bread to a pigeon or two, and soon the sky is bursting with hopeful birds. It's gray out and raining. Bob insists I wear his jacket and holds it for me as I put it on. He buys me a blue umbrella, and the two of us walk arm and arm, sheltered from the storm.

'Do you need money, baby?' he asks. 'You should tell me if you need any money.'

'No,' I say. I pull him closer. 'I don't need any money.'

The evening of the performance, I give Dylan a bath in a huge tub that overlooks the romantic French city. I scrub his back, wash his hair, and even massage his feet.

'I can't think of a place I'd rather be, right now,' Bob says, 'than here, with you rubbing my feet.'

After the show—another superb performance—I tell him I've come up with this brilliant career move for him: the *Biograph* World Tour.

'You could book stadiums,' I say, blotting a dry towel around his sweaty neck. 'Fifty-three songs over five nights. People would have to buy tickets for every performance if they wanted to hear the whole show.'

'Baby, you've got big plans for me,' Dylan laughs. 'When we get home, I'm gonna play prisons.'

If it's Tuesday, it must be Belgium. This is Thursday, and we are spending the afternoon holed up in the hotel. Ernie is due to rejoin the tour in England in a couple of days.

Bob and I are back working on our song, 'You Can Blow My Mind, If You Want To.' It's about a love triangle, two guys and a girl. How on earth did we come up with that? I read him some of the lyrics we have so far.

The odd man out stands by the roadside
What's he selling? What's he got?
The time is right for you at my side
(Let him go now, that's his lot)
If anyone knows about it, we do
And you can blow my mind … if you want to.

'Like in Anna Karenina,' Bob says.

'I haven't read it,' I shrug.

'You haven't read Anna Karenina, and you call yourself a writer?'

He tells me it's the story of a woman who has an affair, and even though her husband knows, he won't give her a divorce, so she goes crazy.

It's my turn to come up with a line, but my confidence is slowly eroding. Dylan has put me on a pedestal, and I'm terrified of falling off. Being with Ernie, I'm coming to realize, may be what gave me the security I needed in the first place to climb out on this tightrope I'm walking.

Hesitantly, I squeak out a few words.

Dylan frowns.

'Come on,' I urge, 'help me out here.'

'*Da da da da da da da,*' he teases.

'*Bob!*'

'I'd rather read than write,' Dylan squawks.

October 8 1987. Brussels, Belgium. Vorst Nationaal. Before yet another brilliant concert, Bob presents me with a gold-foiled box of Belgian chocolates and the most exquisite flowers I've ever seen. He opens the show with 'Desolation Row.'

In the hotel elevator on the way up to our room, we share the car with a stylish couple, very *modern*, à la Annie Lennox and Rupert Everett.

After they exit, Bob says, '*Hmmmmm*, maybe we should've invited 'em up.'

The long ride from Dover to London. Now, *I'm* sick. In the morning, we stop for breakfast at a roadside cafe, but I stay bundled in Dylan's bed in the back of the bus. When I wake up, he is sitting on the edge of the mattress, stroking my hair with one hand, holding an odd-shaped, ill-wrapped package in the other.

'For me?' I smile.

Inside are two long, beautiful handmade candles, black and magenta—semi-psychedelic—by an artist who waitressed at the restaurant.

'A get-well present,' he says, kissing my forehead. 'For my baby.'

That afternoon, Bob orders all the buses to stop along a rustic strip of country road so that just the two of us can take a three-hour stroll. The Heartbreakers get pissed off and go on without us.

Ernie's scheduled to meet us in London and re-join the tour. Bob confesses that he's sorry he's coming back. He's upset that I'll be doin' all the same things with *him*.

'You've got too much going for you to be with just Ernie,' he says, torturing me with the notion that the two of us could actually have a life together.

During the walk, Dylan snaps a photo of me from behind. Later, when I have the film developed, I will find out his camera has also captured an unlikely assortment of other images—a closed gate, a fence with the number thirteen hammered on it, and a sign painted with the international symbol for 'No!'

October 9 1987. The Mayfair Hotel, grand dame of London. Bob has flown in a bimbo, and I hit the ceiling. She's dark-haired, chunky, overly made up, but not stupid.

'What did he fly *me* in for?' she wants to know, as soon as she susses out the situation.

Dylan and I are inseparable now. The plans must have been in the works from before we'd even left on tour, I'm thinking. Probably he'd forgotten about them. For long hours, the three of us will lay on Bob's big bed in his hotel suite, him holding me, her fuming.

'What about all three of us?' Bob asks me.

'I've done my experimenting,' I tell him.

He makes a call and has someone get the bimbo a room of her own.

After she's gone, and it's just the two of us again, he asks, 'What would you think about you, me, and Carole?'

'No way!'

In the morning, the phone in Dylan's suite awakens the two of us. It's Sara. Somehow word has gotten back to her about this baby Bob's been buying clothes for. It's the baby he's had with one of his backup singers—another Carol, Carolyn Dennis—but this is the first time I make sense of it.

Sara's worried that news of an 'illegitimate' Dylan will upset the five children who rightfully carry his name. She's angry that Bob didn't tell her and the kids himself, instead leaving the gossip to be dropped on them like a bomb. All I hear on my end is Bob telling

199

her over and over to calm down, although once he hangs up and explains the situation, I can understand her point of view.

'A whole lotta women in this world have had my babies,' Dylan huffs.

Tonight's the premiere of *Hearts Of Fire* in London at the Odeon Marble Arch. I beg Bob to escort me. A party will follow at the Astoria.

'Do you wanna go, baby?' He hugs me on the couch. 'We can go. It's just all those photographers ...'

In the meantime, we hang out in his room, smoking pot and drinking and bemoaning the fact that Ernie will be coming back soon. Dylan rants that Ernie's betraying him by flying over on a Friday night.

'What's he gonna do for me? Get me food? Buy me things. I don't need that!'

We decide to just stay in and have a romantic dinner.

'I can give you things, he can't,' Dylan says.

He asks me to call the front desk and have them send up some candles. We order lamb chops from room service—one of our shared delights—and a bottle of champagne.

The girl who Bob has flown in does not technically meet the definition of a bimbo. She's educated and funny, and we actually get along fairly well. The next day, the two of us go to see *Hearts Of Fire*. The film is ghastly, though we agree that Bob looks pretty cute in most scenes.

We're in some London dive, eating stale pastries and drinking bad coffee.

Her purple eye makeup is bleeding as she scarfs down a second croissant.

'Did Bob tell you he and I write songs together?'

'Why *did* you fly her in?' I ask Bob as we tumble into each other on the English equivalent of his big brass bed. It's beginning to feel like Bob moves people around like chess pieces.

Afterwards we just lie there holding on for dear life.

'Because you're gonna be with Ernie,' he says.

October 10 1987. National Exhibition Centre, Birmingham, England. It's hard to imagine a better show. After a slow start, with 'Señor,' Bob's harmonica is in excellent form for a long, *passionate* intro to 'I Want You.' I stand on the stage, watching nearby, enraptured by his every move. Without warning, he segues into 'Pledging My Time.'

Dylan wants to see *The Big Easy* because his friend Ellen Barkin is in it. I tell him I've already seen it and I didn't think it was that hot, but Bob's made up his mind, and that's that. Bob, I'm discovering, has the weirdest tastes in movies, or maybe our motivations are just different. I only like to see good movies. He only likes to see movies where he knows someone who's involved in the project.

Back in LA, Ernie and I had been forced to suffer through the Paul Schrader debacle *Light Of Day* with Michael J. Fox because Bob's friend Joan Jett was in it. I'm sure he also wanted to see it because of knowing Paul, who directed the 'Tight Connection To My Heart' video in Tokyo in '85, but afterwards, all Bob could say was, 'Michael J. Fox … now, *that* kid can act!'

Bob and I wander into a nearly empty London theater in the late afternoon. Somehow *The Big Easy* doesn't seem so bad when you're holding hands with Bob Dylan.

Dylan and I window-shop on our way back to the hotel. We're on Moulton Road near William Blake's house. He halts in front of a pricey storefront window and points to these hand-carved, high backed, richly upholstered chairs with tassels and lavish fringe trim—furnishings straight out of *World Of Interiors*.

'Those are the kind of things we could buy for a place of our own,' he says.

Is this guy trying to give me a heart attack, or what?

Bob's starting to freak out.

'Baby, what are we going to do when Ernie comes back,' he asks?

He's pacing again, this time outside the tour bus. The engine is running, puffing white clouds of stinking exhaust into the cold London air.

'I don't know,' I say. I'm looking to him for the answer.

Most of the people on the tour are on to us now. There's just no getting around how much time we spend together. More than once, I've noticed Bob's backup singers giving me consoling looks in the bathroom mirrors, backstage.

'Let's face it,' I say to Dylan, trying to be realistic, trying to protect myself, trying to curtail the damages before they even occur. 'It's not like you and I are going to be riding off into the sunset together.'

'Why not?' Dylan scowls. He stops dead in front of me. 'We're ridin' along pretty good, so far. Who are you to say when the sunset is?'

Victor can tell I'm scared about losing Dylan.

'Why don't you have Bob's baby,' he suggests. 'Then he'll be in your life forever. Bob always takes care of his kids.'

'I'm not that kind of woman,' I explain, tearfully. 'I want Bob to love me for just me.'

After one of the shows, Benmont and I and a couple of others encourage Dylan to have dinner at this restaurant where the owner says he'll hold it open for us no matter how late we show up.

'Come *on*,' I implore Bob, who hates this kind of celebrity treatment. 'We'll have a good time.'

'I always have a good time with *you*, baby,' he tells me.

Later, back in his suite, he's brooding. I've flung myself into an overstuffed armchair to watch as he parades back and forth over the short yellow shag carpet. Dylan always wears this strange rectangular-faced lump of a gold ring that I'm not too crazy about. *An Egyptian ring*?

All of a sudden he pulls out a velvet jewelry box from his suitcase and flips it open. Inside, on a bed of blue, is another ring with nearly the identical setting, though I think this one even has diamonds.

'Do you like it?' he asks, holding the incredibly expensive if not particularly attractive piece of jewelry in front of my nose.

I think I'm supposed to say 'yes,' but I'm shocked by the gesture, having a hard time interpreting it. I'm still not feeling well, and I'm always so insecure about matters of taste with him, like he's testing me or something, and I am definitely not into taking things from him just for the sake of taking.

'It's OK,' I say weakly, but before I can respond fully, he's snapped the box shut and put it away.

October 11 1987. National Exhibition Centre, Birmingham, England. Due to all the stress I'm feeling, my cold has gotten worse. I'm taking Nyquil, Sudafed, Contact, and Coffee, and as if that's not enough to give me an otherworldly experience, Ernie's back. I'm able to fend off any physical advances he makes because I'm obviously under the weather.

Dylan comes to my room to visit me.

'You're sick as a dog,' he says, perched on the rumpled bed, massaging my back and neck. 'That walk the other day didn't do you any good. Stay in bed. Don't do nothin'. You deserve it. You've performed like a champ. I've been working you too hard. If Ernie doesn't make it up to you, I will. Do you need anything?'

'Ernie's on his way to the pharmacy,' I tell him.

'Store-bought medicines? Oh, baby, you know what to do. Drink lots of soup with garlic in it. As soon as I get back upstairs, I'm gonna send the doctor down to see you.'

Ernie drags me back to the leather district with him to shop, and I buy this long black leather duster that I know for sure Bob will like. It's the second show in Birmingham, and instead of riding on the bus with Dylan and Ernie, I sleep all afternoon, trying to get well, and take the train up to the venue shortly before showtime.

As soon as I arrive people warn me, 'Stay away from Bob, he's on a rampage.' He's supposedly been in a black mood and yelled at everyone on the bus.

I find him backstage. He's kneeling on the floor, rummaging in the leather valise he carries with him that looks like an old doctor's bag. When I come in, he smiles, but I can tell he's upset.

'Did I buy you that?' he asks, noticing my new coat.

'No.'

'Why not?'

He shakes his head. I shrug.

'Oh baby,' he says. 'I was so taken out when I didn't see your face on the bus. I can't bear the thought of him and you!'

'What are you doing?'

I walk over to him, bend down, and rub his back and shoulders.

'I'm looking for your picture,' he says.

Tonight's so-so show is short, but to me it seems interminable. Later, Bob will tell me that he made up the set list as he went along. For *me*.

''Cause you came all the way up to see me, and I didn't want you to be disappointed …'

The ambience on the bus on the way home is stilted. All the passengers except Ernie know what's been going on with me and Bob, and Dylan is sulking in his private quarters, alone. I'm in my own world, torn between Jupiter and Apollo.

After we disembark, Ernie is lagging with the luggage by the bus when Bob comes up behind me at the street corner across from the hotel. He rustles his face in the hair at the back of my neck and whispers.

'Breeda, Breeda … I love you, I love you …'

On the way up in the elevator, I convince the principal players that we should party in Bob's suite, so that I can at least be in the same room with him for a while. Guests include Ernie, Benmont, Victor, the bimbo, and Doctor K.

After about an hour, Ernie says he's tired and goes back to our room. Talk turns to Dylan's yacht that he keeps down in the Caribbean.

'That's what we'll do,' Bob says, engaging everyone except me with his latest, greatest bright idea. 'After the tour, we'll go down to the Bahamas for a while.'

My heart sinks.

Dylan lumbers over to the table where I'm sitting, feeling forgotten and alone.

'Is that something you'd be interested in?'

He takes my hand.

'What?'

I'm practically crying.

'Will you come with me to the Caribbean, baby?'

'I can't do that.'

'Sure you can,' he says. His gnarly fingers stroke my hand. In the harsh light of the hotel lamp, his hair looks damaged, his eyes sad, his ragged face ravaged.

If I say yes to him, this time, it will end my life as I know it. I'm scared. The whole room seems to be strangled with silence, in anticipation of my answer.

'Will you?' he begs.

I gaze into Dylan's sorry blue eyes. This is my dream come true, isn't it? Riding off into the sunset with Bob Dylan? They have some damn good sunsets down in the islands. I should know, I've been to Fiji.

'Yes,' I breathe quietly, casting my fate to the Caribbean winds.

At this, Bob's demeanor becomes downright ebullient. We order more drinks from room service, and I won't return to Ernie's and my bed until almost four in the morning.

'I love you,' I say under my breath.

Dylan throws me two kisses from the door and I come back.

'I love you,' I say, more forcefully this time.

'I love *you*,' Bob says, smiling.

'You say that to all the girls!' I pout.

'I say it to all the girls?' Dylan laughs. 'No, I don't.'

Ernie is awake. He wants to make love.

'I don't want to,' I tell him. 'I'm sick.'

But no has never been an answer Ernie can hear. And listening to me has never been his strong suit. He persists, thinking, I'm sure, that his forcing me will make me more excited.

I try to conjure up the happy memories with Ernie. There certainly were lots of them. But in the dappled shadow of Bob's love, they all look dark and murky, like old black-and-white photographs after a flood, submerged and sinking as they're swept downstream.

And, why—now that he's invited me to go with him to the Caribbean—is Bob still talking as if he's already lost me, as if it's a fait accompli that Ernie and I will have sex?

Lying naked, in the cold room, with Ernie on top of me, my mind is splitting, tearing off in opposite directions. I've never been the type to have two true lovers at the same time. Nor have I ever been unfaithful.

'Stop!'

I pound on Ernie's chest.

'What's wrong?' he asks as he backs off.

'I'm in love with Bob,' I cry.

Ernie furiously packs his stuff. He rants, but it's not so much about Bob and me as it is about all the things he was supposed to do for Bob that I will now have to take care of. One of the items has to do with a $30,000 fur coat Bob had bought previously in London and had sent to Carole—it's the wrong size.

'When she called the furrier to exchange it …' Ernie snorts, 'the owner asked her, which coat are you talking about? Bob Dylan bought three fur coats that day.'

I rush to Bob in the morning as soon as he wakes up.

'Ernie's leaving!' I tell him.

'How come?'

'I told him I love you … and that we're going to the Caribbean together.'

In his stocking feet, Bob and I are the same height. Evidently pleased by this latest development, he presses me up against the wall of the hotel room.

As Dylan's hard, perfect body pounds madly into mine, Ernie will knock too lightly on Bob's door to say goodbye.

October 13 1987. Dylan wants to see the British movie *Rita, Sue And Bob Too!*, about two teenaged babysitters who do quite a bit more than sitting with the baby when they're left alone with the father of their charge. I find the film fairly appalling, but Bob likes it a lot. Afterwards, he takes me to this incredibly romantic restaurant called Romeo & Juliet in a glorious vine-covered stone building located in a small square off the beaten path, where we sit for hours, nestled upstairs at a small pink-clothed table devouring the delicate food, sipping red wine from crystal goblets and gazing into each other's eyes.

'You've got the magic touch,' Bob says, holding my hand. 'You know that, don't you? A light touch. I've seen it once before. A girl I only seen one time. Then she pretended she didn't know me no more.'

After the lengthy rendezvous, Dylan unexpectedly becomes concerned about the press. When a car finally arrives for us, he sends me off in it, alone.

From my room, I call my best girlfriend in Northern California.

'I've fallen in love with Bob Dylan,' I murmur into the telephone.

'You were in love with him when we were seventeen!' she says.

October 14 1987. At 12,000 seats, Wembley Arena, London, will be Dylan's most intimate English venue in years. The last four shows of the tour. There are a hundred requests for backstage passes, including some for Mark Knopfler, George Harrison, Julian Lennon, Keith Richards, and Randy Jackson, and now that Ernie's gone, the task of handling all of Bob's road business has once again fallen to me.

Bob asks me to call Mark Knopfler to see about arranging a time when the two can get together, and it blows my mind when the Dire Straits luminary answers his own phone.

'You're so effective,' Dylan says pridefully, when I present him with the date and time of the proposed meeting.

He also has me make a note about the Book of Revelation.

In the colorless afternoon light, we walk the fashionable streets of London. There are three hats in one window that he thinks would look good on me. One of them is red.

'For sure, come back and get that one, tomorrow,' he says.

The first of the Wembley shows is strong, and will include a bittersweet version of 'Tomorrow Is A Long Time,' but Bob departs radically from the agreed set list to include 'Frankie Lee And Judas Priest,' with it's depressingly prophetic moral, and the song most worrisome to me, of late: a heated version of 'Man Of Peace.' Maybe it really is a sin, *to know and feel too much within …*

That evening, on Bob's large, lushly appointed bed, as the two of us roll hungrily, unable to fuel fast enough the furious cravings of our desire, Dylan bursts with psychic pain.

'It feels too good!' he moans.

CHAPTER NINE

Seeing the real you at last

October 15 1987. Early in the morning, I lay in Dylan's bed, listening to him snore like any guy would, and I can't help but thinking about the future.

I'm hungry and I'm irritable, and I'm tired of this bag of tricks ...

Perhaps tomorrow is not as long a time away as the title of his song 'Tomorrow Is A Long Time'—the song I've come to think of as our song, the song he plays for me—would imply.

I'm feeling lost. Empty. I haven't written a word in months except those dictated by Him. Instead of finding my true identity on the road with Bob, my association with Dylan has taken me farther and farther from myself. After the tour ends, we've been invited to spend a few days at George Harrison's home in Henley-on-Thames. Then it will be off to the Caribbean for a well-deserved rest.

After that, what? Is this really how I want to spend the rest of my life?

Dylan rolls over on his side, breathing his sour morning breath on me.

I try to picture what it would be like when we've returned to the States, if I were to move into the Malibu house with him. I see myself waking up in the sex-stained covers of his upstairs bed, looking out to the blue water of the Pacific, blinded by the sun.

Suddenly, I feel smothered by his bedroom's musty smell. I pull the covers over my head. Gasping for fresh air, I die there.

The phone rings in Dylan's suite. It's that horrifying European kind of ring that sounds more like a siren or an alarm.

Ring ring.

Ring ring.

Groggily, Bob rolls over to pick up the receiver. Someone's yelling on the other end. Dylan throws his skinny legs over the edge of the bed and sits up, holding the phone away from his ear.

Now I can hear the voice. It's Carole. Hell hath no fury like a woman scorned.

After a few minutes of Bob never getting a word in edgewise, he rests the phone gently in its cradle.

'Where does she get off talking about *you* like that?' he grunts.

'*Me?*'

I scramble out of the sheets to sit on the edge next to him.

Bob's shoulders are hunched. He's groaning, shaking his head.

'Ernie took her out to dinner and told her everything!'

'Oh, my God.'

That *fucker*, I'm thinking. But Bob quickly adds that Carole had a feeling that something was up, so she called him.

My chest is caved, breaths shallowly heaving. Something's happening, and I don't know what it is. But my gut tells me, whatever that something turns out to be, it's not going to be good.

Dylan's mouth is tight. He rests his chin wearily in his hands. He pulls my picture from the end-table drawer and looks at it.

'That's my sweetheart,' he says, glancing up at me.

I rest my hand on his back, then slide it up over his shoulders to stroke his tired neck.

'It shoulda been me you saw walking down Melrose that night,' he says.

My blood stops cold in my veins.

'You should be having dinner with me. You should be doin' everything with me.'

Oh, god, yes! I find hope in my doom. It'll kill me, Bobby D., but baby I will follow you down …

'You should be livin' in one of my houses …'

'Your houses?'

Fuck you, I'm thinking. *Don't you know me any better than that? I'm not just another girl. I'm the best thing that ever happened to you. I'm your fucking sweetheart, for Chrissake! You said it yourself.*

A deafening quiet explodes in my ears as my whole being splinters into a downpour of rubble, bursting into flames and crushing me under its weight.

'What are we going to do, now?' I blurt out.

'Baby,' Bob says, 'you're gonna have to go home.'

The weather has taken a turn for the worse. A cold wind has begun to blow. Outside my window, the red and yellow leaves scatter. I stagger through my day. When Dylan and I come across each other, we're like lost souls. Our words sound hollow. We wear our masks.

I beg his forgiveness, but Bob will have none of it. He's angry, even cruel.

'I can't get a flight out till morning,' I mention tentatively—any excuse to make contact.

'What're you cryin' to me for?' Dylan snaps. 'Elliot Roberts is the one who's holdin' your plane ticket.'

He softens. Holds me. Then sends me away. Was that a tear in his eye?

If only I hadn't told Ernie, I'm thinking. *If only I'd gone ahead and made love with him, that night. If only I hadn't given myself over so completely to Bob.*

If only my mother had named me Carol.

I go back to my room and write a scathing paean to myself and my former hero, entitled 'Thief.'

You're a lizard, a liar, a gargoyle, a thief
The poison pen of your love stabs my heart with its teeth
And as I claw my way up to the top with the best
I ask, is it you I adore or myself I detest?

October 15 1987. Wembley Arena, London. Shortly before showtime, I wander like a zombie backstage. I'm terrified of seeing Bob yet desperate to see him. I steer clear of his backstage quarters, even though I've been told he's not in them. Standing alone in the center of the badly lit room, I can tell by the look on the faces of the tour veterans: I'm an outsider now.

The show is scheduled to start any minute. I help myself to generous portions of booze at the liquor table, but the alcohol has no effect on me. I'm having an out-of-body experience, and while my heart is drunk on gin and love, my mind stands still, watching everything from above with perfect clarity.

A crowd that includes George Harrison and a holy host of other Brit musicians is gathering in anticipation of Dylan's arrival. But from which direction will he come?

Whirling in the throng, I look first toward the liquor table, then at the clock. My anxiousness is overwhelming me, so I pick a spot and force myself to stand in it, giving up on trying to find Him at all.

I close my eyes, and the clamor of the crowd reaches a tumultuous pitch.

When I open them again, directly in my line of vision, Dylan emerges from the mob, walking toward me at the head of a long procession, a veritable pageant of his blessed following, the entourage of which I was so recently a member, a jovial parade of the famous by association and the just plain famous, who have entered from the bleak gray light of day outside the hall to wallow in the wake of the pied piper of the tambourine generation—who, cloaked in his scarves and coats and with his wingy hat, looks refreshed, renewed, his energy replenished, his soon-to-be-sagging skin well-oiled with all the love I had to give him—as he passes right by me, without a look or a smile or even the smallest nod of acknowledgement, as though we never have met.

Dylan's fifteen-song set includes a forceful—even believable—harmonica-laced version of 'I'll Remember You.'

A freak windstorm is terrorizing all of London, holding even old diehard structures like the Mayfair hostage. Wind like a hurricane whistles through the cracks in the windowsills and sets the shutters banging.

In the morning, Carole is flying in, and I am flying out. I go to Dylan's room and beg him to sleep with me. And I mean sleep.

'I'm scared,' I tell him, and I am, but we both know it's not just because of the wind.

Barefoot, he walks me to my room and helps me to make up my bed. He can't stay, he says, because someone's coming over.

'But you know I won't do anything,' he adds. He throws me down on the mattress and crawls on top of me. Hot shivers reignite my flame.

214

As the wind shrieks through the sorry streets below, he holds me and consoles me, even tucks me in, but he refuses to spend the night with me.

'How can I say goodbye to you?' Dylan says, turning out my light.

'Tell me about it,' I mumble dully.

'At least I have your picture,' he whispers, before closing the door. 'What have you got?'

October 16 1987. It's morning, and the City of London is on storm alert. Hundred-mile-an-hour winds still howl. Power lines and old trees are down. Roofs have been ripped off. A car is on its way to pick me up.

I go to Dylan's room to bid my restless farewell.

I feel empty. Used up.

He's sitting shoeless and shirtless on a gold-colored couch.

'Don't go telling people you fell in love with me,' Bob says. 'It's no position to put yourself in. It's weak.'

He's made it clear on numerous occasions how he feels about weakness: 'there's no excuse for it.'

'I don't understand what's going on,' I tell him, though despite my thorough lack of sleep, I think I get it all too well.

'It's a man thing,' Bob says.

'A man thing?'

'Yeah, between me and Ernie. Understand?'

'No, Bob,' I say, shaking my head. I'm sitting on the floor across from him, hugging my knees to my chest. 'I do not understand.'

'Look, you can't just see someone walking down the street,' Bob says, referring again to how Ernie and I first met.

'Ernie owes me ten thousand dollars,' I say grimly.

'Kiss that money goodbye!' Bob bites his lower lip. 'Maybe you should come work for me.'

'I don't want to work for you!' I yelp. 'I'm a writer, too.'

'A writer, huh?' he sucks his teeth.

'Bob, I need an explanation, here. The truth …'

Dylan clutches his gnarled hands penitently over the crotch of his black jeans.

'Sometimes I do bad things,' he says.

There's a three-hour delay at Heathrow Airport on account of the high winds. I don't care. I sit numbly, holding on to the last evidence I have of my relationship with Bob Dylan: a one-way ticket to Los Angeles via Seattle. Business class. And my paycheck.

I wish the fucking jumbo jet would take off in the storm. I wish it would explode in the air.

When the aircraft does finally lift off the runway, I find myself seated next to the window, looking through this small plastic hole, as the big, bad, bustling world below me—to which I no longer belong—grows smaller and smaller. Then everything just goes white. But not quiet white. Noisy white. The kind of white that can cut you up into a million little pieces.

Rabbit white. That's it.

I've been killed, skinned, gutted, and cooked. But not eaten—not yet—because if I'd been eaten, I wouldn't exist anymore, and if I didn't exist, I wouldn't be feeling the pain I'm in. Big pain. Bigger than anything I knew when I was growing up. Bigger than when my husband died. Bigger than me and bigger than the whole damn flat white world outside my window, but not so big it will swallow me up.

The stewardess offers me a drink and I take it. Vodka on the rocks.

I haven't slept … in months really. I'm tired. And I'm alone.

Maybe I should take a Valium? Yeah, why not? A little something to deaden the old pain. The big pain. This overwhelming pain of humiliation. This overwhelming burden of self-hate.

I rummage my overnight bag for the canister. Sometimes I have a hard time finding things in this bag because I store so much in it, but there it is. The smooth vial slips easily between my fingers like Dylan's tongue between my teeth. So easy, it has to be right. And no child-proofing! The cap pops off like one of Bob's hats before he tosses me down on his bed.

And all the little blue pills spill into my hand like …

I sip thirstily from my frosty cup.

Why would all the medicine have dumped into my palm unless I was meant to take it?

I stare at the tiny pellets and try to imagine them with happy faces. They dance in my hand to the turbulence.

Yes.

This is a sign.

If I take all the Valium, my problems will be solved … *forever*.

What is it about me that chooses to persist? According to the therapist I will see when I return to Los Angeles—the one who is a fan of Dylan's—given my background, anywhere along the line I could have easily become a hooker, a drug overdose, or a suicide. But now, like a warrior sent home from the battle, bloodied and beaten, missing most of my limbs, my weary wounded heart finds the courage to take only a single blue pill to ease the horror of my pain.

When the plane stops over in Seattle, I rush to a pay phone and call Elliot Mintz, but his words of comfort cannot console me.

'I want to die!' I cry into the telephone.

CHAPTER TEN

Like a rolling stone

This is about the time I learn the third rule of celebrity: when it's all over now, baby blue, there are no consequences to the celebrity's behavior: you go back to being you, or a hollow shell of your former self, or straight to hell, whichever comes first. And he goes on, in this case, being Bob Dylan.

October 17 1987. I take the Super Shuttle to Ernie's address. The Cougar convertible sits collecting sand and salt-air in the driveway. All the cactuses are withered from lack of water.

Whatever you wish to keep, you better grab it fast.

Ernie, dark-eyed and brooding, rambles silently like a shadow around his amusement-park house. When I pass, he looks the other way. I go to my room to pack. My closet has been decimated, the contents ravaged. My clothes—half of them clothes he bought me—are stripped from their hangers and strewn about the floor like garbage. Even the glass shade on my 1920s deco floor lamp is broken.

I salvage what I can, telling him I'll come back for the rest later.

The phone rings.

Ernie won't answer.

I pick up.

It's Bob.

'You told me you loved me,' I whimper.

'I do love you, baby,' Dylan says, sweetly. 'I'd take you out on the road with me, anytime. Put Ernie on the line.'

Ernie screams at me when he gets off the phone.

'Britta the groupie, that's what Bob called you! He said it was all your fault! That you came into his room wearing nothing but a T-shirt.'

'That's not true!' I howl.

Where does Bob Dylan get off talking about *me* like that?

'He said if Jesse's plane hadn't had engine problems, none of this would ever have happened. He says he keeps his kids around him to keep him out of trouble.'

'He's lying,' I sob. 'He told me I was his sweetheart. He called me his baby.'

'He calls all his women baby so he doesn't get confused!'

I drop onto the bed, quaking, shirts, shoes, underwear slipping from my grasp.

'At least if you two would have wound up together,' Ernie sneers, 'then maybe this all would have been worth it. I'd have wished you both all the fucking happiness in the world. But, for this? For nothing?' Ernie groans, shaking his head. 'I would have taken a bullet for Bob.'

'What?'

'You heard me.'

'Well, that would have been pretty fucking stupid, then, wouldn't it?'

'I would have taken a bullet for you, too,' Ernie says.

'You can stay as long as you need to,' Karla tells me, showing me to her guest room, which outclasses any five-star hotel I might have stayed in with Bob. I'm in that sobbed-out kind of state that I used to get into when I was a kid and my parents had gotten mad at me for something I didn't even do, and the whole world just seemed so unjust. My face is puffy, my teeth are chattering, and my breath is jerking in and out of my chest, as if my lungs are being driven with both feet, one on the accelerator and the other stomping the breaks.

Karla convinces me we should go out to an early dinner.

Melrose. Again. Pasta and red wine and a lot of heart-to-heart gabbing.

'Breeda, Breeda. I love you. I love you,' I say, mimicking Dylan.

'He should have known better than that,' Karla says.

Afterwards she suggests we make a visit to this psychic that she and her girlfriend, who's a shrink, have been seeing. The woman's name is Maura. She's a gypsy, and Karla says she's fantastic.

I'm skeptical. What kind of a Gypsy has a storefront on Melrose Avenue? I grow even more skeptical when I see the pink neon sign that says Psychic Readings.

Maura is a short, brown, leathery-skinned lady with an unidentifiable accent—Transylvanian, perhaps. She tells me to sit down. I ask Karla to stay because I'm so shook up, and she sweetly complies. After performing the usual fortune-teller tricks, palm reading, pick a card, any card, etc. Maura flips up three tarot cards in a row.

'Rome, Paris, London? You've just returned from a trip.'

Karla and I look at each other.

'Yeah,' I say. 'That's true.'

'Who were you with?' the gypsy wants to know.

I shake my head.

'I can't tell you.'

There I go, again, still protecting Dylan's privacy after he's splayed open my life like a pomegranate on a cutting board, leaving me red, raw, juiceless, and totally exposed.

The gypsy flips up another card.

'He's *very* famous!' she says. 'But he's so unhappy.'

Karla and I exchange glances.

'What happened to him?' the woman asks, turning the odd-looking cards face up before coming to the end of the pack, shuffling and starting over.

The Empress. The Hanged Man. Death.

I start to cry.

'I thought he loved me,' I say.

'He does love you,' she says. 'But he's very confused. Right now, he's with friends, but he's miserable. He's drinking, maybe doing drugs. He doesn't know what to do.'

'Really?' I sniff.

It's the closing night of Dylan's best tour in years, and there was supposed to be a big party afterwards. I picture Bob, moody in the midst of all the gaiety, and find some relief.

'What about the ring?' the woman asks unexpectedly.

'What ring?' I shrug.

'I see a ring. Did he give you a ring?'

My jaw drops.

'Well, yes. I mean, no. He presented me with one, sort of …'

But I lost the ring.

I kill myself with regret.

'I think maybe he'll come back to you,' she says. 'He's very troubled, now. I see a lot of turmoil. He's surrounded by people, but he's missing you.'

Hope flickers like a candle in a storm.

Another card.

'Who's this?' Maura's taken aback. 'Another *man*?'

'Ernie!' Karla and I say at the same time.

'And another woman, too,' I add, just to help her out. 'Carole.'

A tiny muscle at the corner of her mouth twinges, then sags.

I'm very sensitive to other peoples' demeanors. It's a product of my dysfunctional upbringing. Being able to read the smallest of human subtleties, a grunt, a grin, the incline or decline in a wrinkle on a person's face was what enabled me to stay just far enough away from the swinging fists of my parents to survive to adulthood. It's one of the reasons I was able to function so well in Dylan's presence. I could read his needs and satisfy them, as I am now convinced, he could read mine.

He knows just where to touch you, honey, and how you like to be kissed …

Now, as I sit in the worn thrift-store armchair of the gypsy who's about to charge me $125 for an hour of her time, I notice the slightest collapse in her expression and know that she has found the obstacle to my happiness.

'Your man can never be with you because of Ernie,' she says.

Maybe she'd just like to have my heart on a plate. I'd never have even met Bob if it hadn't have been for Ernie.

'What about Carole?' Karla volunteers.

'Ernie,' Maura shakes her head. 'Ernie is the problem.'

She slaps a few more cards on the table. At one point she sees a ray of hope.

'Maybe …' she sighs. Now she's depressed, too. 'There could be a chance …'

I'm not that encouraged. If this woman can perceive anything, she's got to be able to see the mental bruises I'm sporting from the psychological battering I've received.

Toward the end of the reading, Maura tells me how, for a thousand bucks, she can do a healing on me with crystals, but I gracefully decline the offer.

When I stand up to go, she shrieks.

'What are those rings?'

Horrified, she points to my left hand.

'Just rings,' I say.

'Take them off. Let me see.'

Wearily, I sink back down into my chair. On top of everything else, I'm still jet-lagged.

One ring is the one Dylan liked—the Janet Feinstein ring Ernie found in the street when he was a kid. Another is my mother's diamond engagement ring to the man she married before my father. She once pawned it to get money to bet the horses. The third ring is Ernie's 'wife's' wedding ring.

One after another, the psychic squeezes the gold hoops in the palm of her hand, then sets them on the table.

'All dead people,' she frowns. 'You mustn't wear these rings anymore. They're bad luck.'

I'd never thought of it before, but she was right. I knew the energy surrounding Ernie's ex and even my own mother was bad, but I'd been so out of touch with my feelings the last couple of years—stoned, tired, drinking, high on Bob—it had never even occurred to me not to wear them, and who knew anything about the man's ring with the initials that Ernie found by the curb in the 1950s except that, by now, the odds were, the guy who'd owned it was dead. Maybe the ring had fallen off his finger when he was run over by a truck.

'Thanks,' I say, scooping the jewelry into my pocket, before rising.

'I could clean them for you …' Maura begins, her gypsy instincts kicking in once again, 'for a hundred … oh, for you, ninety dollars.'

She smiles, and I notice she's got bad teeth.

'I think I'll just get rid of them.'

At the door, Maura squeezes my arm with her wrinkled fingers.

'Good luck,' she sighs, and then stops Karla and I dead in our tracks with unshakable evidence of her psychic ability. '*Musicians* are always tricky.'

On the way back to the car, Karla and I drop into a trendy jewelry store and I pick out a new ring. It's deco, from the 40s, so I suppose its owner too may be deceased, but it's this heavy sterling silver setting, almost in the shape of a chevron, with piano-key ivory showing bone white in the center. A powerful-looking ring with a good vibe. A man's ring.

I place it on the middle finger of my left hand—my 'fuck you' finger—tip pointing outward, and convince myself that this ring will protect me from any and all future evils.

Late October 1987. Rumor has it that the night I left London, Dylan performed—for the first and last time on the Temples In Flames tour—a particularly stirring rendition of 'To Ramona.'

And someday maybe, who knows, baby
I'll come and be cryin' to you.

For months, I wander the Hollywood Hills behind Karla's house with my dog, trying to visualize Bob Dylan coming crying to me, or just coming to me at all, but he never does. When I'd first met him, it seemed whenever I'd had strong thoughts of him, he would just sort of magically appear. Now all the energy I put out into the universe to try to reel him in comes bouncing back at me like an echo.

December 1987. West Hollywood Hills, California. When Karla and I throw a Christmas party, I call up my tour buddy from the Petty band, Benmont Tench, to invite him. He doesn't call me back.

Pouring rain soaks Los Angeles. I'm killing time at Duke's for breakfast before a meeting with my agent. I order poached eggs and a half a grapefruit—Bob's and my usual, sans the french fries. The waitress sings 'A Hard Rain's A-Gonna Fall' as she delivers my coffee.

Outside on the street, I run into Debbie Gold—the one whose idea it was to pair Dylan with the Heartbreakers. We stand in the onslaught, comparing notes. She too claims to have had a fling with the rock star.

'He told you he *loved* you?' she asks. She's incredulous.

'Yeah,' I say. 'And then Carole found out about it, and the next day I was on a plane bound for Los Angeles.'

'What's she got on him, anyway?' Debbie wants to know.

People Magazine runs a story with Marla Maples gracing the cover, claiming that being the 'other woman' in today's world only makes you an outcast if you're not the victor. Ernie says not a day will go by for the rest of my life that I won't think of Dylan.

My therapy bills soar as I try to make sense out of my life's wreckage.

Sitting across from me, munching on an organic carrot, my therapist will state matter-of-factly during one session, 'Bob Dylan's left a lot of dead bodies around this town.'

The fourth and final rule of celebrity is: never fall in love with one, because the *media* won't let you forget that you did.

The *Los Angeles Times* reports a fire on Dylan's Malibu estate. No one is hurt, but the damage is said to be considerable.

January 20 1988. After I suffer through a blue Christmas and a black New Year's, there's television coverage of Dylan at a gala ceremony held at the Waldorf Astoria Hotel in New York City, as he is inducted into the Rock and Roll Hall of Fame. The one-word take away from his acceptance speech is 'forgiveness.'

February 1988. I go see a movie in Malibu, and the title song is a Dylan tune. Afterwards, in the busy shopping center, I run into Bob's personal assistant, Carol Snow. She's embarrassed, torn between the little bit of friendship we had and her loyalty to Dylan. She actually lives in one of the houses on Bob's property, so she's got a lot to lose if she gets caught in a transgression.

I apologize to her for what happened between me and Bob and Ernie. I confess that I owe everyone around Bob, especially his kids, who adored Ernie, and Carole, who was always so nice to me, an apology. I tell her that in therapy I've figured out that one of the main reasons I was so attracted to Dylan in the first place was because he was like the perfect combination of my parents' worst attributes—sort of a schizophrenic alcoholic. I figured that if I could make it right with him, I could make it right retroactively for all the wrongs I suffered growing up.

'Uh huh,' she says. She's picking out dishtowels or something as I babble.

I remind her about my father living in his car in the desert and tell her that someone told me that Sam Shepard's father lives in a car, too, so I'm in good company.

'Are you kidding?' Carol remarks, her tone so forthright it startles me. 'Bob would live in his car in a minute!'

Karla and her pal J.D. Souther write a song for the soundtrack of the movie *About Last Night*, which is directed by my friend Ed Zwick. After the premiere, a bunch of us sit around a landmark Hollywood restaurant called La Toque, eating, smoking dope, and drinking until the wee hours.

When the official closing time arrives, the owner passes the key to the liquor cabinet to the soberest among us and says, 'Don't forget to lock it up before you go.'

'Boy this rock'n'roll thing is really where it's at,' I say to J.D., passing him a roach clamped in the tweezers of a Swiss Army Knife.

'Yeah,' he says, sucking in a heated breath, 'that's why I picked it.'

Through Karla, J.D. expresses interest in getting to know me better. I'm attracted to him, but I don't trust him. I don't trust any man anymore.

Around this time I attend a dinner party at the Pacific Palisades home of Danny Goldberg, the record mogul, and my would-be candidate for first Jewish President of the United States, and his fiancé, Rosemary Caroll, whose ex-husband is Jim Carroll of *Basketball Diaries* fame. The purpose of this party is to fix me up with British rocker Michael des Barres.

'Danny and I think you two would be perfect for each other!' Rosemary gushes.

Rosemary doesn't know me very well, and sadly, I don't know who Mr. des Barres is either, other than that he's the infamous groupie Pamela's ex. Or, as Dylan said about going to Bruce Willis's that time, 'If I'd a known that, I'd a never agreed to go!'

I arrive late, wearing leftovers from the Dylan scene—tight black jeans, black cowboy boots, and the long black leather duster I bought in London—and find myself in a scene from Alan Rudolph's *The Young Moderns*. The other guests at the party include

Sam Goldwyn Junior, his narcissistic actress wife—who I won't name here 'cause I know it'll drive her crazy—the female editor of the Op Ed section of the *Los Angeles Times*, and the hot young film director of *Square Dance*, starring the hot young controversial actor Rob Lowe.

The most valuable tidbit I will come away with from this evening is the news to me that 90 percent of what you read in the *National Enquirer* is true, or else they would have been sued out of existence a long time ago. Bobby Neuwirth will make a late appearance.

Dressed all in black, with a tan that would make George Hamilton green with envy, Michael des Barres, whose good looks have ruined him, sits posing, relaxed, in an overstuffed armchair.

I make an early, if not expedient, escape.

He comes on to me by the door.

'You think it's an accident you and I are the only ones wearing black?'

Spring 1988. My screenplay is hot, and I'm shopping it around, taking meetings with notable development people in town. Cher reads the script, which is this big deal, because she's supposedly dyslexic, but while she likes the character, she passes on the venture, saying she's only interested in doing 'meaningful' projects now.

One of the producers, the son of this huge old-time director, even asks me out on a date, but I'm sure I come across as needy, and as soon as he finds out I'm not the balls-on tough female character I've written, he's no longer interested.

A friend of Karla's gives me Warren Beatty's phone number.

'Just call him,' she tells me. 'He'll love you.'

Somehow, though, a night, a day, or even a lifetime with

Warren—I don't care how good he is in bed—doesn't seem like it's going to wipe out the eternity of pain I feel from losing Bob.

May 24 1988. I've moved back into my apartment in Westwood. There's a writers strike, so my script and any pending deals—I have a proposal for a new story about Olympic ice skaters in the works at Interscope—are on hold.

I'm out in my garden, minding my own business, pulling weeds with the radio blaring, trying to heal myself, when the DJ announces happy birthday to Bob Dylan. I'd completely forgotten. I take this as a good sign.

Still, I suddenly find myself thinking, *I could call him to wish him a happy birthday*. I have his unlisted number …

No, I talk myself out of it. That would be—how had he put it? Weak.

May 31 1988. As I'm coming back from my exercise class, I decide to drop into Tower Records on Sunset, to see what's new. There's a Dylan record playing as I enter, but I've never heard it.

'It's his latest album,' the three-earringed kid behind the counter tells me. '*Down In The Groove*. They're just unpacking it now.'

I head toward the rear of the store and come upon this huge carton with these two kinda familiar-looking guys picking through it.

'Hey, I know you,' I say.

'What's your name?' they squint, each with a copy of Dylan's new CD in hand.

'Britta.'

'Oh … Britta,' they say, disappointed. Not the usual reaction I get from guys.

'I work for Tom Petty,' says one.

'I work for Bob,' the other one says.

As I slap some plastic down on the counter to pay, I ask the kid with the earrings, 'When did this CD come out, anyway?'

'This morning,' he says.

Another day, as I'm driving west on Sunset, between Beverly Hills and Beverly Glen, I find myself in back of this beat-up pale blue Chevy van with New Mexico plates. It's belching exhaust, and when I go to pass it, I notice Victor Maymudes is behind the wheel. Maybe he's coming from Sara Dylan's place in Beverly Hills and going out to Malibu. Maybe Bob's in the passenger seat. When I try to pass him, he floors it. I back off and wait till he's in the left lane, then try to pass him on the right. Now I'm sure I sense Dylan's dark presence in the car—there's somebody in there—but again, the van speeds up.

It occurs to me that the passengers know that it's me behind them—even though I've ditched the Cougar, 'cause it was such a piece of shit, and am now driving a brand new Celica convertible—and that they are trying to out run me. Screw 'em!

When I turn left on Beverly Glen to go into Westwood, I can still see the van up ahead, veering around the curves, careening off in the direction of the beach.

Ernie really is a mensch. Maybe not the right mensch for me, but he's actually making payments on the loan I made him. When I drop by his office to pick up a check, he can tell by my complexion that I've been raked over the coals.

'She was terrific out here on the road,' Dylan has been telling everyone, 'but I just couldn't keep her out of my bed.'

'He had a tear in his eye when I was leaving,' I tell Ernie.

'Yeah, well, if he had a tear, it was something he learned from his acting lessons with Jeff Cory.'

Any fantasies I might have had about getting back together with Ernie are quickly dashed when his latest woman—attractive, tall, and blonde—arrives in a Land Cruiser to meet him for lunch. He walks me outside to my new car—the car he practically invented.

'You're gonna have to fight for Bob, if you want him,' he advises.

'No fucking way,' I say.

I don't want to be like some raven at his window with a broken wing.

May 1988. The couple that owns my fancy exercise studio fixes me up with a divorced, balding, but brilliant Neil Simon. The four of us lunch at Le Dome, and while I will come away with this great story about his writing of *The Out-Of-Towners*, I'm numb and incapable of speech, and he's cold and distant. A week later, he goes back to his ex-wife.

It's the year of my fortieth birthday, and I'm depressed. My writing career is stalled on account of the writers strike—I'm working on some stupid storyline with an off-the-lot producer from Paramount with a Prince Valiant hairdo who's young enough to be my son, I'm running short on money, and the way things look, I'm going to be all by my lonesome on my big birthday.

Maybe I deserve to be alone, I tell myself, given what I've done to Ernie, not to mention all the other people around Dylan that I let down.

Fuck Bob Dylan, I say to myself.

I don't need to be with him. I don't need to be with anyone.

I pinch a nerve doing push-ups at the gym. Sandy, my music supervisor friend, gives me the number of a chiropractor. I have a chiropractor, I remember … David Kearney. I make an appointment to see him that afternoon.

As I drive my white bright new car out of the driveway, I notice this huge, fat black raven picking at the grass by the curb. The roar of my four cylinders is insufficient to ruffle even a single feather, let alone run the obstinate bird off the lawn.

I speed down Santa Monica Boulevard, thinking that's the kind of thing Dylan would call a bad omen.

Doctor Kearney's waiting room is crowded. I pick up the first magazine I see, and within a few pages there's an article on Bob. Fuck! I just can't get away from this guy.

Two seconds later, Doctor K. opens the door to the waiting room and calls my name. It's then, when I see him, that I remember how I even know him, my life's been so amiss.

'Wow!' I say to David, 'I forgot you even knew Bob. I forgot I even knew him.'

I'm trying to suggest that I've gotten over what happened between Dylan and me, but judging by the chiropractor's baffled expression, I'm obviously still a work in progress.

Kearney ushers me to my room and tells me to change into my dressing gown. I say I want to use the bathroom, and he says, fine, but first change into your gown. I think this is odd, but ever obedient, I comply.

When I return to my cubicle, the doctor is waiting for me. The energy in the small room has shifted, though, and even as he addresses me, I find myself standing diagonally in the space, listing toward the south side of the office.

David smiles.

'Bob's here,' he says, 'and he'd like to see you.'

Bob's *here*? In the whole time I was around the Dylan scene, Bob never came to David's office for an appointment—David always went to his place in Malibu. What in God's name is He doing here *now*?

'Uh, sure,' I say, not really sure at all. It will take me a few days to pick up on the significance of me being half-naked as the chiropractor escorts me to the *south* corner of the building for my audience with Bob Dylan.

Why would this be happening at this moment in time, I have to wonder, *when I've just gotten past the point of wanting him back?*

Dylan's fully clothed, so the bastard's actually a couple of inches taller than me in his boots, making me feel even more vulnerable. He's buttoning the cuffs on a pale blue work shirt.

'Hey,' he says, barely looking over at me when I walk in.

'Hey,' I say, trying not to be too friendly.

He turns, stands directly in front of me, but still keeps his distance. 'You OK?'

'Great,' I lie. 'How 'bout you?'

'OK.' Pause. 'You look good.'

I'm cool toward him. Trying to be cool. Trying to be cold. I stare him down.

'You seen Ernie?' he asks.

'Not lately,' I say. 'You?'

'Naw.'

He doesn't tell me what I will hear later in the rumor mill: that Ernie tape-recorded his entire phone conversation with Bob that day when I was at the house—when Dylan was pointing fingers at everyone except himself regarding our liaison—and that Ernie had threatened to send the rambling non-confession in Dylan's unmistakable inflection to all the local radio stations for airplay. Or that Ernie had flown to New York once shortly after our breakup and supposedly confronted Dylan in his hotel room about the affair before being apprehended by security.

Instead, Dylan stands moody-eyed, arms crossed in front of his chest, looking me up and down like he's deciding whether or not it's safe for him to trust me.

Doctor Kearney opens the door. He's ready for my appointment. Bob follows me down to my room.

'We were just gettin' started,' he moans.

The doctor cuts us some slack. When it's just the two of us again, Bob ventures a little closer to me. He's starting to get that dog in heat thing going where his toe's a tappin' and his body's a shakin'.

'What d'ya been doin'?' he wants to know.

'Writing,' I say sullenly.

'You're not writing about *me*, are you?'

'No!'

Why does everything have to be about you, I'm thinking, but he's looking cute in blue and I can feel my defenses plummeting.

'I've been playing the guitar,' I say. 'I've been practicing "Don't Think Twice" but I'm having a hard time with one of the chord changes.'

'Oh, well, see … you got to do it like this,' he moves up in back of me, taking my arms in his from behind and showing me how to play it on his air guitar. 'I'll teach it to you sometime.'

Sometime? Now I'm really falling apart. I pull away.

David knocks on the door.

'Well, you know how to get in touch with me,' I say, with as much bitchiness as I can muster.

'No, I don't,' Dylan says—which is such bullshit, because anybody working for him could easily track me down. *I've* tracked people down for him. The guy's got more resources than the fucking FBI, and it's not like I'm the one with the unlisted phone number.

'You have a card or somethin'?' he asks.

Gulp.

'Yeah, I do.'

It's hot pink and black—a hip card that my Berkeley girlfriend designed for me. Not a card you'd easily misplace.

I pull one from my wallet and hand it over.

'Britta, huh?' he smiles. 'I thought you spelled that with two *i*s.'

Oh, God.

Dylan slips the paper into his shirt pocket.

'Oh,' I say. 'I almost forgot …'

Through the crack in the door, I can see Doctor K. waiting impatiently.

'I got a new ring.'

I hold my left hand out, chevron-pointed finger aimed at Dylan, and it's like I've sent a punch flying at his gut.

He caves at the waist then backs away.

'Uh huh,' he says. He looks confused.

Before reaching for the door, he kisses me on the cheek.

'I'll call you,' he says.

I drive to the beach.

When I was a kid, I once walked all the way from our house in Mar Vista to the sandy shore by the Santa Monica Pier to escape my parents' rage. Now as I trudge northward, barefoot, through the cool foam of the breaking waves, I pray for that same sense of peace. After a few minutes I run into my old friend Bob the Healer and we sit down on a crumbling sand dune to talk. I tell him about the fat black raven on my lawn as I was leaving the house and how I'd felt Dylan's presence at the doctor's office even before I knew he was there. I tell him Dylan told me he'd call me.

Bob the Healer knows this is the last thing I need to speed my recovery from the Dylan debacle.

'It's almost as if he knew you were pulling away from him,' he admits, 'and wanted to get you hooked into him, again.'

Bob the Healer's got a female friend waiting. We part. I continue north along the wet shoreline until I get all the way to the Palisades. Where the hell did I think I was going? The sun has long since dropped below the horizon, and it's starting to get dark.

I turn around to head back to my car, as a battered raven—*what the fuck's a raven doing out here at the beach?*—cawing and flapping it's frayed black wings against the Pacific wind, flies over my head in the direction of Malibu's Point Dume.

June 1988. A month before my birthday, and a month since I've run into Bob—still no call—I'm invited to another friend's fortieth birthday party. Every guest is supposed to bring a photo of him or herself as a child. As I'm standing in my Westwood garage, sifting through faded pictures of my parents, my dogs, my ex-boyfriends, and my bummer childhood, I come across a photo of Bob on the bus in Copenhagen. Shrouded in darkness, despite the sunlight, his gnarled hands make him look devilish; his whole demeanor demonic. I scream.

June 16 1988. In the middle of the night, I wake up gasping for breath. I've been dizzy of late, light-headed. My whole body feels swollen. I can't make a fist. Naturally, my doctor is out of town. At

4am, I'm admitted to the emergency room at Santa Monica Hospital. A blood test reveals I have twice as much oxygen in my blood as I should. I'm told I've been hyperventilating. For weeks. It's just an illusion that my hands are swollen, but my heart palpitations are real.

'Stress,' the ER doctor smiles. 'Are you in the entertainment business?'

I nod.

He hands me a paper bag and tells me to breathe into it.

'We've been overrun with people just like you ever since the strike began.'

I look across the room and see a bearded guy in a Warner Bros T-shirt with his nose in a paper sack. I cup the rough brown paper over my nostrils and mouth.

But the WGA strike has been going on for months, I remember, before sucking in a humid breath. My feelings of unwellness started right after I saw Bob.

Bob the Healer makes an appointment for me with a curly-haired neurologist and acupuncturist friend of his named Richard Apollo. There's a four-year waiting list to get in to see Richard, but Healer Bob just picks up the phone, and I'm in. Like Doctor K., Apollo has an office in Santa Monica, but his approach is worlds apart. For one thing, before he will even touch you, he interviews you for about three hours.

'You've been possessed,' Apollo concludes, bushy brows raised.

Possessed?

'But my eyes are all swollen,' I complain.

'Un-cried tears,' the doctor says. 'What is it you don't want to see?'

'Ha!' I break down.

I don't tell him how betrayed I feel by Dylan, or how I feel that

I betrayed others: Dylan's kids, his girlfriend, all the people that worked for him that trusted me, Elliot, Ernie, Ernie's mother, his sister, his brother-in-law, *myself*—yes, perhaps I betrayed myself most of all—everyone who thought I was a certain person, but I was a living lie, *living a lie,* lying to myself so I could be close to Bob.

Doctor Apollo has too much class to ask who my possessor might be, but he informs me that I'll have to undergo a lengthy treatment called 'The Seven Dragons' if I want to get de-possessed.

'Do I have to make an appointment for it?' I sniffle.

'No,' he shakes his curly head. 'I think it's best if we get started now.'

I lie down on the table. Somewhere around the sixth dragon, it occurs to me: what happened between Bob and me wasn't just my fault. We all had a part in it. Even Ernie. I have got to stop taking all the blame.

July 1988. Fuck finances! Viva la charge card! I fly to New Mexico for my fortieth birthday. I'm alone. I go to museums, eat in great restaurants, stay in an adobe villa.

On the afternoon of my big day I drive to some sacred ruins that are famous for their echoes. Wandering upon the dusty trails through the chaparral until I reach the mouths of the caves, I shout into the abyss, 'I'm forty and it's fabulous!' and the words resound repeatedly, seemingly forever. On my way out, a family of four, on their way in, break into giggles when they see me.

That night, wearing ripped blue jeans and a fringed suede coat, I take myself out to the best restaurant in Santa Fe. A boisterous party of eight enters midway through my meal. I can't help but noticing the smooth-looking fortyish man among them. Jet-black hair, true blue eyes, swarthy dark tan. He's speaking French.

That has to be the best looking guy I've ever seen in my life, I'm thinking. And he's looking at me. My waitress tells me he's royalty—a duke or something, or the son of a duke, the most eligible bachelor in the four corners. He invites me to join his party, but I decline. On his way out—I'm a slow eater—he passes me his phone number, scrawled on a cocktail napkin.

Who says turning forty's a bad thing?

Upon my return to LA, I throw my own fortieth birthday party. To memorialize the event, I squeeze myself into a red-leather lace-up minidress from North Beach Leather—a gift from Karla. The party's catered by an authentic New Orleans soul-food restaurant called Harold & Belle's. In attendance is my friend Stanley Weiser, who wrote *Wall Street* and claims he *almost* brought Oliver Stone to the party. And, of course, Karla and the rest of the unusual suspects, including miscellaneous development, writer, and producer types, as well as those my buddy Lon Diamond will call 'friends and relatives of the rich and famous,' like *M*A*S*H* creator Larry Gelbart's charming stepson, Gary, who I adore. Then just to keep it real, all my everyday folk kinda friends like Nancy and Al and Kris, who you don't know, and therefore won't give a shit about, even though I do. One notable party crasher is Lawrence Bender, who will go on to produce *Reservoir Dogs* and *Pulp Fiction*.

I get laid but I sleep alone.

August 2 1988. Dylan is performing at the Greek Theater. A screenwriter friend of mine, Jorge Arena, insists on springing for fourth row tickets.

'You're going to go down in history as the only girl who never called Bob Dylan back,' he says.

Jorge's already told me I'm the only woman in Hollywood he knows of who doesn't have 'help'—that is, a rich father *in the business* or a boyfriend who's a studio head.

'I can't call him,' I say.

'Why not?'

'It's weak,' I whimper.

We have dinner at Farfalla with Lyn Hemmerdinger, a fellow writer, dear friend, and consummate party-thrower, who's a patron of the arts, and her pal, the architect Jeffrey Daniels, before heading off to the show. Both Jorge and Lyn have been pushing me to write a book about my Dylan days—a roman à clef, they call it, where you don't actually use the famous person's name, but everyone knows who it is anyway.

The backstage area at the Greek is accessible to anybody who knows what they're doing, and I'm astounded to see Elliot Mintz, Doctor K., and Victor all performing their same functions, somewhat robotically. Though less than a year has gone by, my Dylan experience seems a lifetime away. I feel different, I look different, and my life is different: it's changing, growing. This rock'n'roll life, for all its alleged excitement, suddenly seems stifled, stagnant, dead … a never-ending tour of soggy french fries and smashed cigarette butts.

An obscenely short-skirted Sally Kirkland can be seen flailing herself at Dylan's door, trying to get in. I scurry to my seat with no intentions of making my presence known.

The show is adequate, though Dylan looks weary, his performance perfunctory. I can tell his back is bothering him.

Familiar pangs of longing grab at me, but I douse them with newfound self-worth.

'He's not in love with anyone,' I say to my friends.

February 6 1989. *Dylan & The Dead* is released, but I still am not. At least not completely. I catch myself listening to the album over and over again, trying to recapture those few moments in time when I felt complete.

Bob the Healer suggests I join a twelve-step program. I go to a meeting. When it's my turn to speak, I say, to a collective sigh, 'My mother was an alcoholic, my father was a schizophrenic, and I'm an only child.'

May 24 1989. My permanent meeting will be an Adult Children of Alcoholics meeting in West Hollywood. It's billed in the directory as a writer's meeting, but it turns out they mean *writing about the twelve steps*. It's an interesting group: seven or eight people, give or take, including a formerly homeless lawyer, a UCLA professor, and me. At the end of tonight's meeting, the host, the lawyer, stands up and speaks.

'Bob Dylan's forty-nine today. Where does he get off being forty-nine when I'm fifty-four?'

I'm not even safe at an ACA meeting, I realize, once again having had enough recovery to forget it was Bob's birthday. On my way out the door, one of the women shakes her head.

'It's not a good idea to get involved with a famous person,' she says. 'They're everywhere. I saw a picture of the love of my life in the window of a hair salon on La Brea on my way over here.'

'You're kidding,' I say. 'Who was it? I mean, it's none of my business. It's just that what's-his-name just brought up Bob Dylan, and that's who my famous heartbreaker was.'

I've never spoken to this woman in my life, and now the two of us are standing in the prickly shadows of this seedy apartment building, and she's glaring at me.

'Oh, God, I hope yours wasn't Bob Dylan,' I blurt out. 'He's slept with everyone!'

She cracks a crooked smile.

'It was.'

Rhoda is short, plump, and perky. Not someone I would pick as a likely paramour of Dylan's, but she says she met him in Missouri nearly twenty years before, while riding her bike, and describes her late-night liaisons with the rocker as spiritual, borderline cabalistic. I can almost see the two of them—as she describes their encounters—making love amid a sea of candles, bodies aglow with the red flame of a roaring fire.

She is definitely possessed.

We remain on the sidewalk, talking, till 3am.

'You know that song, "You're Gonna Make Me Lonesome When You Go"?'

'Of course,' I nod.

'He wrote that song for me.'

September 22 1989. *Oh Mercy*. 'Man In A Long Black Coat,' 'Most Of The Time,' 'What Was It You Wanted?,' 'Shooting Star.' The album is his best in years.

This latest Dylan record must have been inspired by something. I recognize fragments of my experiences with Bob in some of the lyrics:

Somebody is out there beating a dead horse ...

Trees bent over backwards from a hurricane breeze ...

Even the long black coat itself ...

I wonder, could any of these songs have been inspired by Bob's time with me?

I catch Anthony DeCurtis's review of *Oh Mercy* in *Rolling Stone*. Of 'Long Black Coat,' he writes, 'The song tells of a woman who leaves her man for a demonic stranger, prompting a series of reflections on the nature of conscience, religious faith and emotional commitment.'

Margaret Mazar, this hot clothing designer I know from when I went to school at Berkeley, calls me to tell me about a documentary on PBS about madness.

'It's about six different women,' she says, 'and one of them is obsessed with Bob Dylan!'

January 1990. Hollywood, I decide, is the perfect place for children from dysfunctional homes: it gives you everything you grew up with: rejection, uncertainty, and abuse.

I'm in development hell. The WGA strike has ended, but my once-vital deal at Paramount is now dead in the water. After months of futile script meetings, I apply for a job as a salesperson at LA's classiest real estate office in Brentwood, and I'm hired immediately.

The woman with the desk across from mine—who will later become my sales and listing partner—has a postcard of the young Bob Dylan propped up near her phone.

I run into my old boyfriend, Realtor Bob, at an open house. His sister, Velo, is doing a poetry reading at Cafe Largo on Fairfax; would I like to come?

After her exceptional recitation on lost love, Velo joins us at our table. She's petite, dark, and easy on the eyes—and, as I mentioned earlier, she had her own scene with Dylan in the early 70s.

'Yeah,' Realtor Bob reminds me, 'Dylan wrote that song, "You're Gonna Make Me Lonesome When You Go," for her.'

Between drags on a Parliament, Velo tells me she's been working as the head film reviewer for *Venice Magazine* and thinks she can score me a gig there writing movie reviews. She's also working for Mrs. Roy Orbison on the upcoming star-studded tribute to the late, great Roy, of which I know nothing. Scheduled guests include Bruce Springsteen.

'We think *Bob* might show up!' she sings.

I brace myself. It would make sense, I think, given his connection to the Traveling Wilburys.

'Huh,' I say.

Throughout the evening, various sycophants approach our table and hint that they would like tickets to the tribute.

'Yeah, sure,' Velo laughs, snuffing out another butt. 'You and two hundred of my closest friends.'

February 23 1990. Message on my answering machine from Realtor Bob: 'Mrs. Roy Orbison, my sister, and I would like to invite you to attend the Roy Orbison Tribute at the Universal Amphitheater, tomorrow night. Said invitation to include great seats, all-access passes, and a special ticket for a VIP party, afterwards.'

My message back to Realtor Bob: 'You sure know the way I like to see a show!'

While the question of whether or not Bob Dylan will make a surprise appearance at the Orbison gala is the buzz on the tongues of the uninitiated, it is clear to me from the get go that he will. Backstage, on the lot, is a small camping trailer, and Elliot Mintz, Doctor K., and Victor can be seen buzzing around the temporary dressing quarters like drones around a hive. Realtor Bob, who I think has always been skeptical about my relationship to Dylan, is mildly impressed when I point this out to him. His sister, on the other hand, is well aware of Dylan's presence, and when we run into her, she gushes, 'Dylan's coming to the party afterwards!'

I have a hard time believing this, because I know how difficult it's been in the past to get Bob to attend functions of much greater import than a mere after-party in a tent at the Universal Amphitheater. Nonetheless, I'm dressed to kill in a short skirt, spiked heels, and black-and-white leggy zebra skin stockings, and I feel myself becoming more and more charged at the thought of seeing Bob.

The show is sensational, with everyone from Edie Brickell to Eddie Vedder paying tribute to the canary-voiced, pockmarked legend of Ray Ban's—and leaving the audience 'Crying.' Dylan's 'surprise' appearance occurs at the end of the spectacle, and his somewhat wobbly performance is bolstered by the presence of former Byrds David Crosby, Chris Hillman, and Roger McGuinn. Years later, I will be alone in a movie theater in New York City and just happen to sit in the same row with the guy whose job it was to provide Dylan one Rum and Coke after another that night, before he went up.

Bob staggers through a few of his own songs, then finishes up with Orbison's 'Only The Lonely,' evidently having more than a little trouble reading the words off the teleprompter. I watch longingly from my seat as he's escorted offstage by a massive throng, which includes all the evening's performers.

I still believe he was my twin.

Backstage, the VIP tent is a ghost town. None of the top-billed players has made an appearance. Realtor Bob and I are sharing a glass of champagne when his sister, Velo, rushes us.

'There's Bob!'

I can't believe it. Sure enough, there he is, surrounded by Elliot

Mintz and company—almost as if he's being supported by them—a sunglass-adorned Dylan, is making his way slowly into the too brightly lit tent. He's immediately besieged by fans.

'I've got to talk to him,' I tell Realtor Bob.

'Whatever,' he replies, that old skepticism creeping back into his voice.

'I've never asked Bob for an autograph,' I say nervously. 'I've always regretted that. I'll have him sign my program.'

I fumble around in my handbag for just the right pen. I pull out a camouflage Parker that a friend brought me from Italy—I'm told the only place you can find them is in the back pages of *Soldier Of Fortune*.

'He'll like this one,' I assure Realtor Bob, who simply shrugs and shakes his head.

The two of us get in the circle with the rest of the autograph hounds.

Dylan is signing away like a drudge on an assembly line.

'He drooled on me!' the girl in front of me complains.

I pass my pen and program to Bob. Standing before him, I wait openly, willingly, ready for anything, enthralled but terrified of what his reaction might be. He doesn't blink twice at the pen, or me, just scribbles his name, hands both items back, and moves on to the shabby-chic guy who waits eagerly, next in line.

'He didn't recognize me!' I say to Realtor Bob, who's obviously already noticed. My world's gone silent, and everything around me is moving in slow motion.

Dylan's robotically scrawling away and Elliot's working the crowd. Later, Karla will tell me that this is how the big artists cope in these situations; they don't even look at the person they are signing the autograph for. That way, they don't have to get involved.

'It's OK,' Realtor Bob says, patting my arm. He tries to steer me away but I'm choked up and incapable of even a stumble.

'I can't believe he didn't recognize me!' I blurt out, tearfully.

Elliot spins around in my direction and glances up at me.

'Britta?'

He's apparently identified my voice, if not my visage.

'I didn't recognize you!' he says. 'You look terrific!'

'Bob didn't even know who I was,' I say, defeated.

'Just a minute …'

Elliot spins back toward Dylan. Clasping Bob by the upper arm, he literally walks him in a 360, while notifying his Honor of my presence.

Dylan jauntily peels off like a two-stepper on his way to the next partner.

'Breeda,' he says. 'Who could forget a face like that?'

'You,' I say sullenly.

Bob doesn't take well to confrontation, probably 'cause he's hardly ever had to deal with it. He looks fairly derelict, stubbly beard, shiny skin. I can tell he's had too much to drink.

'Did you get your autograph?' he asks.

'Yeah,' I say. 'And it was real personal, too.'

I hold it up and show it to him.

'Hey,' he moves closer. 'Remember that day at the synagogue in Helsinki?'

'Yeah, Bob, I remember.'

I'm surprised he does, though. I've heard this is the trick of the true womanizer. They don't forget a thing.

'Remember how the sun was barely out, but the light … the light it was so…'

Bob's oldest son Jesse appears out of nowhere. He's bigger than Bob, and his huge paw clamps down on Dylan's bony shoulder.

'We've got a table in the back,' Jesse grunts. He shoots me a look and practically pushes his father away from me.

'A table ...' Bob mumbles, half shrugging. He nods his head—at me—in the direction he's already bound. It's the kind of nod I could interpret as an invitation. I've done it a million times. After all, we were in the middle of a conversation. *We were just getting started.*

The rest of Dylan's entourage gets swept up in the momentum, gathers force, and carries him away.

It would be so easy to just tag along with him the way I used to, I'm thinking, and I can feel myself being pulled that way. Then I could be the unidentified woman you read about in *Buzz* or *Details* who spent the whole night after the Orbison Tribute talking to Bob Dylan at his table. Or would I just be the bimbo you never hear about who latched on to Dylan after the show, the same way that young girl in Costa Mesa, that night, so long ago, tried to latch on to me?

My heart's an iceberg crushing over the breaking bow of Bob's sinking ship.

I can never possess him, I think.

No one can.

I can only be possessed.

As Dylan's disheveled form is swallowed up by the gathering crowd, I wonder if he'll speculate about what happened to me when he finally gets to where he's going. I wonder if he'll even know I'm gone.

Realtor Bob is trying to get my attention. He's looking darkly dapper in his sport coat and tie.

'Wow! That was cool,' he says.

His brown eyes gaze at me with newly found respect.

'He actually knows you!'

CHAPTER ELEVEN

Knockin' on heaven's door

September 11 1990. *Under The Red Sky*. I buy the disc, play it once, and put it away.

February 20 1991. The 33rd Grammy Awards. I'm out on a date with political satirist Harry Shearer, or the head V.P. at Castle Rock—Rob Reiner's movie Company—or the retired President of Imagine Films, or any one of a number of successful, talented guys I've been dating who can't seem to hold a candle, in terms of my interest in them, to Bob Dylan. The awards are held at Radio City Music Hall in New York, and they're televised. I come home to a plethora of urgent messages regarding the show. Among them is one from Karla. I call her back.

'Oh, my god,' she says, 'did you see it?'

'What?'

'The Grammys! Dylan received the Life Time Achievement Award.'

'You're kidding,' I say, torn between relief that I didn't know he was going to be on and sorrow that I'd missed it. 'How was he?'

'He looked awful. I couldn't even tell what he was singing, and when he accepted his award … well, you're just going to have to get a copy of it and see for yourself.'

At work, the next day, my real estate partner glumly confirms

Karla's opinion. Ella, our black receptionist, tells me she's taped the show and will bring it to me before the weekend.

Two nights later, I steel myself with a good dinner, then settle in in front of the TV. I'm immediately thrown by the choice of a blasted Jack Nicholson as the proper presenter for an occasion as momentous as Dylan's Lifetime Achievement Award from a jury of his peers, and I can only imagine that Dylan found the selection even more absurd than I.

Little of my experience with Bob prepared me for what I was about to see next, though I did, at least, recognize the song. Karla had been at a disadvantage in as much as she hadn't seen his recent shows and was unaware of all his new renditions—a sign both of his ever-evolving persona and his staunch refusal, most of the time, to give even his most die-hard fans what they might want. Still, you'd think anyone familiar with his work should be able to decipher at least a portion of a song as synonymous with the Dylan legend as 'Masters Of War.' But Dylan's desultory yet damning, staccato performance nearly defies even me. He looks old, exhausted, edgy. Afterwards, he stands baffled on the stage. Disheveled is too good a word, babe. This guy is flat out disoriented.

When it's suggested that he say a few words, he inadvertently— or so it seems—begins with the phrase, 'As my daddy used to say to me.' While nearly a full minute of prime-time TV goes by in silence, you can practically see in his eyes the wheels spinning around inside his head in search of another phrase to connect to.

'Well, my daddy used to say a lot of things,' Bob says, finally, bringing it all back home, before rattling off another nearly unintelligible paragraph, which will be deemed by the overly kind-hearted Robert Hilburn, in his review of the proceedings, as 'sheer brilliance.'

I soak in a hot tub.

How could he embarrass his children this way? How could he embarrass himself?

I've gotta call him, I think. *Maybe I can still save him.*

No. I slide down the wall of the old bear-claw tub until my shoulders, neck, and head are submerged.

He's too far gone.

February 14 1992. My first date with the cinematographer M. Valere Shain. He's handsome, European, intelligent, and on the same spiritual wavelength as me. He is also, like Ernie, a product of the Holocaust, born and raised in hiding in Belgium, twenty-two members of his family lost to the camps. He suggests we go to see the reprise of this old French film that's playing in Santa Monica called *Les Enfants Du Paradis*.

'*Qu'est-ce que c'est?*' I ask. I've known M. for about a year now, as friends, but we've never gone out before. He speaks fluent French, and I'm trying to brush up on mine.

'You don't know *The Children Of Paradise?*'

My brain freezes as a sense of déjà vu overtakes me. Bob's words come tumbling back.

Oh you have to see that one … you just have to.

'Shot in France during the Nazi occupation,' M. continues. 'It was a miracle it ever got made. About how theater people live … behind the scenes. A love story with four men and one woman.'

'*Quelle horreur!*' I tease him. In real life, M., whose first name is Marcel, has been competing with two other guys for my attention.

He takes a sip from a bottle of Belgian beer.

'*Les enfants du paradis* are the commoners who sit way up high in the cheap seats to watch the play. A smart actor finds it empowering to play to them, 'cause they're the most enthusiastic members of the audience.'

Uh. Oh.

That night, I go with M. to see the film classic that Dylan once said I had to see. A movie that moves seamlessly between truth and lies and back again. A movie that obliterates the line between hope and despair. A movie that uses mirrors and makeup and other backstage tricks to transform real life until, at its end, the performance observed expands to include the audience.

While watching the film, from time to time, M. whispers the actual translation of the romantic tale—as opposed to the somewhat stilted language of the subtitles—into my ear.

October 16 1992. New York. Madison Square Garden. The 30th Anniversary Concert Celebration, commemorating Dylan's thirty years of recording. M. surprises me by buying the pay-per-view tribute Neil Young will dub 'Bobfest,' where everyone does Bob's songs better than he does. Despite the virtual who's who of folk luminaries gracing the stage, all anyone will talk about in coming days is Sinead O'Connor getting booed for desecrating a picture of the Pope two weeks before on *Saturday Night Live*.

July 4 1993. I marry M. Valere Shain in a private ceremony at the Pine Hills Lodge in Julian, California. We've bought a house there in the country, five miles outside of the touristy old gold-mining town, on a mountain high above the Anza-Borrego desert. A funky, crazy house on a rambling piece of property with lots of inspiring places to hang out in, kind of like Bob Dylan's backyard in Malibu, but without the sea or the Malibu charisma. All wood and glass— the house was built out of scraps—like massive hand-hewn beams and antique stained glass—that the contractor had salvaged from his previous jobs to build his own private residence.

I have a black lab/golden retriever mix named Beulah and a malamute Samoyed wolf called Cisco who guard the place. Barky, my purebred Samoyed, is buried under a field of tulips. Every once in a while I fantasize how much Bob would like it here, but I've put away my mementos. I don't tell people I knew him, and I hardly ever play his music anymore.

'Oh, it's your boyfriend,' M. facetiously teases, when a song of Bob's comes on the radio. 'Too bad you don't still know him,' he sometimes says, soulful brown eyes flirting, as he swigs on a single barrel bourbon or puffs on his cigar. 'I'd have liked to have met him.'

Careless Chabad telethons. Depressing *David Letterman* performances—I even catch Jakob, early on, doing his own shtick on *Letterman*. I don't see Dylan's 'Chimes Of Freedom' at the Clinton Inauguration, though I hear it was barely comprehensible.

Good As I Been To You, World Gone Wrong, Unplugged …
I'm told Dylan can routinely be found sparring at Mickey Rourke's unnamed gym on Beverly Boulevard, half a block down the street from my hairdresser's. A friend of Margaret the designer says he tried to pick her up there by telling her he could get her into the movies, but he smelled bad and looked like a derelict who'd wandered in off the street, so she shined him on. Afterwards, the starstruck club attendant stopped her, 'Didn't you know who that was? That was Bob Dylan. He never talks to anyone!'

It's not long before I discover a neighbor of ours at the Julian house has a son named Dylan.

'Oh,' I say, somewhat dismayed. Here we go again. 'Was he named for Bob Dylan?'

'Who?'

I explain.

'Oh, gosh no,' the girl says. 'I named him for Dylan on *90210*.'

This same girl's husband confronts me a few days later.

'Bob Dylan didn't write "Blowin' In The Wind,"' he says scornfully. 'That's a folk song!'

May 18 1995. The Hollywood Palladium, Los Angeles, California. I'm studying writing in a private workshop with John Rechy. If you don't know who Rechy is, think of *My Private Idaho* and remember that Gus Van Sant once said he only made that film because he couldn't get the rights to Rechy's masterpiece, *City Of Night*.

I'm working on an autobiographical novel called *Unsuspecting Heart* about growing up on the periphery of Hollywood in the 1950s in a family tormented by madness and alcoholism. Another member of the workshop is Bruce Haring, the rock reviewer for *Variety*. Bruce goes out of his way to make sure I have excellent seats for the show. In an unusual move, Steven Wright is the opening act before Dylan's uneven and incoherent performance.

During the encore, the 'children of paradise' rush the stage. Among them I see Realtor Bob and his sister.

'I shall be released,' Dylan sings, looking like he's been exhumed from one of the tombs we visited in Egypt.

Not soon enough, I'm thinking.

Everything is broken, including Bob Dylan.

November 19 1995. The Shrine Auditorium, Los Angeles, California. Bob Dylan participates in a star-studded gala to commemorate

Frank Sinatra's eightieth birthday. In a curious PR move, he's slotted to perform last, following a breathtaking lineup that includes, oddly enough, a tour de force by Hootie & The Blowfish.

The only one to perform his own material—that is, not a Sinatra hit—Dylan proceeds to wail his way through 'Restless Farewell'— his very own 'My Way'—as Sinatra's already glassy eyes glaze over, bordering on tears.

Fall 1996. My friend Margaret sends me a clipping from the *Los Angeles Times*. Some woman I've never heard of has crawled out of the woodwork to sue Dylan for palimony, claiming they've been married for twelve years. While this particular lawsuit will prove to be fruitless, I will one day find out that Bob was married to his former backup singer Carolyn Dennis the whole time we were together.

Spring 1997. Since my husband and I have moved permanently to the country, I've had one cold after another. Most recently, I've had a cough that's lasted months. I no longer sell real estate. I'm into dealing antiques, now, and I do pottery restoration. I'm also a co-founder of the Julian Certified Farmers Market, where I sell herbs. My novel, *Unsuspecting Heart*, is sitting, along with a recommendation by John Rechy, on the desk of a powerful literary agent in New York City. I'm in the house, washing dishes, listening to CNN coming over the satellite television upstairs, when I hear the Newsbreak:

'Folk legend Bob Dylan has been hospitalized for a potentially fatal lung infection.'

A corkscrew to my heart.

Panic on a cellular level ensues. Who can I call? M. is in Los Angeles, shooting a commercial. I feel stranded. Alone. Desperate. I haven't even thought about Bob in so long—not in any meaningful way—only when some standup comedian makes a joke about how he looks or sounds these days.

I rush out to the front deck, hoping to get some solace from the leafing oaks or the towering pines. My dogs sense something's up and hasten to my side to comfort me.

I search my most recent phone book for someone who will understand why I'm so distraught. Someone who might even know what's up.

I call Charles Lyonhart, Realtor Bob's best friend in New York City, a musician who hangs with the Dylan band—he's even written a terrific song about Dylan called 'No Heroes'—but he's not in.

I try Karla. She's on the road.

Oh my God, what am I going to do? This can't be happening. Bob's not going to die. That's so dumb. Why didn't I see the signs? They were all there.

I call John Fischbach, Lyn Hemmerdinger's husband. They live in New Orleans now. He's an owner of Piety Street Studio and has recorded just about everybody. In addition to engineering *Songs In The Key Of Life* for Stevie Wonder, John also produced a band called the Freewheelers at about the same time Jakob Dylan's Wallflowers were coming up. No answer.

By now, I have the radio on, as well as the TV. But the story's just broken. Half the stations don't even know about it. And I'm going crazy trying to get more news.

The dogs trail me from room to room as I scavenge the drawers searching for old address books. There's gotta be someone I can call.

Elliot Mintz! Oh, god. He couldn't have the same number still. Could he?

'Elliot Mintz,' the intelligent but weary voice answers the line sharply.

'Oh, Elliot,' I sigh into the phone. 'It's Britta.'

'Britta!' He sounds surprised. 'I *will* call you back. What's the number?'

I have an errand to run in my pickup truck so I can't wait for the returned call. I promised a flower vendor from Brawley I'd sell his load for him the next day at the market as a favor. I try to cancel the appointment, but the guy I'm supposed to meet has already left. I race down the curving back-country roads at about a million miles an hour, hoping to get back to the house in time to receive Elliot's call.

Britta, I rehearse Elliot's words.

I will call you back.

I *will* call you back.

I will call *you* back.

And I wonder if he's even gonna call.

I have the radio tuned to KFWB in Los Angeles—the only station I've found so far that's carrying the Dylan story, but every twenty minutes or so, when they mention Dylan's illness, the truck manages to be in some never-never land of mountains and sky, and the reception just turns to static.

At eight o'clock, when I return, there's a message on the machine saying simply, 'Elliot Mintz called for Britta.'

I call Elliot back and leave word.

Somewhere around nine, the phone rings.

'Is he all right?' I ask.

Pause.

'No. You realize I have to be terribly guarded about what I say,' Elliot tells me.

'Of course,' I say.

'We won't know for sure until the tests come in on Friday,' he continues somberly. His voice is hoarse. Elliot says he's fielded five hundred calls during the day.

'He's cancelled his tour,' he tells me. 'And, you know, he's never canceled a tour before.'

'How old is he now?'

I notice I'm being peculiarly guarded myself.

'Just turned fifty-six.'

Awkward silence.

I don't want to ask Elliot what hospital Bob's in. The news has reported the rock music legend is in an undisclosed location, and I don't want to carry the burden of knowing where he is without being able to confide it in one of my friends. I also don't want to sound like just another of Bob's groupies. But mostly, I realize as I'm flopped down on my mattress, in front of the silent television's flashing news images, I don't want to know, because I'm afraid if I find out, I may wind up knock, knock, knockin' on Dylan's door.

'He must be terribly proud of his son,' I say, nearly crying.

Just this week, darling Jakob's face graced the cover of *Rolling Stone*—his band, The Wallflower's latest album having sold more copies than all of Bob's records combined.

Silence.

'What can we do?' I ask, sensing Elliot's sobriety.

'Pray for him.'

Charles Lyonhart calls me back the next morning.

'You spoke to Elliot?'

'Yeah.'

He's very impressed. 'What did he say?'

I realize I have hardly anything of substance to report. 'He says we have to pray.'

258

'Yeah, well I'm not surprised,' Charles says, between drags on a joint. 'He was smoking three packs of cigarettes a day.'

'Three packs!'

I'm gonna start again.

Charles says he saw Dylan in New York the week before, at a show, and he looked like hell. He says Bob flew back to California for some event and had to be escorted from the stage. After a day or two at home, refusing to go to the doctor, he was rushed to the hospital.

'The doctors told him he had a fungal infection a year ago, and he was still smokin' like a chimney.'

Neither of us has a clue where he's hospitalized. The *Los Angeles Times* says New York. The New York papers are all reporting that Dylan's in LA.

By the time I hear back from John Fischbach—my friend in New Orleans—there's a nationwide debate as to whether Dylan's difficulties lie within his lungs or his heart.

'Well, I guess the old man had to do something to top the recent attention to his youngest son,' John chuckles.

Eventually—it feels like it takes forever—CNN reports that according to Dylan's spokesman, Elliot Mintz, the folk legend has been released from the hospital and is recuperating comfortably at home.

Fall 1997. *Time Out Of Mind*, Bob Dylan's first truly impressive album since *Blood On The Tracks*, is released. I hear a cut on public radio and I'm first in line at the local record store to buy it.

Once again, Dylan is in stride with his times, but this time he's talking about death. An entire generation, the generation he spoke to so long ago with his songs of protest, hope, and disillusion—my generation—is about to face its mortality. They say the lyrics were written before he was ill, but it's obvious to me he was feelin' his sickness comin' on while he was writin' 'em.

It's a dark album. Almost black. I play it over and over, remembering what attracted me to Bob Dylan in the first place.

November 1997. Margaret Mazar calls me from her design studio in Santa Monica to tell me that it's just been announced over the radio that Bob Dylan will perform five nights in a row at the El Rey Theater. Tickets will go on sale Saturday morning for what I will come to call 'the concert of the century.'

I call Charles in New York and tell him I need tickets and/or passes. He calls me back.

'Phone me when it gets closer to the gig,' he says. 'Buy tickets anyway, even if they're terrible. You can always get rid of them later when my connection comes through.'

I'm going to LA on Monday to meet with John Rechy, so I figure I'll buy the tickets then.

Margaret calls me on Sunday night to tell me the Dylan show sold out Saturday morning in two hours.

December 1997. As the dates for the El Rey concert approach, I come down with yet another cold. It snows, and I stay inside a lot listening to the radio. The DJs up in LA go on and on about what a great show it's going to be.

'Even the dude from the Black Crows can't get tickets,' one DJ says, '*and* it's his birthday.'

I call Charles to remind him about the passes, but I know it's too late. He says he'll make a call. I have too much pride to call Elliot and beg for tickets. Charles never gets back to me. Later, he tells me it's because his contact never got back to him.

Throughout what feels like the longest, most tortuous week of my life, I will hear over the airwaves unprecedented adulation for Bob Dylan. You'd have thought Bob had arisen from the dead, and I guess in a way he had.

'The best concert I've seen in my life,' reports veteran disc jockey Jim Ladd. Another DJ brags he's got tickets for every night. Opening acts include Sheryl Crow, Joni Mitchell, and Willie Nelson. I wander the cold house, gazing at frozen rain, blue in the moonlight, as it hangs in spike-like icicles from the wooden eaves. I try to rationalize that it's better that I didn't get to go to the show because I'm still sick.

The concert of the century goes on without me, but not without affecting me. And I'm shocked at how deeply I'm still bound.

Late December 1997. The Kennedy Center Awards. One of the highest honors in the country has been bestowed on Bob Dylan, and it's televised on network television. It's the first time I've seen his image in ages and I'm revolted. His face is all puffed up and white like he's wearing a molded death mask. His actions are contrived and inappropriate. Out of time. Out of mind.

The next morning, my girlfriend in Julian says, 'He looks like he's had the life drained out of him.'

'He looks like he's been embalmed!' I retort.

I can't get over the depth of his self-destruction. I'm devastated.

'Yeah, well he's had a hard life,' Charles explains, when I speak with him next. 'All that booze and those wild, wild women.'

New Year's Day 1998. I spend the day doing things that make me feel good. I hike the mountain, sit upon a rocky slope, and watch my dogs romp gleefully through muddy streams. I enjoy the sunset. I take a hot bath.

As I'm soaking in the mineral-filled water, relaxing, breathing, feeling halfway decent again, I think about how sad it is that such a big part of me is still so tangled up in Bob Dylan. I remember Ernie telling me once that his association with Bob was all that kept him from just being some schlub who owned a printing press. I realize I'll never be able to love anyone truly again, even M., unless I can free myself from Bob. My tears fall into the bath water till it feels like I've cried the whole tub full.

January 2 1998. Desert Hot Springs, California. Sky's Haven Mobile Home Park—M.'s Mother's desert hideaway. Late. In bed.

I tell my husband I've decided to write *The Bob Dylan Book* now. I'm going to be fifty this year, and it's time to shit or get off the pot. I'm only here this one time on the planet, and what if I *don't* write about Bob? What if I don't tell my story that I was in love with, and traveled around the world with, the most famous genius of our times? What am I supposed to do, just roll over and die?

I remind M. of the most recent rejection letter for my latest novel—I received it on Christmas Eve. I tell him I don't want to write a kiss-and-tell book. It's not like I'm gonna come out smelling like a rose. I tell him I want it to be a valentine.

But most of all, I say, I need to write it for myself.

M. sighs, nodding his approval before nodding off.

That night, I dream I run into Bob.

'When did you start acting like that?' he asks, referring to my newly forthright, confident manner. 'If you'd acted like that when I knew you, we'd be man and wife, right now.'

January 4 1998. I tell writer friends I'm thinking of pitching a memoir about Dylan to my soon-to-be new agent. They think it's a great idea.

'I know what you'll be doing this year,' one of them says.

'That's the kind of book you can get an advance for,' another concurs.

'It's not going to be a tell-all,' I say to the first.

'Are you crazy?' she nearly swears at me. 'That's what'll get you your deal.'

I write a letter to the agent on my computer, reminding her about my current project, and pitching the Bob Dylan book, at first calling it *Temples In Flames*, the story that the spurned lover in me wants to tell, then changing it to the more positive *Bob Dylan: Seeing The Real You At Last*, which also gives me the opportunity to use Dylan's name, twice—once underlined—so in case she isn't reading carefully, I'll have more than one chance at getting her attention.

I don't mail the letter right away. I want to think about it. I want to think about what it will mean to Bob, if I write a book. And, more importantly, what it'll mean to me.

January 7 1998. Dennis Miller on the Jay Leno show: 'What happened to Keith Richards and Bob Dylan? They're not even guys anymore, they look like old wallets that mumble.'

Later, on his own show, Miller takes a query from a caller named Dylan.

'Let's hope it's not the real Dylan,' he laughs, 'or we won't be able to understand the question.'

January 9 1998. I dream that Bob has died. I'm terribly sad. A part of me—the part that will always be connected to him—will have to die now, too. I can't believe it.

In the dream, I tell my husband, 'Well, we didn't get to go to the El Rey concert, but I'm pretty sure we can go to the funeral.'

It's a three-day deal—probably inspired by the recently televised Sonny Bono services. On Friday night, Joni Mitchell and others will pay tribute. On Saturday, Willie Nelson. Then, on Sunday, there will be this huge open-air memorial that's open to the public.

M. and I go on Sunday with Craig, this other writer friend of mine who's a music supervisor in film and television, and his wife, Judy. In real life, I've just given Craig a copy of *Time Out Of Mind* for helping me out with a computer problem.

It's a bizarre venue, kind of like the Greek Theater, but more primitive, almost prehistoric, with rocks and boulders for seats. I'm dressed stupidly, in high heels—even though, in reality, these days I mostly wear hiking boots—and a tight outfit that makes it difficult to negotiate the rocky stairs.

At the very top, above the stage, sits a large wooden casket with Dylan's body in it. I convince everyone in my party that we should make the pilgrimage to the coffin because there might be some performance or something, but it's most crowded toward the top and we immediately have to split up, sitting next to strangers.

From my seat, I keep looking up and seeing people who never even knew Dylan walking up to the front of the casket and touching it, almost like they're more interested in the wood it's made of. Many people are pressing Kleenexes to their noses, crying. It's beginning to sink in that there won't be anyone noteworthy playing this event. This is the service for the fans ... *les enfants du paradis*. Once again, I've missed the real deal. I'm just an ordinary person who happened to have known him and therefore not worthy of the more intimate gatherings held previously to honor him, the gatherings of his peers.

Off the back of the seating area, I notice a heavy wooden door made of rough planks and rusted iron, and I wonder if that's where the important people are hanging out. I ask a waitress if I can go there, telling her I used to be a friend of Bob's. She shrugs.

The room is cavernous—dirt floors, curved rock ceiling—and part of Bob's casket is jutting into the space. People are milling around but I don't recognize any of them.

I order a coffee, and while I'm waiting for it, I become more convinced than ever that I should walk up the rock steps to visit the coffin. I've endured this much; to do otherwise is like leaving without completing the journey.

The coffee arrives just as I'm getting up to leave. It's a very small ceramic cup of terrific-looking espresso. I sip from the cup, and it's so good that I sip again, and with a third sip, which the waitress warns me might be too much—it's very strong coffee—I finish the drink.

Balancing the small cup on a jagged tray, I move awkwardly through the crowd toward the left of the stage to join the procession, which is moo-ving like cattle up the craggy steps toward the casket. My tall shoes, along with all the stuff I'm carrying—a purse, a program, a leopard-skin shawl—make it a perilous climb.

I remember the whole time being aware of people watching me. But when I get to the top, I realize I've somehow gone past the casket and missed it. The only direct route down is to climb over a rail, and in my tight skirt and high heels it's a real attention-getter.

Within seconds, I'm alone, kneeling at the back of Dylan's coffin, and, to my shock, I discover the lid is open a crack. I can see Bob's face and body covered in a badly wrapped gauze job, and I think he must have died in a motorcycle accident. His nose is poking out through the cloth. I can see his left eye.

'Bob,' I say. 'It's Britta.'

Did his eyelid just twitch?

'I love you.'

I think I see him move.

'I will always love you.'

He *is* moving! His eyes are open! His gnarled hand reaches out through the opening and shoves away the casket door.

'I love you, Bob,' I say.

Dylan's body rolls toward me as he begins to crawl out of the box.

'He's alive!' I shout.

My love for Bob Dylan has brought him back to life.

February 26 1998. The Grammys, again. For the first time ever, Dylan's been nominated for three. I'm taking a memoir workshop at the home of a professor who is the head of the center for autobiographic studies at USC—where I'm … uh … writing this book—so I won't be home to watch, but Realtor Bob, still a good friend, says he'll tape it for me.

When I do finally see the show, Dylan's stuffed into a tuxedo that looks like it was rented in East LA. He's still wearing his death mask, but he pulls off a masterful performance. Some idiot in production must have thought that he needed a cheering section to liven up his bit, so there are all these actors in the shadows behind him, faux-clapping to the beat. One of the more over-zealous hired hands decides any recognition is better than none, so he strips off his shirt and does a hairy, writhing fat-bellied dance, with the words 'Soy-Bomb' scrawled across his torso, next to the nonplused Bob Dylan. Later, I will read that the jester who nearly ruined the show is a frustrated performance artist who, as a result of his outlandish behavior, has landed a three-record deal.

I can hardly bear to look at Dylan's face for the ravage of pain that must have brought him here. He's blown up and blown out. His skin is greenish white, almost chartreuse. His red eyes rimmed with black liner.

'He looks like hell,' M. says.

'He looks like the devil,' I say.

As Leno will report in the days following the performance, 'Dylan looked like one of the bodies floating in the water after the Titanic went down.'

Realtor Bob chimes in: 'If Dylan dropped dead right now on stage, they wouldn't have to do a thing to him.'

When Bobby D. sings 'I'm sick of love,' I know he means it. I'm pretty sure he means he's sick of life, too.

His son Jakob is a no show tonight, even though he, too, was a nominee. Bob scores all three Grammys, including the one for best album. In his final acceptance speech, he credits Buddy Holly for the album's success. It's the kind of thing he used to say totally in jest, like one time on the plane when he told the stewardess who asked his name that he was Neil Sedaka. Little fictions. But his fans hang on his every word.

Charles will tell me that, after the ceremony, Dylan was uncharacteristically jovial and partied way into the night.

The next morning, Stanford University announces it will be offering a new course focusing on Bob Dylan, the man, the poet, the legend.

March 1998. Once again, it's announced that Bob Dylan will be performing in the Los Angeles area—this time at Pauley Pavilion at UCLA. His opening act will be Van Morrison. Even though we know we blew the concert of the century when we missed the El Rey shows, my friend Margaret and I decide we should get a group together and go. I call New York right away and tell Charles to alert his sources. He virtually guarantees me backstage passes this time.

The day the tickets go on sale, Realtor Bob is first at the ticket window with his Platinum card, but it turns out they'll only take cash. By the time he gets back with the green, all the good seats are gone. The vendor insists he can only sell six tickets at once, and we need eight. After waiting in line at a second place for two more seats—he's probably lost two real estate deals by now—Realtor Bob figures what the hell and buys up another six, knowing we can always unload them. So, by lunch, we've landed twelve ninety-dollar tickets for the May 22 show—and these are the cheap seats!

A day or so later, Van backs out, due to 'creative differences' with Dylan, I'm told—more like an ego clash—and is replaced by Joni Mitchell. A few days and a few apologies after that, Van is back on the program, so now the Pauley Pavilion bill reads Van Morrison, Joni Mitchell, *and* Bob Dylan.

Maybe this will turn out to be the concert of the century after all.

April 1998. I'm called to New York on an emergency. My mother's sister—my last living relative—is dying. I'm forced to blow off a scheduled and long awaited trip to Yosemite with dear friends, but I'm positive I'll be back in time for the Dylan show on May 22.

Robbie Robertson guests on Charlie Rose. About Dylan, he says, 'Something happened to him in his youth where he just decided to write off all the rules.'

Robbie's talking about Dylan's music—how Bob redefined freedom in terms of the structure of songwriting—but I believe his statement also applies to Dylan's life.

April 22 1998. The Third Millennium Evening at the White House: *The American Voice In Poetry*. As I flip through the cable stations on my aunt Maggie's vintage TV in NYC, I come across President Clinton's conference on poetry at the White House.

It's an incredibly inspiring affair, featuring rap artists and street poets, as well as the present and former poet laureates. At one point, Hillary takes a question from the Internet and addresses the panel.

'Suppose that in the next millennium poetry becomes the medium of shared vision and American community—there's a reading beginning at midnight, 2099. What lines from American poetry of the twentieth century might be recited 1,000 years or so hence?'

Most of the panelists squirm uncomfortably in their seats, except for Bob Hass, a former Poet Laureate, who grins.

'Probably someone would get up and sing Bob Dylan's "The Times They Are A-Changin'."'

When my husband arrives in New York toward the end of the month, he says, 'Think about going to Paris.'

He looks more handsome than ever since he's given up drinking. I'm proud of him. He's in good company: I've read recently that Eric Clapton and Lou Reed are all clean and sober, now. M.'s skin is the color of aged bronze from all his tennis playing. His body's in great shape.

'Paris?'

'Yeah. My cousin's getting married there at the end of May,' he says, snuggling up to me. He smells good. We kiss. 'He's invited us to stay at his house. His place is cool. You'll love it. It's four hundred years old.'

A flicker of panic strikes.

'When?' I ask.

'I'll look it up.'

He does. I wait arms folded.

'The wedding's on the ...'

'Twenty-second,' I laugh, and shake my head. I remember back to when I almost passed on going to Japan so I could see Bob at the Forum with Al Kooper sitting in.

'How did you know?' And then the realization hits him. 'Oh, yeah,' he shrugs. 'I guess we'd have to miss the Dylan concert.'

May 10 1998. Stretched out in my aunt's aging recliners, M. and I catch *Imagine*, the John Lennon documentary, on cable. Outside our window, the Manhattan traffic honks as it passes. In the film, John's clean and sober, too, way back when in the late 70s.

'I don't believe in Jesus,' the song goes.

Or Elvis.

Or Kennedy.

'I don't believe in Zimmerman,' he adds.

I just believe in me.

May 22 1998. Bob Dylan performs at Pauley Pavilion. My husband and I sit at a quaint outdoor café in Paris, soaking up the architecture and sipping espresso from small cups, while a busker goes table to table singing 'Heaven's Door' in French.

Writing about my experience with Dylan has helped heal the rift that's existed inside me for too many years—that terrible split between what was right with me and Bob and the rest of the world and what I can't help thinking was fate. The fact is, if I had it all to do over again, I would.

I tell M. I've finally forgiven myself.

'Hell,' M. says, with a smile and a wink, 'don't be so hard on yourself. I'd have run off with the guy myself.'

I love Paris in the springtime.

It's not dark, yet ...

Spring 2001. The memoir that started out as a journal entry to save my life and my marriage is lying dormant in a filing cabinet in the garage under a light dusting of insects and dirt. I receive a call from Margaret Mazar's boyfriend, now husband, who is naturally named ... Bob. He is in great spirits, though I haven't heard from him in a while, and cheerily asks if I've ever looked myself up on the Internet.

'Of course not,' I say. 'Why would I do that?'

'Well, you're on there,' he gushes, barely able to contain himself, 'as Bob Dylan's *girlfriend*!'

It's not like the Internet has been around forever at this point. This news is disarming, and, at the same time, alarming. Why would I be on the Internet? I'm nobody.

Now, suddenly, I find myself terrified. That night, I Google myself for the first time and am shocked to discover that while I've been living in the middle of nowhere in Julian, California, in recent years, immersed in nature and music, I have a whole other persona online, warped in a netherworld of verbiage, some words drafted by others, some my own, and many, indeed, derogatory.

Within minutes—thanks to dial-up—I am able to trace the

source. Somehow—it is unclear to this day as to exactly how, although I have my theories—one of Dylan's biographers had gotten ahold of my unpublished manuscript and mined little jewels from it. Ninety-two of them, to be precise.

'A loss … any loss … brings up the pain of all losses for those who have not yet been healed,' my therapist tells me. In an instant, the abuse I experienced as a child, the death of my first husband, the grief of losing my friendship with Bob and having decimated my relationship with Ernie, all come crashing down on me with the force of a derailed train jumping its tracks. I am annihilated.

'Did you, by chance, copyright the book?'

The attorney in Marina del Rey is dressed in a black T-shirt and jeans. He has a small sand box with a rake on his desk—a little Zen garden—to keep his waiting clients occupied in his absence. When he arrives, he is the essence of calm. He sings the praises of copyright, tells me how if the book is copyrighted, I will be immediately entitled to a fixed amount of damages.

'It's my life story,' I say, dryly. 'It never occurred to me someone could steal it.'

The attorney sighs. He tells me it will be hard to prove damages since I'm an unknown author. In the next breath, he says I've made myself a public figure by having written a book—even though it was never published—and that people can now say whatever they want to about me without me having any recourse. On the other hand, he states that this is one of the most flagrant cases of plagiarism he's ever seen. He will do the only thing he can for me: he will write a letter to the publisher of the author in question, asking them to cease and desist.

As the door closes quietly on this chapter of my life, I will be left to wonder if it wasn't me who stole my story from someone else.

At some point, I pick up the guitar again for the first time in many years. Within a short while, a chant I am using as a mantra, given to me by this phenomenal yogi up in LA named Guru Singh, morphs into the first song of at least a hundred I will write.

Karla's longtime musical partner and dear friend, the now late Kenny Edwards, who co-founded The Stone Poneys with Bobby Kimmel and Linda Ronstadt, had become a buddy of mine in the late 80s, when we were both trying to be screenwriters. Kenny had gone to the same high school as me, Venice High, with him being just a couple of years ahead; and now, as he was embarking on his own solo career as a singer-songwriter, he would become my songwriting mentor.

By the early 2000s, I had co-founded my own small-town band, a San Diego County ensemble called the Howling Coyotes, and was one of three singer-songwriters who fronted the group and played regularly to a faithful fan base in Julian, California, and its environs for several years in a row until the inevitable self-combust in 2008.

'Even The Beatles broke up,' I reminded myself, as I walked out the door.

Kenny, who I would come to remember as 'my big brother in song,' was elated by the news. He encouraged me to attend these epic music conferences for folk musicians that took place all over the country and to sign up for a songwriting camp called Summersongs that he taught at in California and occasionally in New York. When I played out, he would sometimes accompany me, and once I opened a show for him at a fairly good-size venue up in Santa Barbara in front of a big crowd.

By 2010, I had made my first solo record, *Between The River And The Road*, produced by Kenny's best friend, multi-instrumentalist and music producer Freddy Koella, who, among other musical triumphs, had toured with Dylan in the mid 2000s, and was touted by many Dylanophiles as the finest musician to have ever played with Bob.

The CD got positive reviews in minor publications and wound up enjoying airplay—on a limited basis, of course—across the country and around the world, in Australia, Canada, Israel, and the Netherlands. It was surprising how often a song of Dylan's would be played on the same show as one of mine. Sometimes even in the same set. On at least one occasion, I know for a fact our songs were played back to back.

When the first track on the CD, 'Lay Your Body Down,' turned up on Roz Larman's playlist for the seminal, syndicated folk radio show *Folkscene*, I sent out an email to friends: 'I have arrived.'

After years of not knowing who to be, or what to do, I had finally found my calling. Screenplays and books were great, but they took years to write if they were going to be any good, and even then the odds of them ever seeing daylight were so slim that, most likely, they would wind up ruined relics in a bottom drawer for my husband's relatives to discover after I transitioned to a better place. With songs, I could engage my friends with them almost immediately.

In the early days, post–Temples In Flames, when the memories of my adventures with Bob were freshest, people would beg me to tell them something, anything, about my experience with Dylan. By the end of a story, I would feel almost as drained as I did at the end of the tour itself. So I stopped telling anyone. Once my book and my reputation had been sullied, it was easy. I just wanted to be me. To be seen for who I was, and not in association with anyone else.

In the mid 2000s, after a long, relatively quiet period of anonymity, I was inadvertently outed by a close friend, a quirky, ingenious singer-songwriter out of Austin who had fostered my early playing and songwriting. He had written a rave press release for the Howling Coyotes' upcoming concert in the *Julian News*—the local paper where I was still living at the time—using phrases like 'touring with Bob Dylan.'

Unintentionally, he'd made it sound as if, I, as a musician, had gone out on the road with Bob, not realizing that, aside from being misleading—since I wasn't a musician then—most people in the small town didn't know I had any connection to Dylan, at all. The never-ending wound was once again, ripped open.

Even as recently as 2014, in Stanley, Idaho, a couple of good old boys strolled up to me while I was signing CDs after a gig and said that 'someone' had read online that I had been Dylan's girlfriend. Was it true?

The blood drained from my head to my stomach and puddled there. If I said yes, without going into my side of the story, I would essentially be admitting to the sleazy slant on things to which I'd been subjected on the Internet. Was there ever going to come a time when I would be able to take responsibility for my own truth and set the record straight?

'Guess you'll just have to read my book,' I stammered awkwardly.

Just a week or so before the Stanley show, I'd been up in LA, playing a gig, when I was approached by a likable character out of Nashville who I'd never seen before. He was new to town and would prove to be a formidable talent. After I finished my set, he came up and told me how much he enjoyed my songs and my performance. He said he was going to be playing that same venue the following week. I said I would try to make it.

A day or two later, I received the announcement for his show. His only accompanist would be a female fiddle player—the world-renowned violinist Scarlet Rivera, who Dylan had discovered walking down the street, violin case in hand, in the mid 70s, and whose distinctive style had landed her not only recording sessions on *Desire* and *Hard Rain* but also a highly coveted invitation to join the Rolling Thunder Revue.

Their show was phenomenal, to say the least. Afterwards, when my new acquaintance introduced me to Scarlet, he enthused, 'This is Britta. She's like a female Bob Dylan.'

And no one flinched, except me.

Through music I have met many friends who have become my family. At this writing, I am in the studio working on a second CD with a dear soul and fabulous musician, songwriter, and producer who sees me for who I am and has known my history from the beginning. The new CD will be called *What The Heart Wants* and will feature a cover of Dylan's latter-day hit 'Make You Feel My Love.' It will also include a song I wrote for Bob called, 'Too Much Fame,' as well as the song he and I wrote together in 1987, 'You Can Blow My Mind (If You Want To),' to which I've added a verse and some music.

Some of my newer friends will no doubt be surprised to learn of my association with Bob Dylan, perhaps even startled.

Hey—even at this late stage, I'm surprised by it myself.

But those who do know have urged me to come forward, to speak up for myself and tell the truth, my truth, and nothing but the truth (except, for the occasional change of names to protect the innocent). With the interest and help of some fine prose-writing songwriters I know, this book has been significantly enriched over the years and is a much more thorough and resonant examination of my experience than was portrayed in the original draft.

Not that long ago, at the FAR-West Folk Alliance in Mesa, Arizona—one of those big music conferences that Kenny Edwards would encourage me to attend—I confided my story about Bob to a more recent friend, a gifted multi-instrumentalist who had played with Bonnie Raitt in the mid 70s and who generously accompanied me on occasion with his guitar and harmonica. During our brief friendship, we had determined that he had been born the same month and year as me. We had also been at Berkeley in the 60s at the same time. Besides Bonnie, he had played and/or recorded with Jerry Garcia, Spencer Davis, and Little Feat, to name a few, and during the pivotal years, he'd been the MC for the legendary Monday Night 'Hoot' at the Troubadour, a breaking ground for emerging artists where folks like Tom Waits and Rickie Lee Jones and my still good friend Karla Bonoff, would show up to take the stage and overwhelm the crowd with their brilliance.

Joel had seen it all. He, I decided, would make the perfect advisor for me at this juncture in my life.

As we sit talking in the sweltering heat on the sun-bleached patio of the Phoenix Marriott-Mesa, relishing an intermittent sprinkle from a cooling fountain, I tell him more than I would tell most about my Dylan experience.

I tell him how I had known that if I didn't write it out of me at some point, I would be forever taunted by and tethered to the past. I tell him of the pain and extraordinary violation of having my intellectual property not only stolen but reinterpreted and turned against me. And I tell him that, in the present moment, I am being encouraged by someone we both know, a mutual friend in the music biz, a powerful woman, to reconsider publishing my book as a way of righting the ship and clearing my name.

He listens intently. He is encouraging.

But as soon as he departs, the old feelings of being sucked dry of all of my self-worth overtake me. I wonder if I haven't said too much. I fear that when he gets home, he'll go online and read about me and suddenly he won't like me anymore.

A few long weeks later, I stand strumming my guitar in the yard of my desert home, staring out over a garden of cactus and Carob while a cloud-studded sunset paints the sky in turquoise, pinks and purples. The phone rings. It's Joel. After returning to Seattle and settling in a bit, he tells me he's taken some time to comb the Internet on my behalf. He's evaluated the situation after rooting out some of the less than complimentary characterizations that I have been so worried about for so long.

I brace myself. The sky is blazing red now.

Nearly shaking, I ask, 'And?'

He laughs.

'I read that stuff, and I thought, wow! Those people sure don't know Breeeeeeeeeda very well.'

Acknowledgments and picture credits

SPECIAL THANKS TO

Paul Zollo, author of industry favorite *Songwriters On Songwriting*, for reading my decades-old manuscript, asking me the hard questions, and then championing my work all the way to publication!

Robert Morgan Fisher, award-winning prose writer and writing consultant extraordinaire, for his encouragement and talent in bringing my manuscript into the twenty-first century.

My publisher, Jawbone Press in the UK, for believing in me, and taking the leap.

My brilliant editor at Jawbone, Tom Seabrook, for '*getting*' me and my work, and then painlessly transforming my words into the best book I could ever hope for.

Karla Bonoff, a consummate songwriter of our time, for her gentle spirit and deep and enduring friendship.

Penny Nichols, musicologist, vocal coach, and founder of Summersongs Songwriting Camp, for creating a safe environment for me to explore my music.

Kenny Edwards, one-of-a-kind musician, songwriter, and beautiful soul, for being my big brother in song.

… and to my husband Marcel, who once, after I facetiously quipped, 'It must be difficult being married to a creative genius,' said, 'I wouldn't know.' *Without your love I'd be nowhere at all …*

RECENT TITLES FROM JAWBONE